D0297300

Book No. **03527981**

30121 0 03527981

Studying Audiences

Studying Audiences provides a critical overview of two decades of research into the television audience. With the development of ethnographic research methods, hailed by Stuart Hall as 'a new and exciting phase' in audience research, researchers turned their critical attention to groups of 'ordinary people' watching television, combining interviews and participant observation with textual analysis of television programmes. This early research attempted to document the premises of theories of spectatorship and reception.

In a comprehensive analysis of the origins and achievements of the 'cultural studies audience experiment', Virginia Nightingale evaluates five projects which helped to shape the field of television audience research, including Charlotte Brunsdon and David Morley's work on *Nationwide*, Ien Ang's *Watching Dallas* and David Buckingham's study of *EastEnders* and its audience.

Nightingale traces how central tenets within audience studies were challenged by discourses of post-colonialism, fan activism and new theories of writing, arguing that audience research is necessarily a complex activity.

Virginia Nightingale is Associate Professor in Media and Cultural Studies at the University of Western Sydney, Nepean.

Studying Audiences

The shock of the real

Virginia Nightingale

London and New York

STAFFORDSHIRE
UNIVERSITY
LIBRARY

First published 1996
by Routledge
11 New Fetter Lane, London EC4P 4EE
Simultaneously published in the USA and Canada
by Routledge
29 West 35th Street, New York, NY 10001

© 1996 Virginia Nightingale

Typeset in Times by Routledge
Printed and bound in Great Britain by TJ Press (Padstow) Ltd, Padstow, Cornwall

All rights reserved. No part of this book may be reprinted or
reproduced or utilised in any form or by any electronic,
mechanical, or other means, now known or hereafter
invented, including photocopying and recording, or in any
information storage or retrieval system, without permission in
writing from the publishers.

British Library Cataloguing in Publication Data
A catalogue record for this book is available from the British Library

Library of Congress Cataloguing in Publication Data
A catalogue record for this book has been requested

ISBN 0–415–02447–1 (hbk)
ISBN 0–415–14398–5 (pbk)   **03527981**

Thompson

14 JAN 1997

(iwk)

302.2345

Contents

Acknowledgements

This could not have been written without the care and concern of my partner Garry McDougall and of my children Jim and Ben Nightingale and Anna McDougall.

I also thank the academic friends and colleagues who encouraged me – in particular, David Sless for believing in my ability to write a book before I did myself, and for commissioning it, and Phillip Bell for supervising its early life as a PhD thesis, now much revised. John Frow, Meaghan Morris and Graeme Turner encouraged me more than they perhaps realised when they enjoyed the work I extracted from this project as a journal article in 1989 and subsequently included it in their respective Australian Cultural Studies readers.

Anna Gibbs, Cate Poynton and Lesley Johnson, and my colleagues and friends at the University of Western Sydney, Nepean – where we write in spaces stolen from other acts of creation in the context of a new and developing university – have been extremely important to me as theorists and researchers who generously discussed ideas, shared jokes and know-how, and provided encouragement. I thank Diane Dickenson and Justine Lloyd for their editorial assistance.

Virginia Nightingale

Preface

At the beginning of the 1980s, when in the USA Stanley Fish was introducing the concept of interpretive communities (Fish 1980), researchers in Britain were already drawing on a different academic tradition to explore his most radical proposition – the idea that meaning was not contained within cultural works, but made through them as the discursive work of an interpretive community. Fish's position was informed by the history and theoretical preoccupations of the international academic communities which studied writing in English and literary theory. The radical British work to which I am referring, by contrast, positioned itself initially as 'audience research', and by doing so brought a quality shared with literary theory to this field. The British work had links with literary theory – Raymond Williams and Richard Hoggart were its forefathers – but it chose to pursue its theoretical project through social science and empirical research methods. This hybrid history – the combination of literary and social theory and methods – produced audience research about theoretical issues rather than social problems, and substituted broad questions of social influence and control for the positivist preoccupation with causal effects and their social implications which had defined the practice of mainstream audience research. The radical quality of the British perspective remains, in my view, its commitment to the empirical work that literary theorists, including Fish and Jauss, hope someone else will do.

The early cultural studies audience research chose popular television programmes as its cultural works, and sought to establish their meaning as discourse by uncovering a co-determinacy of ideology in the text (deconstruction) and meanings in the audience (reconstruction). This cultural studies research was imagined as a new approach, which led Stuart Hall to anticipate that 'there seems some ground for thinking that a new and exciting phase in so-called audience research, of a quite new kind, may be opening up' (Hall 1980a: 131). The contemporaneous developments in literary theory outside the British context were to give this research a significance never imagined by its researchers and theorists because it accepted the challenge of empirical research, rather than damning it with the faint praise so evident in Jauss:

> Since I still do not yet suffer from having become an empiricist, I can calmly put up with the fact that my solution does not yet provide the model for the overdue empirical research into reception.
>
> (Jauss 1982: 144)

By addressing the production of just such 'overdue empirical research into reception' from a combination of audience research and textual analysis, the research became an exploration of the extremes of reader-response criticism, where it had at first imagined itself as a new direction in audience research and social science (Nightingale 1986).

Hall's excitement about the new audience research seemed to be confirmed when in 1980 David Morley published the sequel to *Everyday Television 'Nationwide'* (Brunsdon and Morley 1978), *The 'Nationwide' Audience* (Morley 1980). Morley's research inspired others to follow in his footsteps, and during the 1980s many similar projects were published – Dorothy Hobson's *Crossroads: the drama of a soap opera* (1982); Ien Ang's *Watching Dallas: soap opera and the melodramatic imagination* (1985); John Tulloch and Albert Moran's *A Country Practice: 'quality soap'* (1986); and David Buckingham's *Public Secrets: EastEnders and its audience* (1987). In Chapter 4, I have treated these works as a group of projects which exemplifies the radicalism of the British approach because they share so many features in common – each addressed the popularity of a particular television programme; each used some form of qualitative or ethnographic (certainly empirical) research methods; each dealt with politics through discourse; and each asserted the value and importance of research about popular culture. The projects challenged the separation which had divided audience research from the study of texts – films, television programmes, books – and promised to consolidate a new era of 'balanced' cultural criticism, in which equal weight was to be accorded to text and audience. The research took the concept 'audience' and tried to shake it loose from 'mass audience' preconceptions and general survey methodologies. It tried to make room for the audience as 'real' people engaged in the production of their culture, rather than as abstract generalities, and each tried to integrate the audience in a critique of popular culture. Some early cultural studies audience research, particularly Radway (1984), Walkerdine (1986) and Hodge and Tripp (1986), has not been counted as 'exemplary' for trivial reasons of comparability – Radway wrote about reading romance novels; Walkerdine's research was not of a television programme, but a film on video; and Hodge and Tripp chose a relatively obscure children's cartoon. I consider these three studies of equal, if not greater, consequence than the focus projects, and have used them as comparisons and contrasts.

Compared to the volumes of research that testify to the cultural importance of television programmes, industry and production, this research may at first appear inconsequential. I argue that it has been extremely important for audience research because it pioneered multi-genre media research as hermeneutic method, affected a didactic mode of address to its own audiences/readers, and tried to speak beyond that constituency to a readership unfamiliar with the language and the means to interpret its own significance. In this respect, the projects pursued a political project in regard to the audiences for popular television which 'answered back' the pursuit of media effects. Instead of measuring the effects of the media on people's behaviour, the effects were proposed to lie in people's lived relationships with popular texts.

Yet by presenting itself as audience research and addressing the audience paradigms which informed it ('uses and gratifications', effects and subculture/deviance research), cultural studies audience research sought legitimation from the most social-science-literate, least textual-theory-literate sector of the media studies community: audience research. Perhaps this is why so much of the research pursued secondary pedagogic aims. The researchers felt the need to teach potential readers about textual analysis or industry ethnography because, as interdisciplinary researchers, they were speaking across disciplinary boundaries. With hindsight, the presentation of the research as audience research can be seen, in my view, to have been a mistake, because it led to the work being undervalued. As social science, the cultural studies audience experiment is weak, but as an experiment in textual research it is much more significant.

In Chapter 1, the convergences and misunderstandings that characterised media studies in the 1980s are examined and the tendency to define common ground, rather than to explore theoretical inconsistencies across the field, is noted. The common ground in the world of audience research was formed with concepts like the sender–message–receiver model, the 'active audience', and repeated assertions of the importance of popular culture. But this symptomatic similarity disguised fundamental differences in orientation between Anglo and American ideas about culture. The American preference for exploration of the realism of consumption as statistics and demographics is juxtaposed with the British preference for social realist accounts of the 'authentic' lived experience of the British working classes. This Anglo-American scenario sets the stage for critical consideration in Chapters 2 and 3 of two seminal articles written by Stuart Hall in 1980 – 'Encoding/decoding' and 'Cultural studies: two paradigms' (Hall 1980a, 1980b). These articles usefully summarised the theoretical project that informed the cultural studies audience research and the scope of the new field of study proposed. Hall's articles are taken as a guide to the value positions which informed cultural studies at the time the audience research began, and as a source of explanations about why the research privileged, ignored or closed off ideas which might have proved useful to it.

In Chapter 4, five examples of cultural studies audience research are examined in detail, with broad emphasis on the ways concepts like text, discourse, ethnography and popular culture are used. An account of my reading of the projects, and of what I consider most striking about each, is followed in Chapters 5 and 6 by analysis of what was sacrificed to the pragmatics of research process. The cultural studies audience research required expertise in textual and ethnographic research, as well as interpretive skills for reading the psycho-dynamics of viewers and the signs of texts. My main criticism of the five projects concerns their failure to grasp the significance of the radical character, and the changes inherent in their projects, and the complacency with which they borrowed the rhetoric, assumptions and rationales of mainstream sociology and social psychology without questioning the political assumptions of such borrowed research practices. The compromises which concern me most cluster around definitions of text and discourse which perpetuate research practices that objectify audiences and refuse them the right to determine research agendas or theoretical analysis.

In Chapter 7, I look to new horizons: changing theoretical interests, a changing world, the cultural studies audience experiment itself – all have changed the ways we think about media audiences. Interests have developed in cultural criticism which refuse the very word 'audience', while integrating what was formerly referred to by this term into more complex research agendas. While the cultural studies audience research did not present itself as an experiment in translation, my analysis convinces me of a multi-layered translation process at work. Viewers translate their viewing experience into the sorts of stories they believe the researchers will find interesting. The researchers translate the stories they are told into a form of popular academic writing. In turn, academic readers, like me, translate it all into a meaning for future popular culture research and theory. Translation appears to be a unifying characteristic of cultural studies research, a way of explaining the combination of editing and interpretation, academic reproduction, which points to an agenda for a type of research which will succeed the early cultural studies audience research described.

I suggest that one of the unexpected consequences of the early cultural studies audience research is the identification of new objects of research which are relational, rather than objects in the traditional social science sense. According to this argument, the cultural studies audience experiment marked the beginning of audience–text research and the identification of a new research object, the audience relation. Work which integrates such understanding has already begun, especially in recent fan research (Jenkins 1993; Lewis 1992; Fiske 1993) and writing about impersonation (such as Nightingale 1994a). I argue that the audience–text relation operates along a continuum from impersonation to improvisation, where people find ways to enact the themes and discourses of the stories they experience (genera presented as media narratives) within the problematics of their lived everyday (particularities). Chapter 7 considers what the characteristics of such a relational object might be, and begins an exploration of the prototypical relation which subsumes audience–text – that is, self–everyday life. 'Self' and 'everyday life' are symbiotic, simply inseparable, in the same way that 'audience' and 'text' are analytically inseparable. As a result, several key theorists of everyday life were forced to articulate relational metaphors in developing theories about either one or the other. For example, Goffman used the 'actor–stage' analogy for the relation; Agnes Heller used the relation between 'the particularity' and 'the individuality' as types of consciousness to explain the ways people are inexorably linked to superstructural ideals. Lefebvre made a similar point by linking modernity and everyday life as dialectical opposites, and claiming that the bureaucratic society of controlled consumption produced by modernism will be undone only by mobilisation of the guerilla tactics of everyday life. Michel de Certeau, by contrast, located theory of everyday life in the cultural environment of the metropolis and explained its operationalism, so that at last it is obvious that the dialectical rationality of Marxism can be replaced by a logic of operation based on personal trajectories, spider webs or life lines which weave a fabric between base and superstructure.

The book finishes by pointing towards improvisation as an unexplored territory for the future. Its research future will depend on careful consideration of key processes of cultural production, like memory, translation, and cultural transposition, and the ways they are elaborated in performances of audience. Such research will still construct viewer activities as cultural production – as 'the particular living results of all the elements in the general organisation' (Williams 1975: 63) – and it will prepare us to identify and research policy action to promote the 'jouissance' of cultural engagement to enable us to distance the ennui of the entertainment industries' management of everyday cultural life. More importantly, it should promote an understanding of audience activity as cultural production not limited to reception or to intellectual activity (like thinking, evaluating, etc.), but as reaching beyond into a performative dimension where the discourses of everyday life are enacted in a landscape scattered with monuments from the past.

Chapter 1

An audience perspective and media criticism

Interdisciplinarity is not the calm of an easy security; it begins *effectively* (as opposed to the mere expression of a pious wish) when solidarity of the old disciplines breaks down – perhaps even violently, via the jolts of fashion – in the interests of a new object and a new language neither of which has a place in the field of the sciences that were to be brought peacefully together, this unease of classification being precisely the point from which it is possible to diagnose a certain mutation.

(Barthes 1977: 155)

As a result of the sort of interdisciplinary ferment which inspired the above observation by Barthes, debate about the nature of the audience, the nature of culture, the best ways to research each, and the ways in which they might be linked evolved as core knowledge for critical writing about the power of the media and the arts (Foster 1987). In this book, the questions this interdisciplinary discourse raised about audience research and how it should be practised are explored. [As literary theory, film theory and art criticism added new ideas and theories about audience activities previously understood in limited sociological or psychological terms – as audience behaviours, attitudes and preferences – questions about the nature of reading, listening and viewing, questions about the extent and limits of interpretive activity, gradually began to challenge the older social science paradigms.] Understanding audience through indicators of consumption and direct effects became intolerable as the urgency of questions of interpretation pushed the quantitative measures aside.

In this book I turn back the clock to reflect on the ways this change was enacted in the British cultural studies audience research of the mid-1970s to the mid-1980s, and to consider where audience research might usefully direct its future efforts. I will describe how the previously accepted position that people and audiences were phenomenologically the same was shaken as theories about the cultural embeddedness of audience developed. The realisation that audience is not adequately explained by researching either the people of the audience or the texts they like, but that audience is distinctively inflected by the nature and cultural significance of the interaction between audience activities and textual character (understood in the widest possible sense) causes a reconsideration of the very nature of audience. My purpose in turning back the clock is not only to reconsider and explicitly describe the changes brought about by the British research of the 1970s and 1980s, but also to propose a project for the future which does not reinvent the past as the future, as seems to be occurring in the too-easy substitution of the term 'public' for 'mass audience' in the 1990s, but better identifies the significant advantages of a post-modern approach in audience research.

SETTING THE SCENE FOR INTERDISCIPLINARY CHANGE

Interdisciplinary change in audience research cannot be understood without at least recognising that the research ideals pursued, and the sort of work desired as a result, were reactions to widely felt concern outside the United States over the post-World War II dominance of US popular culture. The 'American-ness' of mass media culture – especially of film, television, and popular music was considered threatening primarily because of its material proliferation, globally, in the life experiences of ordinary people and because it challenged and frequently displaced older more communal or oral cultural forms. Popular culture was suddenly distinguishable from both 'folk' and 'populist' culture by the signs of its foreignness – its 'American-ness'. For this reason, the concern about imperialism generated an imperative outside the USA for the invention of theoretical and philosophical perspectives from which to critically evaluate the meaning of such imported and commercial culture and the social and cultural changes it promoted. This imperative produced some of the great media theorists – Richard Hoggart and Raymond Williams in Britain, Henri Lefebvre in France, Harold Innes and Marshall McLuhan, and later Dallas Smythe, in Canada – not to mention the earlier critical theoretical concerns of the Frankfurt School. Inside the USA, of course, concern about the changes in popular culture produced continuing debate about the processes of influence and the psychological and social impacts of media effects – demonstrated in the work of symbolic interactionists like W. I. Thomas, sociologists like Robert E. Park, Robert Merton and Paul Lazarsfeld.

Four aspects of popular culture – its identification as 'American'; its production by commercial imperative; the standardisation and quality control of its production conventions; and the widespread patronage it has always attracted – have come to characterise the collective and global experience of 'American' popular culture. The experience of American popular culture as imported and commercial culture and the widespread popularity of commercial media as entertainments justified the continuance in popular discourse of the analogy that audiences are the same as the masses, the mob, the crowd – and that audience enthusiasms for particular texts can be equated with fads, follies and obsessions (for example, see Panati 1991). The idea this analogy suggests – that media interests are akin to perversions or addictions – sticks like glue in a context where the development of a language for a more sophisticated analysis is neglected, or psychologised. In this changing popular cultural landscape, criticism was pursued with a distinctively social science inflection, cut off from the philosophical and literary genres of criticism which characterise high culture. [A criticism which could encompass the lived experience of popular commercial texts and expanded definitions of the 'textual'[1] could begin to develop only when the tendency to compartmentalise, to put audiences in a box separated from texts, authors, industry and politics had been revoked.]

The recognition of the limitations of understanding communication as a compartmentalised and linear process began to gather momentum in mid-twentieth century Europe, when scholars like Lefebvre, Hoggart and Williams prepared the groundwork for an idea later succinctly expressed in Eco's 1968 essay, 'Towards a semiological guerilla warfare'. In this essay Eco sketched, too briefly, a project in which audience reading would be integrated with cultural criticism. Eco anticipated the possibility of a transatlantic critique of modern mass media in which the 'variability of interpretation' and the authority of specific audience readings might be integrated with the contemporary realities of the consumer society (Eco 1986b). He not only recognised the role of the 'reader', but also assigned reading activity a significant place in the explanation of mass communication. For Eco, both the context in which the message was encountered and the identity of the reader possessed the power to change the message. The 'variability of interpretation' based in discourse, in the historico-social situation of the reader/viewer, promised to explain the power of the mass media and its influence. Eco's imagined example of two viewers' reactions to a refrigerator advertisement located meaning in the ongoing life of a complex modern nation with a history actively affecting the sense of identity and place of each viewer. For Eco, the context of lived social and political realities was accepted as an essential component of media criticism.

In US writing, by contrast, such an understanding was assumed as inherent in the processes which make mass US culture. Stuart Ewen (1976) demonstrated the changes advertising had made to everyday activities such as grooming, cleaning, personal demeanour. The European immigrants whose experiences Ewen recounted, his equivalent of an 'audience', were presented as vulnerable (because of their poverty, homelessness, non-Anglo background, etc.) and not just open to media influence, but desiring it, accepting its terms of reference as the key to becoming less obviously 'European' and more visibly 'American'. The insecurity which resulted from immigration created an acceptance of an imagined community greater than the petty realities of everyday encounters in the ghetto. That imagined community existed in the material world as advertising and popular mass culture. Ewen's 'immigrant audience' aggressively bought the media image, and conformed to the individualist ideals which signified 'American'.

As a result, contrasting theories of the viewer/reader have always informed the difference between American and European approaches to audience research. Eco's imagined viewer transformed the media message to confront 'his' environment. The refrigerator advertisement was simultaneously evidence of affluence and oppression. The ad could be imagined to inform both the urgency of political agitation and the luxury of a big ticket shopping spree. Ewen's immigrant, by contrast, transformed 'her' self to fit the imagined America of the media image, making herself 'American' in accordance with its recipes. Eco's viewer transformed the image into political rhetoric, while the newly Americanised viewer embraced the image and pursued its realisation in her everyday life. Both viewers engaged actively with the media, but the political significance of that action is differently inflected. The European viewer found in the image hope in reform; the newly American viewer, hope in conformity.

The 'receptive' US consumer continues to be evident in Gitlin's (1978) analysis of the modes of audience research informed by Katz and Lazarsfeld's 'personal influence' model (Katz and Lazarsfeld 1955). For Gitlin, audience research when divorced from an understanding of both the politics of mass communication and texts was necessarily 'administrative': designed to manage audiences for media industries rather than to explain their developing, changing, dynamic and formative nature, or to explore the quality and meaning of the media experiences encountered by audiences. In other words, he noted that the administrative nature of most audience research actively precluded its co-optation as cultural critique. It was designed to serve the needs of media policy makers or industry interests, rather than to provide the audience with knowledge. Gitlin presented a critical Marxist perspective on the mass media. Unlike his predecessors, however, Gitlin centred that critical perspective on the hegemonic control of prime time by media management, where the Frankfurt School critique had centred on the cultural form and its standardisation, and where Lefebvre had concentrated on the enactment of processes of bureaucratic management through contemporary media.

The audience as 'consumer' is an assumption which recurs implicitly and pervasively in much North American analysis. It appears beyond question, in just the way that class assumptions were beyond question in most British writing. The consumer usurps other identities. It is not just the basis of 'the fundamental ideological difference between cultural criticism based upon a Marxist critique of capitalist society' and 'the critical position of some social scientific inquiries' (Hardt 1992: 113), it has become an 'American', and increasingly a global, way of understanding national identity. In the 'American' context, consumerism is the shared understanding of the way the world should be. It represents a higher calling than class or ethnic affiliation, as Veblen (1899) indicated almost one hundred years ago. It is a sign of 'American' culture – a culture where place is earned not allocated; an amnesiac culture which has 'forgotten' slavery and the definitional role this assumed in relation to situation. This consumerist 'logic' is evident even in Meyrowitz's exploration of 'place'. Meyrowitz (1986: viii, 308), in close imitation of Goffman, defined 'place' situationally, as a space taken up by an interaction, rather than as the place where a community finds itself (as a non-white person might) or as a geographical site which explains a reason for being (as an indigenous person might). The loss of a 'sense of place' occurs, Meyrowitz proposed, with the displacement of interpersonal situations by mass mediated ones – in the world of mass media, place has become a transaction not an interaction.

[In Gitlin's criticism of the 'personal influence' model, mainstream, quantitative audience research became a reminder of the distance which still existed between television criticism and television audience research.] While some US television criticism attempted to place the texts of television within an arts and culture framework (Newcomb 1974, 1976), television audience research operated in the realm of sociology and psychology, impervious to the vigour of the developing cultural critique based in semiotics, and also to the value of integrating an analysis of the texts of television with the more sociological or psychological interests of audience research. Until the mid to late 1980s (particularly in the work of Mellencamp and Grossberg), the sociological orientation to media studies allowed little room for connection with extremely important North American developments in literary and culture theory (Fish 1980; Said 1983). There was no cross-over between media sociology and film theory (Allen 1983; de Lauretis 1987), literary theory (Radway 1984) or the post-modernist criticism of Reaganism (Foster 1982) until the 1980s.

The lack of interest in texts and cultural criticism among traditional audience researchers (whether from the US or Europe) left a gap in the field which, by the early 1980s, British cultural studies theorists and researchers were moving to fill with hermeneutics-based rather than social science research skills (Hall 1980a). In British cultural studies, the effects debate was marginalised by more textually relevant issues such as the dominant ideology of the text or its 'cultural meaning'[2] and (later when literary and feminist theory began to make an impact) by the search for the locus of textual pleasure. Theorists proficient in the cultural interrogation of television or film texts tried initially to find ways of extending their cultural critique to embrace the television or film audience (see particularly Elsaesser 1981) and subsequently to produce cultural criticism of television, or modern mass media in general, from an audience-oriented perspective (Radway 1984, 1988; Ang 1985, 1991). The textual aspects of their work directly challenged the established, social science audience research traditions like 'effects' research (for a more recent exposition of the effects project see McLeod et al. (1991) and 'uses and gratifications' research (Katz et al. 1974) remain the most thorough exponents), which explicitly ignored or generalised the nature of the text.

In the 1970s and early 1980s small groups of media researchers throughout the world began to experiment with interpretive and qualitative methods of audience research based in cognitive psychology and symbolic interactionist theories (Halloran 1970; Noble 1975; Wartella 1979; Halloran and Nightingale 1982). Gerbner's 'cultivationist' research (as well as Newcomb's 'humanistic' critique of it) are examples of North American applications of a cultural perspective to the problems of television audience research within mainstream, quantitatively grounded sociology and social psychology. Gerbner's work stressed the ritual dimensions of television viewing and defined the implications of the content/viewing nexus in terms of socio-cultural, rather than textual, impact – quantitatively measured, of course (Gerbner and Gross 1976; Newcomb 1978). The idea that television representation should be as close to 'reality' as possible was a founding assumption of Gerbner's mid-1970s US research, which exemplified the social science understanding of texts as representations or replications of reality and has been so influential in popular media debates about television. Nevertheless, the moves towards convergence, in which researchers moving from psychology to interdisciplinary studies found themselves, was the first softening around the edges of the hard 'social science' approach to audiences which made it possible to identify the common ground in which the drama of interdisciplinary change would occur.

Common ground

The concepts and theories which I believe constituted a treacherous common ground for interdisciplinary convergence in the 1970s and 1980s included the appropriations of Shannon and Weaver's 'sender–message–receiver' model; the proposition of the 'active audience'; and, to a lesser extent, the critique of the 'mass audience' and its related defence of the popular. Such concepts and theories enabled researchers to hear, if not to listen, across disciplinary boundaries, and to begin to negotiate definitional changes. The sender–message–receiver model,[3] for example, was axiomatic in media studies[4] among the protagonists of British cultural studies, among European cultural theorists (see Eco 1986b) and in the US market modelling and communication theory approaches. Transposed in the 1950s and 1960s to the terrain of human communication, the model proposed a conceptualisation of media audiences which is always reactive, always over-determined (Hoggart 1973a: 133–62; Eco 1986b; Hall 1980a; Morley 1980). It is an intensely technological model of communication, carrying within itself two splits – initially the 'split between perceiver and world' which Crary (1992: 145) links with the technology of the camera obscura, and secondly a split between the message and the world, made technologically necessary by the invention of the telegraph. In Crary's account:

> Over the course of the nineteenth century, an observer increasingly had to function within disjunct and defamiliarized urban spaces, the perceptual and temporal dislocations of railroad travel, telegraphy, industrial production and flows of typographic and visual information. Concurrently the discursive identity of the observer as an object of philosophical reflection and empirical study underwent an equally drastic renovation.
>
> (Crary 1992: 11)

The relation between the model's elements was hypothesised as a specified linear relation which actively supported research differentiation. It provided common ground – neutral territory where the ideological differences between hermeneutic, Marxist and consumerist perspectives could be conveniently ignored, without reflecting that they were covering up the iron glove holding the hypodermic syringe which delivers the perjorative evaluations of the audience as the narcotised, lobotomised and powerless masses.[5]

The active audience

As problems with the static structuralist nature of the appropriation to social science research of the Shannon and Weaver model began to be recognised, research problems which could not be articulated using the language of the model began to be heard. The most significant, at least for this discussion, was the 'activity of the audience'. At first the inadequacy of the model was compensated for with more and more complex sender–message–receiver models – 'noise', 'channels', cultural difference, all sorts of 'interferences' and boundaries were added. The audience activity in such revisions was called 'feedback', and taken as an endorsement of the enhanced versions of Shannon and Weaver. But some of the things that audiences do are clearly of a different order than the concept 'feedback' allows. The simultaneity of everyday activities – for example, the combination of television viewing, domestic labour and childcare commonly practised by mothers of young children – dramatically affects the quality of viewing and, in sociological terms, is intrinsically interesting as contemporary knowledge of childcare practices and family relationships.

The idea of the 'active audience' was initially considered radical. It enlarged the audience research agenda by including everything from attitudes and motivations, to actions and speech, to the generation of ideas and meanings. In the USA it appears to have operated as a sort of rebuttal of recurrent moral panics over media dependence, and as an attempt to use social science to contain ideological criticism of consumerism in its own terms (Postman 1982). During the 1980s, however, theoretical differences about the origins of 'activity' were sometimes wilfully ignored in an entrepreneurial celebration of global academic mobility and international prestige generated by Reaganism in the USA and Thatcherism in Britain. The academic entrepreneurialism of the 1980s included legitimate shared projects, like the demand for serious academic research about popular culture, as well as less noble projects such as the need to generate academic credentials built on a denial of the incommensurability of beliefs held.

In the uniting anthem of the active audience, *symptomatic* aspects of audiencehood (its signifiers) were confused with its phenomenology and with theories about its origin (its signifieds). The symptoms of audiencehood, misunderstood as conceptual common ground, extended well beyond the active audience, as will be detailed in later chapters. The confusion of symptomatology with diagnosis is obvious in the comparison of sender–message–receiver and 'uses and gratifications' (Katz, Blumler and Gurevitch 1974). The 'uses and gratifications' model insisted that social utility is a necessary precondition for mass communication. From this logical condition, a second term was deduced – the activity of the audience (Katz et al. 1974: 21). The commonsense understanding which attracted protagonists to the approach was the utilitarian idea that audiences exist only because broadcast information is useful. Audiences, therefore, are active users of media messages by definition. The uses and gratifications model was important for a second reason – it reversed the sender–message–receiver communication hierarchy by insisting that the exploration, in their own terms, of audience orientations is an essential precursor for 'value judgements about the cultural significance of mass communication' (Katz et al. 1974: 22). While audience activity and its priority as a source of cultural criticism are only two of the five assumptions of 'uses and gratifications', they can be seen to presage some of the more radical aspects of textual theory that the cultural studies audience experiment explored, even though the uses and gratifications model's adherence to functionalism is unacceptable to culturalism.

The idea of the active audience was also particularly attractive to symbolic interactionist researchers, who championed the idea of activity, either because it allowed them to talk about the rule-following activities of audiences (Lull 1990), familial and personal performances (following Goffman), or in general to focus on the ways families integrated mass media like television into their everyday activities (Lindlof and Meyer 1987). The tendency noted earlier in Ewen as characteristic of North American ideas of the audience persisted. This research implicitly defined audiences as feeling vulnerable to media (otherwise why would they need to monitor and limit television viewing by their children) and as wishing to be influenced (otherwise what is gained by being selective). A desire for identity, for synonymity, of the 'dramatic world' of television and the tiny everyday corner occupied by a particular family, is strongly conveyed. The symbolic interactionist audience research expanded the repertoire of audience activities considered relevant for media research, but did not materially change the definition of the audience used.

The active audience motif was invoked repeatedly, as we shall see, by the research I focus on in later chapters, where I call it the 'cultural studies audience experiment' (see particularly Chapter 4). The active audience allowed them to situate their research in a social science context and to enter into discussion and disputation with researchers holding very different understandings of communication and culture. It enabled all to believe they were speaking the same language. The 'activity' of the audience resonated in an uncanny, if largely unsuspected, manner with the emergence in literary theory of reader-response approaches to literary criticism (see Tompkins 1980). The interest of culture theorists in television audiences, essentially a phenomenon of the 1980s, led to an amplification of the concept of audience activity to include interpretive activities for which social or psychological utility bore little relevance. In retrospect, the issue of active or passive reception of media messages by media audiences can be seen to have provided a pivot for the swing to toleration of alternative theories of audience and the problems of reception.

Psychoanalysis

The use of psychoanalytic concepts in media audience research also provided common ground, where yet another set of symptomatic similarities could obfuscate the discussion of theories of audience. In the 1950s and 1960s, media audience research based on identification and catharsis, concepts derived from psychoanalytic theory, was common. In such research, behavioural evidence of identification and catharsis was measured. These concepts remain popular as explanations of the effects of the media, even though this post-war use of psychoanalysis demonstrated all the features of the 'operationalisation' now so thoroughly despised and discredited by contemporary Lacanian writers (e.g. Žižek 1992). Such behavioural psychoanalysis was virtually abandoned as a mainstream psychological research method by the mid-1970s because of the difficulty of operationalising 'identification' and 'catharsis' to yield quantifiable results.[6]

[At the moment when psychoanalysis was being discarded for its clumsiness as an 'effects' method, it re-emerged in cultural studies as a theory of spectatorship[7] (Mulvey 1981), as an approach to cultural and textual analysis (Elsaesser 1981), and as a means of demonstrating the ideological nature of film texts as gender and political discourse.] At that time, there was no forum for the multi-disciplinary meeting of these two currents of activity, but together they ensured not only that the new research would 'make sense' but that it could be linked to older research traditions. Again a terrain was mapped out for recognition of psychoanalysis as an approach for integrating audience research with cultural criticism (see Walkerdine 1986) and as an approach to understanding the power of discourse (Žižek 1992; Walkerdine 1990). [In the early psychoanalytic research, identification and catharsis had been understood as processes of personality formation, not culture. Personality development, in turn, had been understood as individually rather than culturally authored, as it is now interpreted.] In the complex context of contemporary cultural debate, personal utilitarianism again waits to be confused with social and cultural phenomena.

What is an audience?

The nature of audiences, either as a conceptual or a theoretical issue, went unquestioned until almost the mid-1980s when speculation about alternative theories of 'audience' began[8] as part of a critique of the mass audience. Before the 1980s, the category of 'the audience' had not registered as a culturally significant one. Audiences were not considered significant in the way that 'class' or 'nation' are. In the absence of explicit theoretical work about the nature of audiences, particularly television audiences, it was simply accepted that the application of the term 'audience' to anyone using any of the broadcast media, in whatever circumstances, made sense. The research strategy was to research the person, not the culture. For this reason, McQuail's (1983: 150–4) discussion of the differences between the audience as 'aggregates', as 'mass', as 'public or social group', and as 'market', demonstrated an attention, unusual for the time, to the differentiation of what could be meant by the term, even though for each of his categories 'receiving' still constituted 'audiencehood'. McQuail's analysis articulated the more European thematic of constituency theories of the audience, of people as citizens, as having civic responsibilities and as deserving fair and honest reporting and representation from the press. His perspective drew attention to the unduly neglected matter of citizenship, to its rights and responsibilities, to the political dimension of audience activities.

While in Europe academics like McQuail redefined old ideas of the public and the public sphere to embrace contemporary media audiences, some US researchers were applying more statistically sophisticated social science to the commercial reality of media audiences. Frank and Greenberg (1974),[9] for example, proposed the definition of audiences by 'lifestyle' groups, identified by sophisticated statistical factor analysis of the mass audience. This type of media research has given the world yuppies and DINKS, and no doubt countless more market categories. It demonstrates a commercial realism in its apprehension of audiences. The commercial reality is that people are always potential audience material. In such a scheme, textual pleasure is an outcome of consumption-driven lifestyle choices – a reward for spending money. The more you can be relied on to spend, the more you will find programmes you like on television. The audience assumed is the consumer society and the culture celebrated is the culture of narcissism (Lasch 1980). The goal pursued is entrepreneurial opportunity, a celebrated characteristic of the Reagan/Thatcher years.

The logic of such strategic and managerial diversity encouraged greater attention to the basis of audience definition (Allor 1988) and renewed efforts to prove false the assumptions on which 'the mass audience' and its political evolution as the 'silent majority' depended.[10] It also inspired the negativity and pessimism of post-modernism expressed in Baudrillard's lament:

> The whole chaotic constellation of the social revolves around that spongy referent, that opaque but equally translucent reality, that nothingness: the masses. A statistical crystal ball, the masses are 'swirling with currents and flows,' in the image of matter and the natural elements. So at least they are represented to us... Everything flows through them, everything magnetises them, but diffuses ultimately without a trace. And, ultimately, the appeal of the masses has always gone unanswered. They do not radiate; on the contrary, they absorb all radiation from the outlying constellations of State, History, Culture, Meaning.
>
> (Baudrillard 1983: 1–2)

Within the critique of Reaganism, pursued most by post-modernist writers, the beginnings of a recognition of the audience as a politically meaningful category, can be heard,[11] even if initially as lament or strange curiosity (Eco 1986a). Where Baudrillard lamented the political role attributed to the mass audience in the 1980s, those searching for alternative theories looked for ways of creating distinctions within the mass. They opted initially for older sociological categories, like subculture and community, or developed new concepts like interpretive community or social formation. The debates about the activity of the audience stimulated interest again in the political power of audiences and the micro-politics of its expression. Many of these ideas had their genesis years before Reagan and niche markets.

An underlying problem of audience research initiatives in the 1980s is a conflict between incommensurable audience research goals – between a consumerist perspective directed towards capturing the realism (perhaps even 'pragmatism') of consumption – versus a culturalist perspective directed towards capturing the realism of cultural experience. Preoccupation with defining the realism of media experiences as cultural experiences has a long history in British research, and it is difficult to understand why it became confused so easily with the US preoccupation with capturing the realism of consumption. In the writing of Richard Hoggart and Raymond Williams, appreciation of the pertinence of arguments based on the realism of consumption appears as an imperative for the analysis of the realism of consumption (see particularly Hoggart 1973a). I would argue that the two approaches were not initially confused because, in the British context, structuralist explanation based on a class analysis was more highly valued and more sharply distinguishable from the managerialist perspective of US consumerism. This distinction was overwhelmed in the late 1970s by the emphasis on the populist politics of popular culture and by post-structuralist approaches to the pleasure of the text.

Critique of the mass audience

The emphasis on the context which produces audiences is the reason why Raymond Williams stated unequivocally in *Culture and Society* (written by 1958) that there was no such thing as 'the masses', only ways of imagining people as masses (Williams 1985b: 289). [The masses are an imaginary category – a way of dealing with the proximity to the large numbers of unknown and unknowable people encountered on a daily basis from about the early nineteenth century.] Williams pointed out that in Britain industrialisation and urbanisation in the eighteenth and nineteenth centuries broke up local communities and forced people to congregate in urban centres. The new context for cultural expression that these changes created as lived experience was identifiable by the mid-nineteenth century. Chambers described it as 'the metropolitan experience' (Chambers 1986) and, analytically, it has been understood as a class phenomenon in British writing. In the USA, as in Australia, however, the immigrant experience combined with, and at times eclipsed, the significance of class and rural dislocations as reasons for the discomfort of the metropolitan experience, though these were both also present. Discrimination was considered to have occurred more because of ethnicity, or the maintenance of dress and food preferences linked to country of origin, than because of class (for example, Hoffman 1989, Travaglia 1993, and others). As explanations of the metropolitan experience, both consumerism and class are produced by the same phenomena in different (Old World versus New World) contexts.

What Williams clarified in his critique of 'the masses' is that he believed British people, like himself, were heirs to a history characterised by experience (or, at the very least, folk memories) of community. The metropolitan experience Williams referred to is reminiscent of the ways rural and ethnic affiliations are represented as structuring allegiances to organised crime in contemporary Hong Kong gangster films (Berry 1985). It is not just British – the metropolitan experience is international and always experi-enced with the historical specificity of a particular nation or international structure. Even though some of the poignancy of historical connection to rural or ethnic communities may weaken after two or three generations of metropolitan life, some of the predispositions generated by communal life persist through generations of urban experience. These community postscripts, cultural remnants and residual cultures directly informed the 'cultural studies audience experiment' and provided inspiration for the development of new understandings of audience.

A dialectic of community

Williams proposed a dialectic of community which swings around the opposition of solidarity and service. Williams' own working-class background enabled him to explore differentiation where others saw only homogeneity. His, perhaps sentimental, certainly nostalgic, understanding of 'community' was endowed with ideals against which the social, economic and cultural poverty of the new metropolitan experience could be gauged (Williams 1985b: 287–306). However, as with all dialectical analysis, the recognition of the dialectic was followed by identification of one pole (solidarity) as the positive or good model and by disinterest in the other, regressive pole (service). In 'solidarity' there appeared to be hope for social change and for improvement in the conditions of the working class. In 'service' there was only the maintenance of the *status quo*. This dialectic provided the basis for the predisposition within British cultural studies to value whatever appears as 'resistance' and to doubt whatever appears to endorse the dominant culture – even if the endorsement of the dominant culture is a resistance of consumerism.

In explaining his dialectic, Williams worked within the usual class analysis, yet implied that the expression of working-class consciousness would differ according to the way the ideals of 'community' had been experienced and were interpreted. Where solidarity could generate the class awareness of itself which would result in unified class action or revolution, the notion of service was taken to denote a sacrificial relation to the wishes of others, an acceptance of the prior claims of another class – whether bourgeoisie or aristocracy. While in the 1990s it is possible to better understand the ways in which a sacrificial relation can generate social action, particularly in the light of contemporary Lacanian analysis (Lacan 1977; Žižek 1992), such a perspective was found infrequently in academic work at the time. The focus in the 1970s was on the types of experiences available to a working-class person, the ways those experiences locked him or her into reproducing the patterns of class, and on the identification of minor rebellions or resistant skirmishes, which were taken as signs of the inherent resourcefulness of a working class faced with massive exploitation.[12]

As far as mass communication is concerned, it was as though the concept of 'community in service' was forgotten and 'community in solidarity' alone maintained (perhaps because of its resonance with the social changes of the 1960s and 1970s). When applied to media audiences, the community analogy implied, at one pole, a group of people who share a common interest in a particular media product, such as the fans of Madonna, and, at the other, a group of people who pre-exist 'as a community' – for example, the residents of London's East End; or perhaps more problematically, a spectacular youth subculture with its service to cult icons and its self-generated communal experiences. Fans can be considered to demonstrate service, whereas subcultures demonstrate solidarity.[13]

The impact of modernisation on an idealised working-class life is a recurrent motif in the work of British post-war academics like Hoggart and Williams. The interest was pursued by the next generation of British academics during the late 1960s and early 1970s. Hoggart, for example, speculated on the likely impact of television, the motor car, and more money in the pocket on working-class attention to the development of personality, family, neighbourhood and locality (Hoggart 1973a: 45–61). He understood the mass media as precipitating social and cultural changes which appeared to improve life conditions, but actually robbed the working class of the possibility for solidarity. As Hoggart saw it, if the masses did not already exist as a feared 'other', then if left unchecked, consumerism threatened to transform good working-class folk into just such a fearful entity.

> It would be better if we could combine some of the strengths of the old life (tolerance, nonconformity, neighbourliness, responsibility) and some of the new (flexibility, greater emotional and intellectual disinterested-ness). Otherwise we could move from the inarticulate 'lower classes' to the conformist classless mass in one easy stage. It really depends at bottom on how we look at one another.
>
> (Hoggart 1973a: 61)

British researchers looked for the continuation of working-class solidarity wherever they found evidence of spontaneous group affiliation – in spectacular youth subcultures (Willis 1978), drug cultures (Cohen and Young 1981), music cultures (Hebdige 1975; Chambers 1975; Hall and Jefferson 1975) and political activism (Halloran, Elliot and Murdock 1970). The idea of community and of culture as the materialisation of common forms of organisation was supported with elaborate and convincing theoretical argumentation (Hall and Jefferson 1975). The class and subculture research consolidated the theoretical preconditions for an approach to media studies which included media experiences of all kinds and culminated in the uniting of text and audience in the one research project – the encoding/decoding model (Hall 1980a: 128–38).

A good example of the subculture research which inspired the encoding/decoding model is Hebdige's work on punk. Hebdige (1979) interrogated a youth subcultural phenomenon, punk, in the 1970s. This spectacular subculture was categorised (inappropriately I suspect) as a youth community which expressed itself stylistically through punk iconography. Hebdige demonstrated that the particularity of punk genres in music, argot, dance, behaviour, lifestyle and fashion, expressed the relation of this subculture to other youth subcultures (like Rude boys or Rastafarians) and to the dominant culture. He demonstrated that such forms function for the subculture as expressions of subcultural style and as statements of subcultural solidarity and opposition to the dominant culture. As a contribution to 'cultural' audience research, his work is important for its analysis of what he terms 'reception aesthetics': 'the attempt to account for the variable significance of objects and images as they are circulated in different consumer markets' (Hebdige 1979: 59).

[Hebdige's work is important in offering an example of how a particular group of people can constitute both a media market and a subculture simultaneously. He demonstrates that consumption is not necessarily just a matter of timeless self-interest but can incorporate elements of subcultural affiliation. The objects, words, sounds and stances that a subculture adopts – the signs of its difference – reflect both the group's experiences of, and its location within, the dominant culture. [The expression of subcultural difference and resistance is both a threat to the dominant culture and a source of innovation and creativity for it.] The mass media record the resistance and explain it from the dominant perspective. They popularise the threatening ideas of the subculture in a 'defused' version. In what superficially resembles a 'uses and gratifications' account, Hebdige claims media audiences adopt as significant to themselves those objects and images which offer a coherent account of their lived experiences of the culture and promote a sense of community or solidarity with significant groups within it. However, unlike 'uses and gratifications' accounts, Hebdige demonstrates that the symbolic value of the objects and commodity forms selected by the subculture are accessible through semiotic analysis. His emphasis is less on the effects of the media on audiences than on the roles played by the media in maintaining the dominant culture through 'recuperation' and 'incorporation' of the dissident meanings generated by the subculture.

It is worth noting that Hebdige's research involved 'reading' the subculture rather than engaging with it ethnographically. When compared with Morley's (1980) study of the ways in which groups of people interpreted given episodes of the programme Nationwide, a change can be noticed in the way the audience-as-community is constituted in regard to television. Morley used the encoding/decoding model to demonstrate the differences that social position makes to the interpretation of the programme and to the perception of its ideological status. For Morley, the audience was still 'everyone', stratified according to classic demographic principles, yet his 'mass audience' is a general public within which diverse, discursively structured groups mingle. [In Morley's work, diverse audiences are treated as 'communities' in the sense of sharing 'direct common concerns', especially socially and politically.] For both Morley and Hebdige, the audience has a dual existence – it is part of the mass audience and also part either of subcultural or communal relations with others.

Two rather different results of Morley's study are of particular relevance to the extension of 'community' concepts to audiences. Firstly, Morley demonstrated that social position does make a difference to the way a television programme is decoded, and secondly he established that a programme's 'mode of address', the way it talks to its audience, is crucial for the establishment of decoding patterns among the audience. These two potentially contradictory findings – that what the audience brings to the programme and that the way the programme speaks to its audience both affect the way a programme is 'read' – have had important implications in cultural studies research. This idea is touched on by Mary Douglas in her mention of Turner's insistence on the relevance of 'community', on a sense of communality, for the sharing of ritual jokes:

> In 'community' the personal relations of men and women appear in a special light. They form part of the ongoing process which is only partly organised in the wider social 'structure'. Whereas 'structure' is differentiated and channels authority through the system, in the context of 'community', roles are ambiguous, lacking hierarchy, disorganised. 'Community' in this sense has positive values associated with it; good fellowship, spontaneity, warm contact. Turner sees some Dionysian ritual as expressing the value of 'community' as against 'structure' ... Laughter and jokes, since they attack classification and hierarchy, are obviously apt symbols for expressing community in this sense of unhierarchised, undifferentiated social relations.
>
> (Douglas 1991: 303)

Morley's *Nationwide* findings (as opposed to his later work, for example, Morley 1986) strategically shifted the emphasis of audience research from concentration on the medium (television) to concentration on the text (the television programme); from audience–medium interaction to audience–text interaction (see Nightingale (1984) for clarification of this distinction). The findings also extended the notion of audience-as-community to include a grouping better described as a constituency – a constituency comprised of the community of users of the sign, where the television programme is the sign and the community of users is a political grouping with common socio-economic status. Douglas's observation reminds us that the entertainment media are likely to offer ritualised opportunities for experiences of community which celebrate good fellowship over class distinction.

Dispersed communities

This new conceptualisation identified the audience as in a symbiotic relationship with the text, and the construction of meaning as dependent as much on the audience as on the text. But it created other problems which have become obvious only in subsequent research. Perhaps the most telling include the problems of determining the 'knowability' of the 'community' theorised, and the variability of the senses of community invoked, especially in empirical terms. For example, Hobson (1982) assumed the priority of community in her study of women watching *Crossroads*. For Hobson, women constitute a 'community' which pre-exists the text and shares some 'materialisation' of 'common forms of organisation', but which can also be defined by a 'sense of common interests'. Her study, which grew out of prior research about housewives, women's culture and the media (Hobson 1980, 1981), focused on the work patterns women create to integrate watching a particular television programme with their everyday routines. Using participant observation and other ethnographic research techniques, Hobson noted points at which the programme, the characters, the production team and the programmers' decisions figured in the ways the audience talked about the programme, both to her and to each other. She explored the basis for understanding an established audience as a community sharing common interests and concerns in a television programme, and common ways of talking about those shared interests. The sense of community was, in some senses, artificially bolstered for Hobson's research by a threat to the programme (see Chapter 4) which became the centre of a public outcry. At this crisis point, the press and the television station became sites where the *Crossroads*' 'community' could express itself. A dispersed community seized the opportunity to engage in communal action to take control of the story direction of the programme. In Hobson's research, pre-existing communities of women and aged viewers materialised to provide a corpus, the living bodies to inhabit the 'textually' conceptualised audience imagined by the programme's production team.

By contrast, Janice Radway (1984) began her research not with working-class women, as Hobson had done, but with women who subscribed to a romance readers' newsletter. In other words, she used the text – or more precisely, an expression of commitment to the romance genre – to identify an audience of real readers. In line with my earlier argument, the reality of their consumption defined them as a culturally relevant group. The importance of romance reading as a source of solidarity among her readers, and the importance of the novels themselves as sources of personal confirmation and hope, were central concerns in her research. The real reader affirmed the social meaning of the literary form. Radway's research included three levels of investigation: the production and distribution arrangements governing the availability of the romance novel as a cultural commodity; individual and group interviews, as well as written surveys, with women who regularly read romances; and a structural (textual) comparison of 'ideal' and 'failed' romance novels. She explored the relationship between the repeated themes and ideas of the most popular romance novels and the role the romance plays in the lives of women who read them regularly. She concluded that while the romance novel may appear to endorse traditional views of relationships and marriage, the experience of romance reading offers participation in an imaginary world where the heroine is powerful, competent, desirable and successful – characteristics often suppressed or repressed in the reader's own life. For this reason, she claimed that the romance could be subversive of traditional relationship patterns by keeping alive a version of self which is often contradicted in the everyday realities of the reader.

Where Hobson started with women in the community and demonstrated the role of the programme in providing a focus for shared discussion and 'gossip', Radway started with the text and ended with the shared experiences of women in the community. In these examples of feminist research, the commonality of women's experiences of oppression in capitalist society provided a unifying sense of 'community' around which the attachment to texts is explained. The studies work on a fluid definition of community, a definition which moves like the ebb of the tide as the researchers' focus moves from production, to audience, to text, to domestic context, to audience or text generated meanings. The significant break with Williams' theories of community is in the breaking of expectations that community involves a geographical boundary, ethnic affiliation, or shared experience other than that of metropolitan life. The search for audience-generated cultural criticism leads back to everyday life in the metropolis as the neglected origin of a critique of modernism.

[Such audience research shows that a sense of community can be generated by particular mass-produced media commodities (such as the romance novel, the television soap opera, the television news magazine programme, or the computer video game). Each form constructs its own audience through providing opportunities for the audience to use skills of interpretation and analysis developed over years of schooling or media use.] The pleasure of the text may reside as much in the delight of being able to participate in the symbolic system of the text as in its personal or social significance. In other words, this body of work suggests the importance of developing a theory of audiences as media communities over and above their allegiances to personal/domestic and social/cultural groups. Such research pioneered a cultural critique which has led to the inclusion of popular cultural texts in debates about social meanings and the media, debates which endorse the value of the pleasure of the popular. It has also, significantly, suggested as problematic the relationship between media communities and social communities.

As Henri Lefebvre (1971) noted, everyday life is likely to be the source of an audience-generated critique of culture, the origin of a critique of modernism. The construction of a texture for everyday life, the attempt to textualise the mundane, to render it accessible for discussion and description, to make it classifiable and so to inscribe it in the realm of academic discourse, has provided a recurrent theme as accompaniment to the study of popular culture. One could say that everyday life is a necessary, if often unacknowledged, accompaniment to the study of popular culture. Everyday life is, epistemologically, even more important than just another concept, another set of categories and classifications to be devised, discovered, invented. Everyday life is the ground for the study of culture. The recognition of its necessity in the study of culture and of audience marks an epistemological transition from the preoccupation with the extra-ordinariness of 'man' (Foucault 1970) to a preoccupation with 'life' as the object of scientific enquiry.

In the work of Lefebvre and de Certeau the study of everyday life contextualises people and texts in the same field, in the activity of writing – reading. As de Certeau has suggested, we cannot reproduce ourselves without textual involvement. Textuality is part of our make-up – as the current rash of Elvis, Marilyn and Sherlock Holmes impersonators and rock-and-roll tribute bands demonstrate. Everyday life is the common ground in which the particularistic and the homogeneous meet. Everyday life is spatial, temporal, emotional, part of every life and yet identically experienced in no life. It is in everyday life that the precipitation of the organisational strategies adopted to administer metropolitan life accumu-late. It is in everyday life that the necessity of textual symbiosis proliferates.

NOTES

1   For example, Michel de Certeau (1986) *Heterologies: discourse on the other*, Conclusion, pp. 225–33.
2   This shift is evident in the collections of articles selected for Section III (the audience section) of the Curran and Gurevitch reader (1991). While this book still follows an S–M–R model, identifying the audience as 'receivers' in the very conceptual structure of the book, and denying the audience a role as producers of culture, the articles in its concluding section demonstrate the confusion caused for effects researchers by the more textual approaches (McLeod et al. 1991: Chapter 12), and the confusion about relevant methods for a textual approach (Livingstone 1991: Chapter 14). Effects researchers seem confused over the significance of the textual orientation and the textual theorists seem to have lost the plot.
3   See Fiske's explanation of Shannon and Weaver, circa 1947, in Fiske (1982).
4   And reluctantly I must admit that the sender–message–receiver model remains axiomatic in media studies, even though the point of this book and work like Crary (1992) chart the beginnings of a new technological necessity for a reappropriation of sensation and affect to the 'techniques of the observer'. The acceptance and simplistic appeal of Shannon and Weaver's model assist the maintenance of discourses which assert that senders and messages matter more than the culture. In its more bizarre interpretations audiences are even separated from 'culture'.
5   This model and its implications are dealt with in depth in Chapter 2.
6   For an heroic attempt – Howitt and Cumberbatch (1975); an older, though more characteristic example is Maccoby and Wilson (1957).

STAFFORDSHIRE
UNIVERSITY
LIBRARY

7   Spectatorship is a way of describing the literary concept, the reader-in-the-text, when the text is film or television.

8   Ien Ang (1991: 13–14) provides an account of this moment in the introduction to her book, *Desperately Seeking the Audience*. The book is a continuation of the quest for an understanding of 'audience' appropriate for contemporary cultural criticism. Allor (1988), Grossberg (1988) and Radway (1988) also contribute usefully to such discussion. I, too, began trying to solve the puzzle in 1983 (see Nightingale 1984, 1986).

9   Frank and Greenberg (1974) used factor analysis to identify significant lifestyle and income groups and their television and other media preferences.

10 In *Dependency Road*, Smythe (1981) tries to shock the audience by his disclosures of the falsity of the free lunch. Smythe accepts the idea of the audience as mass and stops short of pursuing the type of socio-political action which people might engage in as audiences.

11 Said (1983) considered the relationships among the terms, opponents, audiences, constituencies and community, and their political significance in the production and control of knowledge.

12 The work of Paul Willis (*Learning to Labour* (1977); *Profane Culture* (1978)) and Halloran, Elliott and Murdock (1970) are examples of this type of work.

13 It is my view that this distinction becomes untenable when applied to fans.

Chapter 2

Encoding/decoding

Althusser's innovation, and his break with a classical aesthetics of representation, is to argue that the basis of identification and affective behaviour in audiences is not primarily psychological, but social and ideological.

(Sprinker 1987: 279–80)

A plan for the integration of audience research with cultural criticism was presented as a research initiative in Stuart Hall's 'encoding/decoding' essay written in the early 1970s. By the late 1980s five published research projects which demonstrated the method had been completed. The research was based on popular television programmes *Nationwide*, *Crossroads*, *Dallas*, *A Country Practice* and *EastEnders* and it pursued a conviction, developed from a combination of Althusserian aesthetics and British culturalism, that the hegemonic power of the media would be disclosed by the study of social and ideological processes rather than by individual psychology or personal experience. It was a first attempt at bridging the 'apparent distance separating aesthetic theory from other regions in historical materialism' (Sprinker 1987: 269). The research demonstrates the problems of method which result from the artificiality of the separation of theory and research praxis, as well as the hopefulness generated by the excitement of discovery.

The emphasis on the audience–text process distinguished this new research from studies of the process of television production popular in the 1970s and early 1980s (for example the work of the Glasgow Media Group on the news production process; Elliott's work on the professional practice of journalists; the production process of popular television programmes like *Dr Who* (Tulloch and Alvarado 1983), *Hazell* (Alvarado and Buscombe 1978), *Bellamy* (Moran 1982) – all characteristically named for the focus programme). Where the production process research was considered to 'explain' the cultural meaning of popular television programmes through analysis of the structures of production, the cultural studies audience experiment added the study of audience and/or the so-called 'structures of reception' to this agenda. The commitment to empirical investigation of media audiences marked its difference from theoretical and non-empirical work about popular television (such as Dyer et al. 1981; Modleski 1982;

Kaplan 1983). The research produced a rather uneasy liaison between textual analysis and audience research, semiotics and ethnography, later to be recommended by Fiske (1987a: 272) as the way forward for cultural studies. Fiske understood better than many others the importance of audience research for cultural criticism of the entertainment media, but the over-simplification of Hall's encoding/decoding model he recommended severely limited its potential.

The encoding/decoding model

The encoding/decoding model was proposed in 1973.[1] It outlined a research agenda which united what Hall (1980b) described as the 'two paradigms of cultural studies', 'structural' culturalism and the 'European' structuralisms, and then double exposed this amalgamation with the sender–message–receiver account of mass communication. This superimposition obscured the potential for the encoding/decoding project to reference, incorporate and/or freely explore fields of social science ferment which have since emerged as theoretically relevant – like reader-response theories of 'text'; discourse and the nature of subjectivity; and the role of ethnography in the production of cultural criticism. The initiative was tagged 'communication' research rather than 'culture' research by this link with 'sender–message–receiver'. In the early days however, when first presented in the encoding/decoding model, its agenda for a materialist aesthetic grounded in audience experience was radical and exciting.

The model can be understood as a guide to a meaning-centred semiotic study of mass communication. The essay summarised an emerging conviction that semiotics could explain the audience. It was prescriptive in that it outlined a project. It was methodological only to the extent that it explained the theories that might be applied to empirical problems. It did not explore its own ideological stance or potentially politically exploitative methods – a tragic shortfall. The essay is reminiscent of Eco's conjecture on the fruitfulness of applying semiotics to problems of mass communication. Themes like the concentration on the 'communicative act', on the 'variability of interpretation', and on the usefulness of comparing the 'codes at the source' with the 'codes at the destination' of the message (the codes with which the audience interprets the message) (see Eco 1974, 1986b: 137–42) were affirmed. The promised benefit of the encoding/decoding model centred on its situating structures of production, text, and audience (reception) within a framework where each could be read, registered and analysed in relation to each other. It proposed that class categories be substituted for the psychological perspective which had dominated audience research, in which 'the individual' was aggregated as receiver.

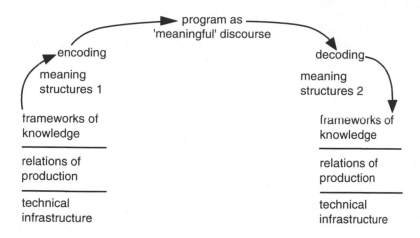

Figure 1 Encoding/decoding model (Hall 1980: 130)

Mixing methods and research genres

The vision pursued in the 'encoding/decoding' project suggested an analytical equivalence between utterance in dialogue (the research interview) and media discourse. This is evident for example in Hobson's research where each of the housewives interviewed by Hobson (1982) was considered to 'speak' her culture in talking about Crossroads. This type of utterance was considered as valid a production of discourse as Dickens 'speaking' his culture in his novels (see Williams 1984: 28–59). This type of emphasis on discourse drew attention to its genres as objects of research – genres which might include such diverse phenomena as the novel, an interview, gossip, an impersonation, or an opera performance – and generated renewed interest in the relevance for media research of socio-linguistics and social semiotics. When later Fiske (1987a) advocated semiotics for the study of texts and ethnography for the study of audiences, a mode of practice was recommended which mixed research methods and genres in a very new way. The boundary which had hitherto divided text from audience as research objects was softened, though not demolished. However, the expedient use of research methods to suit the genres of cultural production combined in the project overlooked the political assumptions inherent in the practice of research, and the hierarchical structure necessitated by the research method. The aim to produce an audience generated aesthetic was for this reason compromised from the start.

Hierarchies of discourse

There are senses in which encoding/decoding bore similarities to a two-step flow (cf. Katz and Lazarsfeld 1955). A hierarchy in the production of discourse was implied, based on different relations to the means of cultural production. The articulation with the sender–message–receiver model intensified the implied hierarchical structure, legitimated initially by the Althusserian preoccupation with 'determinations' and later by the Gramscian notion of 'hegemony'. The ideas of the dominant culture were assumed to be reproduced in television. They came to be synonymous with 'the sender'. The reduction of cultural production to discourse production encouraged an expectation that discourse would be self-evident in dialogue. The production of television was doubly articulated in the 'cultural studies audience experiment' – both as programme and as dialogue. Production staff, situated in an institutional context, were understood to produce a television programme which is 'meaningful' as discourse – its meaning ultimately pronounced by the audience in the lived continuum of the everyday. The encoding/decoding model generated assumptions that the progress of discourse could be traced, and the power of institutions like 'the media' could be documented as they permeated the real life experiences of the people who make the distributed product and of the people who engage with it. While it was recognised that texts must be interpreted for their meaning to be proclaimed, utterance/dialogue was considered transparent. The work of the researcher was to explain the 'message as meaningful discourse' and then to trace its meanings out into the community of viewers. By listening to and reporting people's talk, the researcher could expect to discover the destination and final meaning of the 'message'. These assumptions of hierarchy in meaning production/message transmission distinguished this work from reader-response understandings of interpretive community where the community ultimately 'authors' the text. The cultural studies audience experiment could have taken up the 'authoring' challenge of audience activity, but did not.

Links to subculture and deviance research

'Culturalist' assumptions and perspectives which had informed the subculture and deviance research (Hall and Jefferson 1975) were integrated with the assumptions of the 'encoding/decoding' project. The knowledge it assumed included:

- that by definition, culture and subculture and the relations between them consolidate the hegemonic dominance of one group of interests and ideas;
- that the use of 'ethnographic' methods is appropriate to such research;
- that alternative and deviant subcultures are appropriate objects for cultural study;

- that the aims of the research are to identify the forms in which class consciousness and cultural resistance are manifest.

The research presented in Hall and Jefferson was not media centred but subculture centred.[2] Working-class subcultures were the preferred objects of study. They were seen as the besieged remnants in Western culture of authentic cultural resistance; the problem to be explained; the challenge to the dominant culture to be protected. British media research of the early 1970s followed the subcultures and deviance agenda. It began from a preoccupation with the representation of cultures and subcultures, especially in the news media (see Halloran, Elliott and Murdock 1970; Cohen and Young 1981; McQuail 1972: Parts 4, 6) – a concern which remains a significant cross-over point between sociology and the more hermeneutic perspective of cultural studies today. In method, vigour, and orientation the research echoed the early days of the Chicago School.[3] The links with journalism and journalistic practice resurfaced and led in this case to an alternative reportage – an academic account of what 'really' happened and why (Halloran, Elliott and Murdock 1970, for example) – to counteract the perceived totalitarianism of the mainstream manufacture of news.

Williams' theory of cultural totality was assumed, particularly the

> ...anthropological and sociological senses of culture as a distinct 'whole way of life', within which a distinctive 'signifying system' was seen not only as essential but as essentially involved in all forms of social activity.
>
> (Williams 1981: 13)

Williams' definition encompassed the 'artistic and intellectual activities' which constitute the practice of the culture. It advocated the 'reading' of subcultural practices as signifying practices – practices which demonstrate the relation of the group to the dominant culture. In this respect a position of resistance – as either negotiation or opposition, was assumed. The subculture research sought to uncover the relations which structure the 'whole way of life' of the culture. It demonstrated the active presence in the precursors of the cultural studies audience experiment of the characteristic cultural studies discourses of 'social commentary' and 'ethnography' identified by Tolson (1986: 148, 149). As a development of the subcultures and deviance research, the 'encoding/decoding' model marked a significant moment in the appropriation of European structuralism by British culturalism (see Chapter 3). It is important to bear in mind however that the particular character of this appropriation was shaped and authored by the preferences and logic of British culturalist research.

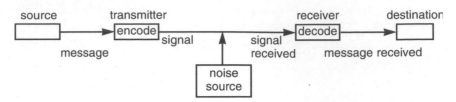

Figure 2 Sender–message–receiver (Shannon and Weaver Model, 1949)

Encoding/decoding and sender–message–receiver

Although the encoding/decoding model was developed within Marxist aesthetics, it adopted a compromising position towards the then popular sender–message–receiver model of mass communication. In an uncanny quirk of fate, sender–message–receiver proved amenable to a variety of incommensurable theories, including Marxist materialist aesthetics. The 'encoding/decoding' model echoed preoccupations familiar from 'sender–message–receiver' and accepted by American (De Fleur and Ball-Rokeach 1975; Schramm 1954), British (Hoggart 1973a) and European (Eco 1974, 1986b) scholars of disparate persuasions. 'Encoding/decoding' translated sender–message–receiver for an audience context in which class, not consumerism, was the prime analytical concept. An argument for how and why semiotics could account for mass communication, was fashioned from the problems with sender–message–receiver, though the model itself remained sacrosanct, natural, obvious, commonsense.

The primary concerns of sender–message–receiver models of communication are with accuracy and effectiveness. They are about the sending of messages, and ways of doing so more accurately or effectively. Fiske has pointed out that three levels of analysis were addressed by the original 1949 Shannon and Weaver model (1982: 7) . The Shannon and Weaver model was concerned with accuracy at the technical level, technique at the semantic level and effectiveness at the outcome level. It was designed to account for, to detect, and to diagnose problems in message construction or distortions caused by the technology of transmission, to encourage evaluation of techniques of message construction (how to say what you want to say most clearly), and to determine whether what the sender meant to convey had successfully reached its destination (that is, could be parroted back by the receiver).

It is immediately apparent that 'sender–message–receiver' is a simplification in practice of the Shannon and Weaver model. It remains the fundamental assumption of communication studies, and has been most widely applied to situations of interpersonal interaction. 'Source' and 'transmitter' became the sender. The idea of message was extended to encompass both 'content' and encoded form ('signal'), and the receiver included 'receiver', 'message received' and 'destination' (or outcome).

The problems Hall recognised with the sender–message–receiver model included its linearity, its concentration on the 'level of message exchange', and on its absence of a 'structured conception of the different moments [of mass communication] as a complex structure of relations'. Yet, significantly, Hall's encoding/decoding model is a curved line which maintains a hierarchical dimension; the 'different moments' of encoding/decoding mirror the sender–message–receiver chain; and it deals with a variation of the message, with less than the message in fact – with the message as only 'meaningful discourse', and sometimes as ideology.

The last of Hall's criticisms, the understanding of mass communication as a complex structure of relations, is the most salient. It pointed to the administrative purposes pursued by the sender–message–receiver model. Hall proposed that instead of seeing mass communication as a means of achieving administrative aims, such as designing faster and more efficient systems of information dissemination, or designing messages which make 'receivers' act in the desired way more consistently, 'it is also possible (and useful) to think of this process in terms of a structure produced and sustained through the articulation of linked but distinctive moments – production, circulation, distribution/consumption, reproduction' (Hall 1980a: 128).

'Sender–message–receiver' was accepted as description rather than as a proposition by the encoding/decoding scholars. Their acceptance of the model placed the institutions and personnel nominated as 'sender' under a new scrutiny because the tacit assumptions of sender integrity and intention could be interrogated by a new logic, that of the audience. The practice of 'sending' was considered hegemonic and ideological by its very nature. In the field of reproduction (reception) it was assumed that the crimes of 'the sender' would be demonstrable, documentable, like political victimisation by the USA in South America or like the dumping of infant milk formula by multi-national companies in Africa. It was assumed that the accounts of the media produced by its 'victims', the audience, would complete the case against media monopolies and initiate a new era of representative, fair and just mass communication. This perspective justified again the focus on working-class audiences, rather than on middle-class or wealthy audiences.

For such reasons, it was advocated that the study of mass communication should not concentrate on matching what the 'sender' intended with what the 'receiver' understood, but should examine the forces at play in the moments when the 'message' was 'produced' both as 'message' (encoding) and as 'reading' (decoding). In other words it was thought that 'reading' the significant moments of media production would open the process of political hegemony to scrutiny (for example, the work of Glasgow University Media

Group; Philo 1990). The encoding/decoding model proposed that this assumed politics would be confirmed by the patterns of audience readings.

The work of the researcher was foreseen, therefore, primarily as the analysis of discourse. Because the production of discourse was assumed to be determined in the distinguishing moments of 'production–distribution–production' and this process of mass communication was in turn assumed to be homologous to the 'skeleton' of Marx's explanation of 'commodity production', mass communication was considered homologous with the structures of economic production within capitalist society. Hall used this homology to assert that the 'messages' of the mass media always support the dominant culture. The homology was accepted as both explanation and account of the operation of power within mass communication. A study of the political economy of mass communication was therefore considered redundant because the hold over people's hearts and minds was considered to be adequately explained by the study of ideology. Or vice versa, the study of ideology by definition would disclose the vested interests in the propagation of certain ideas. Tracing the ideology in discourse was to be the important research activity. Particular practices (involving encoding and sometimes decoding) were deemed significant because they produced 'meanings and messages'. The circulation of the goods/commodities so produced was believed to be more significant in 'the discursive form' (Hall 1980a: 128) than in their commodity form.[4]

Such a formulation of the research agenda is possible only by adopting the linearity and interactional level of the sender–message–receiver model. At the level of what Fiske (1982: 7) has described as its application to 'effectiveness problems', 'sender–message–receiver' permitted the substitution of 'the discursive form of the message' for the message, or any other way of describing mediated information. The versatility of the sender–message–receiver model has always been the source of its popularity. Where the change in focus from the formal structure of the message to its meaning or ideology has required major theoretical justification in literary theory it appeared, through ignorance of the complexity of the literary debates, a relatively minor change in emphasis in communication theory. If anything, the promotion of the discursive form of the message in encoding/decoding further privileged 'messages' and their meaning over the structures of production and the structures of reception in communication, where its main application had been in interpersonal therapy or managerial diagnosis.[5]

As Eco (1974: 54) has pointed out, such preoccupation with effectiveness can engender fallacies about the audience (addressee). Firstly, it can imply that if the addressee is unable to parrot back the message accurately, then he or she is using 'imperfect and obsolete codes' (in other words, there is something wrong with the 'receiver'). Secondly, it can imply that the inability to parrot the message means the addressee has understood nothing at all of the message, or has 'understood' it incorrectly (again there is something wrong with the 'receiver'). As Hartley (1987) has usefully noted, the outcome of such misunderstanding may include changes to the production of 'messages' (which are simplified to be more accessible), and to a complete underestimation of the audience. According to Eco, the second fallacy confuses what has been understood with what can be put into words. It assumes that people will always be able to find words to express what they think and have understood. It assumes a viewer orientation of detachment rather than involvement in relation to media texts.

Hall also rejected the concern with accuracy and effectiveness, but for slightly different reasons. He began by problematising the necessity of 'matching' the sender's encoding with the receiver's decoding. The point he made was that no amount of accuracy of encoding or efficiency of transmission can deliver a particular meaning, interpretation or reading. As Hall put it, 'the value of this approach is that while each of the moments, in articulation, is necessary to the circuit as a whole, no one moment can fully guarantee the next moment with which it is articulated' (Hall 1980a: 129).

'Decoding' was considered a 'distinctive moment' because in decoding, in the interaction of reader and text, reproduction of the dominant culture was ensured. The other 'distinctive moments' suggested by Hall are 'production', 'circulation', 'distribution/consumption'. Each of the distinctive moments involved both transformation and translation of, for example, an event into a news story, a television news story into ideas and opinions etc. They are the moments when discourse is produced and reproduced, when it lives through those involved in its production (as television programme, meanings, or both). Mass communication for Hall was about reproduction of the meanings, ideas and interests of the social formation, and in this sense the 'message' of mass communication was both problematised and politicised. Commitment to demonstrating this process of reproduction involved an investigation of how the 'sender' or source, which in this case was taken to point to the influence of the dominant culture, convinces others – people who do not necessarily share those views – that they are commonsense. It also commits the researcher to a variety of forms of translation (see Chapters 5 and 6). The social science and cultural research required demanded an understanding of translation in its broadest senses, and a relation of (self-) sacrifice to the people researched. In encoding/decoding, influence was to be demonstrated in the pervasiveness of dominant ideology and in the ways it incorporated dissident ideas. This task was not fully understood at the time as one of cultural translation.[6]

The ambiguity of encoding/decoding is evident in Hall's summary of the distinctive moments of mass communication (1980a: 128). He claimed for the distinctive moments the potential to challenge the tenets of sender–message–receiver and to bring about a radical change in the notion of 'agency' in televisual communication (and communication in general). The conceptualisation of message sending as encoding 'production', message receiving as decoding 'production' and message as 'televisual discourse' was intended not only to dismantle the notion of communication as 'correct understanding', but also to allow the model to transcend the limitations of individualism which encumbered it. Hall's model allowed, among other possibilities, for communication to be understood as an act of community, as group action, or as culture speaking through the work and leisure practices of ordinary people in community. It suggested the possibility of 'agency' as 'subjectivity' and 'discursive community', rather than individualism. But this challenge was based on the proposition that sender–message–receiver could be turned back to front – that the process of communication made sense from an audience perspective. This was, however, the possibility destroyed by the uni-directionality of the encoding/decoding model which in this sense broke with the Marxist base–superstructure understanding of culture as cyclical even if characterised by lags between base level production of ideas and experientially authored cultural production, and the circulation and transformation of that production at the level of superstructure. Like the sender–message–receiver model, the encoding/decoding model is uni-directional. The apparatus for the production of television must exist before there can be a programme as discourse; there must be a programme as meaningful discourse before there is decoding – necessarily. There is no suggestion in the way the model is presented that the 'programme as "meaningful" discourse' depends on decoding. The model stops well short of the reader-response view that the reader determines the message. The programme is considered discourse – the discourse of its production personnel and their lived experiences of producing the programme each week and of their culture in general.

The claim that the audience is both the 'source' and the 'receiver' of the television message referred to the ways in which both the audience and the production personnel participate together in the 'wider socio-cultural and political structure of which they are a differentiated part' (Hall 1980a: 129) and implies that the structures of production yield a 'message' which requires a reader in whom to live, but which exists independently of that reader. The reader realises (makes real) the text in the process of everyday life. The encoded 'message' of the programme, not the programme itself, has differing meanings for different audiences. For example, in *Everyday Television* (Brunsdon and Morley 1978: 30) a *Nationwide* item about married couples choosing not to have children was demonstrated to convey the 'message' that 'the failure to conform to the nuclear pattern' poses 'an explicit and threatening problem'. Encoding resulted in a 'message', in a position or stance which could be determined by the researcher/reader. In decoding, on the other hand, the encoding/decoding model proposed that the audience is free to agree with this 'message', to disagree with it or to choose a middle ground, depending on the politics of the message and on the class relation of the audience in relation to it.

Reading process

The reading process (decoding) was under-theorised in encoding/decoding. The appropriateness and meaning of the researcher's reading was unquestioned. The viewer's 'reading' was not interpreted. It is likely that O'Sullivan et al.'s (1983: 238) definition of 'text' was considered acceptable at the time.

> **text/message*** These two terms are frequently used interchangeably, and refer to a signifying structure composed of signs and codes which is essential to communication. *This structure can take a wide variety of forms, such as speech, writing, film, dress, car styling, gesture, and so on.
> (O'Sullivan et al. 1983: 238)

O'Sullivan et al. included no entries for 'reading', 'decoding', 'interpretation' among the key concepts in communication they define. They understood text and message as interchangeable terms which 'refer to a signifying structure composed of signs and codes'. Reading was discussed endlessly, but never as a viewer activity of significance. The problem with this definition for encoding/decoding is most evident when we ask for whom the message/text/'programme as "meaningful" discourse' was thought to be 'meaningful'. Clearly it cannot be the audience. Given the linear sequence of the model, the audience can interact with this discourse to incorporate it into their frameworks of knowledge only after it has been deemed 'meaningful'. To be 'meaningful discourse' the programme had to be produced by one of two different groups: the production team or the academic researcher, or both. The production team created the programme as 'televisual discourse'; the researcher created it as the ideological product of the institutions of television. But when a viewer is interviewed, is he or she likely to be speaking about either of these 'programmes'? In encoding/decoding, no room was made for the viewer's text.

An alternative account of reading, related to the encoding/decoding position, has been proposed by Sless (1986). Writing from a communication perspective, Sless preferred to retain a commitment to the relevance of the intentions of the sender/author, and suggested that the reader actively constructs the author's position in order to position him/herself in relation to it. In Sless's terms, both production team and researcher are producing 'author's texts' (the text the author intended) in the encoding/decoding model. Yet we are still left wondering why these accounts of the 'author's intentions should be any more acceptable than the readings by the viewers. Sless's proposition that there is an orientating author's text inductively constructed by the reader/viewer does not resolve the variability of the author's 'message'. The two texts it compared are both generated by the reader/viewer – (i) the viewer's account of what the programme was meant to be and (ii) the viewer's account of what the programme was. These two texts become the field where the text is made. While Sless displaced the researcher's text, he replaced it with an even more variable concept – the viewer's account of the author's intentions. Nor did he establish how the author's 'message' is deducible and whether it varies according to the reader. Belief in the determinacy of the message, in its predictability given the structures of production and frameworks of knowledge which produced it, suggested its amenability to semiotic and discourse analysis and empowered it as discursive intervention. Belief in the 'message' was necessary for ideology to be demonstrated using signs and codes.

The 'programme as "meaningful" discourse' called into play other concepts relevant to the audience–text relation. For example, Barthes's distinction between 'work' and 'text' usefully draws attention to the instrumental understanding of text used in encoding/decoding (Barthes 1977: 155–64). Barthes idealised 'the Text' as a new field of study, and celebrated its non-determinacy. As an object, the Text implied engagement/ involvement. In Barthes's view 'Text' is plural. It is inspired by a metaphor of network, and exists in a relation of symbiosis with the reader – its pleasure depends on the non-separability of reader and text. The text is Text in its interplay with its writer/readers. Barthes prefigured de Certeau's (1984: introduction) account of the vitalism of writing–reading in everyday life. Text is the interaction which produces culture. It is human life. As Barthes put it

> ...the discourse on the Text should itself be nothing other than text, research, textual activity, since the Text is that social space which leaves no language safe outside, nor any subject of the enunciation in position as judge, master, analyst, confessor, decoder. The theory of Text can coincide only with a practice of writing.

> (Barthes 1977: 164)

From the perspective of encoding/decoding, 'textual activity' is the enigmatic term here. To this term encoding/decoding gave a mass audience perspective, but in so doing the terms 'text' and 'research' were precipitated into the separate boxes of 'sender' and 'message'. Barthes's understanding of 'text' was pinned to an equivalence with 'the sender' (or at best the 'structures of production') and his understanding of the 'research' dimension of Text was reduced to the researcher's analysis of the 'message as meaningful discourse'. Nevertheless, because of the ways semiotics was articulated in encoding/decoding, a theory of writing was ambiguously entwined with a theory of mass communication. The 'programme as "meaningful" discourse' encouraged an understanding of text as signifier, as a polysemic entity, but not as 'textual activity'.

Televisual sign – televisual message

Hall's description of the complexity of the televisual sign seems in retrospect most concerned to delineate the parameters of the television programme as 'work'. The encoding/decoding proposal for the formal analysis of the televisual sign combined 'two types of discourse, visual and aural' (Hall 1980a: 131). Hall argued that the visual discourse of television 'is an iconic sign' which acts to 'naturalise' the televisual message, to reproduce in the viewer the (illusion) of the conditions of perception occurring at the televisual event. Two important points about the visual discourse of television are made here. The first was that 'visual signs' are' 'coded signs'. As Hall put it:

> Discursive 'knowledge' is the product not of the transparent representa-
> tion of the 'real' in language but of the articulation of language on real
> relations and conditions. Thus there is no intelligible discourse without
> the operation of a code. Iconic signs are therefore coded signs too – even
> if the codes here work differently from those of other signs. There is no
> degree zero in language. Naturalism and 'realism' – the apparent fidelity
> of the representation of the thing or concept represented – is the result,
> the effect, of a certain specific articulation of language on the 'real'. It is
> the result of a discursive practice.
>
> (Hall 1980a: 131–2)

And secondly, that even though visual signs may 'appear not to be constructed', the very 'naturalism' of such signs bears testimony to the type of coding in operation:

> Simple visual signs appear to have achieved a 'near-universality' in this
> sense: though evidence remains that even apparently 'natural' visual
> codes are culture-specific. However, this does not mean that no codes
> have intervened; rather, that the codes have been profoundly naturalized.
> The operation of naturalized codes reveals not the transparency and
> 'naturalness' of language but the depth, the habituation and the near-
> universality of the codes in use.
>
> (Hall 1980a: 132)

Visual signs were considered both 'coded' and 'naturalized', constructed to ensure that what is seen and heard on television 'makes sense'. The aural codes of television seem to have been equated with the written script, with little concern for the difference between an indexical code of sounds, and language (cf. Guiraud 1975). This underestimation of the contribution of sound, sound effects and music in the construction of televisual discourse, as well as the interaction between visual and aural codes, resulted in an oversimplified project for the textual analysis required by the encoding/decoding model. The lack of specificity about the ways in which the term 'code' is used, and the elision of verbal and non-verbal codes, indicate points of weakness in the model. More importantly, by approaching the television programme as 'work' rather than 'text', the pleasure of the text was compromised – the reason why, perhaps, so many of the 'cultural studies audience experiment' projects tried to recover 'textual pleasure' in their research design.

At the level of connotation the televisual sign was believed to acquire its full ideological value – 'appear[s] to be open to articulation with wider ideological discourses and meanings' (1980a: 133). While the televisual sign was proposed as 'structured in dominance' and so taken to represent the interests of the dominant cultural order, it was through connotation that connection with 'the wider universe of ideologies in a society' was thought to occur, and that the sign became 'meaningful discourse'. In other words the televisual sign was considered to be constructed in 'dominant' ideology at the level of denotation. The popular television text was a 'closed' text, in the sense suggested by Eco (1979: 8),[7] in that at the denotational level it seems straightforward, 'natural', unexceptional – except that it works with an 'open project of the reader'. At the level of connotation, the text was 'open', available to all as a site for the projection of the personal as interaction with the generic. Such connotational 'openness' is highly significant because:

> it is at the connotative level of the sign that situational ideologies alter and transform signification. At this level we can see more clearly the active intervention of ideologies in and on discourse: here, the sign is open to new accentuations and, in Volosinov's terms, enters fully into the struggle over meanings – the class struggle in language.
>
> (Hall 1980a: 133)

The 'openness' of the televisual sign at its connotative level signalled its ideological significance in the class struggle, situated it in the struggle between discourses, the struggle for the hearts and minds of the people, and justified it as a proper object of study.

I suggested earlier that the encoding/decoding model was both prescriptive and methodological and that at the level of method the model was problematic. The televisual sign was identified as complex, as made up of visual and verbal codes. But in pragmatic terms little guidance as to what counted as a 'televisual sign' was provided. It could have been the programme, an episode of the programme, a segment within a programme or the whole evening's viewing. All vie for consideration. While it is possible to claim that the choice of 'sign' is a matter for the researcher, the methodological problem does not disappear with this sleight of hand. The verbal text of a television programme can be transcribed, written out, pored over and analysed, treated as a written text, but the visual text cannot be reduced to a series of still photographs. The verbal and visual texts share little analytical equivalence, they are as symbiotically linked as the audience is to the text. Like film, the televisual text lives in the moment(s) of its broadcasting (or viewing). The televisual sign possesses such a degree of visual complexity that the method of analysing the sign by its verbal and visual codes, and of analysing the operation of codes by examining the denotation and connotations of the signs, seems extremely inadequate. Some 'meta-code', capable of linking the visual and verbal codes, or even an 'audio-visual' code seemed called for. But then, perhaps the problem was, as Corner (1980) has suggested, that the concepts, 'sign' and 'code' were being called on inappropriately, and to do more work than was possible. 'Code' seems now to have been replaced by 'discourse' as the means of tracing ideological thought. It is interesting in this regard, that Brunsdon and Morley (1978) felt they had no option but to ignore the visual codes of *Nationwide* and analysed only its verbal codes. The very limited definition of text used in the encoding/decoding model, and mostly ignored by the research that followed limited the overall feasibility of the model.

The variability of interpretation

The difference of encoding/decoding from 'sender–message–receiver' was addressed by Eco's (1986b) explanation of the 'variability of interpretation of the television message':

> The mass communication universe is full of these discordant interpreta-
> tions; I would say that variability of interpretation is the constant law of
> mass communications. The messages set out from the Source and arrive
> in distinct sociological situations, where different codes operate. For a
> Milanese bank clerk a TV ad for a refrigerator represents a stimulus to
> buy, but for a peasant in Calabria the same image means the confirmation
> of a world of prosperity that doesn't belong to him and that he must
> conquer. This is why I believe TV advertising in depressed countries
> functions as a revolutionary message.
>
> (Eco 1986b: 141)

The emphasis on the 'variability of interpretation' in Eco's work diverged sharply from the perspective of the sender–message–receiver model in the very moment of his affirmation of it. In contrast to the encoding/decoding perspective, Eco had brought the chain of communication suddenly into focus, but visualised it from the 'receiver's' perspective. He recognised as integral to the interpretive work of decoding the 'distinct sociological situation' of the 'receiver', the context of reception and its cultural relevance. As I have pointed out in Chapter 1, an active and protagonistic model of the receiver – as politically situated in a context larger than that of the media and its messages – was substituted for the managerially appropriate consumerist model. The politics and national significance of the consumerist model was not examined. On the contrary, Eco attempted to recast the model in a more familiar European political context – that of the class struggle. Consumerism is a regime available to the employed and to the wealthy, but it ignores those disenfranchised by their lack of spending power. It was as though consumerism could make sense in a European context only when situated within a European class structure.

Role of the researcher

The development of a decoding perspective also defamiliarised the role of the researcher, implying a commitment to self-reflexivity in regard to the cultural difference between researcher and researched. By accepting that variability of interpretation occurs, cultural difference could be accepted as an indication not of stupidity or ignorance on the part of the audience, but as an indication of diversity. In the early days, the researcher took on a rather patronising role, usually (Willis 1978) but not always (Hebdige (1979) on research as bricolage) with the supposed interests of the subculture at heart. But more was and is required. A patronising researcher may be tolerated by the research participants even though, out of a sense of personal pity or an intuitive understanding of the strategic importance of the project, they comply. The researcher with sensibility, on the other hand, may find the research situation completely intolerable (see Walkerdine 1986). The ethnographic initiative of encoding/decoding demanded a transcultural approach to audience research – an imperative which was not understood at the time. An ethnographic initiative capable of bridging the gap between the culture of the researcher and the audience needs informants and collaborators and requires negotiation and bargaining over the ideas discussed and described.

This is the dark side, the difficult terrain encountered once reception is approached from the audience's perspective. In the formulation of the old sender–message–receiver model, the researcher occupied a limited number of infinitely more comfortable role possibilities. If the researcher interrogated the technological proficiency of the communication chain, the 'sender' and 'receiver' would be machines, and encoding and decoding mechanical activities. The activity of machines could be empirically tested by output, measured, and observed. However, at the semantic level, an identification of 'sender' and researcher had always been assumed. The researcher was thought of as the servant or proxy of the sender, someone who explained what was right or wrong with the message through consultation with the recipients. In the development of reception the researcher was identified with the 'receiver' – an identification unfortunately invalidated not so much by the practice of research as by the act of analysis. At some point the researcher has to write, pronounce, speak, define, categorise, and limit the researched other. An assumption of identity of researcher and researched was attractive to researchers who, like Buckingham and Tulloch, were trained in literary analysis and the sociology of culture because criticism and reading were considered the same activity. But in the context of literary criticism, reading was not envisaged as part of the sender–message–receiver model. The problem of the role of the researcher for the cultural studies audience experiment appears and reappears as a significant theoretical and methodological motif.

While recognising the audience as already discursively structured appeared to assist research of the audience and its discursive activities, the explanation of that structuring should be questioned. Hall suggested the interplay of three codes of reception: the dominant, negotiated and oppositional codes. These positions originated from Frank Parkin's (1971: 79–102) proposition that dominant, subordinate and radical value systems explain the acceptance in Western societies of class inequality by those adversely affected by it. Hall, by contrast, wanted to know why people accept as commonsense ideas and meanings which are manifestly not in their interests. The projects are related but by no means identical. While adopting Parkin's conceptualisation justified the idea of a discursive structuring of the audience, I believe the superficiality of this appropriation actually under mined the possibility of a theory of structuration.

Parkin's argument was that while the dominant value system finds adherents throughout the social structure, the subordinate and radical value systems originate in working-class communities and the mass political party based on the subordinate class respectively. Social location, according to Parkin is therefore a broad indicator only of where people adhering to the subordinate and radical meaning systems may be located within the social structure. He made it clear that class and other demographic variables are no guarantee of adherence to meaning systems, since members of the subordinate classes frequently adhere to the dominant value system and construct either deferential or aspirational interpretations of it in order to lessen the burden of their subordinate status within it. Clearly for Parkin, the three value systems are simultaneously shared social knowledge and competing discourses within the social formation. While Parkin's 'value systems' are determined by the social structure, his description of adherence to them suggested a freedom of choice, of political choice only, consistent with consumerist definitions of the individual. In other words, Parkin worked with a definition of the historical subject which is individualist rather than culturalist. For Parkin, 'individuals' chose freely among available discourses on the basis of aspirations and needs. Choices were assumed to be made 'rationally', after careful analysis of all available data, rather than as an expression of socio-cultural positioning. Choices resulted from 'logical' appraisal of where self-interest lies. The theory was not a theory of discourse but political values and decision-making, and in particular it was a theory of the limits on such decision-making. In Parkin's formulation, the 'sovereign individual of capitalism' (see Abercrombie et al. 1986), free, active, rational, self-motivated and male, chooses among diverse interpretations of his world. 'Individuals', in Parkin's sense, were not discursively structured. They were citizens exercising their freedom to act with their own class or against it.

Hall's appropriation of Parkin jeopardised the ground gained in the formulation of the relationship between discourses and subjectivity, and so of the relation of people to their culture. Parkin's 'value systems', the rationalisations produced to explain social inequality by major political parties, were transformed into decoding positions for the television message as 'meaningful discourse'. The dominant-hegemonic position was proposed to operate through the dominant code, the negotiated position through the negotiated code etc. While this formulation might have worked to demonstrate that there is no necessary correspondence between encoding and decoding, it raised other problems such as what was meant by the term 'code' (see Corner 1980), and how these 'audience' codes differ from those of the televisual sign. The links between 'codes', 'discourses' and 'language' are particularly unclear, and from a methodological point of view, unspecified by either the model or the essay which explained it. However, in suggesting that audiences are already structured in dominance, positioned in relation to the meaningful discourse of the media according to social location and experience of social practice, the possibility was created for researching audiences as discursive formations. The relevance of the 'individual' for cultural studies audience research was questioned. Hall's work on 'decoding' made it possible for us to conceptualise audiences as communities existing within social/discursive formations, and 'speaking' their experiences, including media experiences, from that positioning.

The encoding/decoding model suggested a way to research ideology in the audience by proposing that the audience is already 'structured in discourse'. The model set an agenda which looked beyond television programmes. It encompassed in addition structures of production and of reception, not as separate and isolated research endeavours but as integral dimensions of the one project. The television programme was considered a site where meaningful social and political 'conversation' occurs. This is to move beyond the notion of 'effects' to a different vision of mass communication – a vision centrally concerned with contestation over meaning, specifically political conflict. As Tolson suggested, it constructs a narrative of 'culture in crisis', demonstrated in a 'discourse of social commentary' (Tolson 1986: 148). The role of the researcher implicitly advocated was that of commentator or news anchorman.

NOTES

1 Morley (1980: 166) referenced a CCCS mimeo called 'Encoding and Decoding the TV Message' as 1973. I have used the more readily available 'Encoding/decoding'

version, Chapter 10, in Hall, Hobson, Lowe and Willis (1980) *Culture, Media, Language.*

2 Though Hebdige (1975: 135–53) and Chambers (1975: 157–66) did focus on music as a medium for the expression of cultural and subcultural experience (Hall and Jefferson 1975).

3 Atkinson (1990: 28) has noted that the background as a journalist of Robert Park influenced the early practice of sociology at Chicago. British researchers had an even older example in Henry Mayhew, a nineteenth-century journalist and social reformer (Bennett 1981).

4 Much later, this separation was explained by Fiske as two separate economies – the financial and the cultural economies of the media.

5 The use of sender–message–receiver in behavioural social psychology is well known.

6 In *The Predicament of Culture*, James Clifford (1986) deals with the problem of ethnography as cultural translation and its requirements for collaboration and negotiation with participants (see also Chapter 6).

7 It is noted that Fiske (1982: 85–6) uses the term 'closed text' differently, referring directly to what Eco defines as the 'project of the reader'.

Chapter 3

Key concepts and alternative rallying points

The problem Althusserian theory poses for the concept of art is as follows: what is the relation between aesthetic practice and ideological practice? Or, more narrowly, what is the concept of art in the theory of historical materialism?

(Sprinker 1987: 269)

Althusser's innovation, and his break with a classical aesthetics of representation, is to argue that the basis of identification and affective behaviour in audiences is not primarily psychological but social and ideological.

(Sprinker 1987: 279–80)

Stuart Hall's paper, 'Cultural studies: two paradigms' (Hall 1980b), offers a useful overview of the key concepts and 'alternative rallying points' in general contention within the field when the search for a 'new audience research' was under way. In this chapter the definition of the emerging field, British cultural studies, offered by Hall is reconsidered. Some aspects of the philosophy of its delineation have been dealt with by others (Hardt 1992; Grossberg 1988). My focus is on the implications of Hall's evaluations of theory for the cultural studies audience initiative because researchers (as opposed to theoreticians) frequently find themselves caught in a web of compromise fashioned at the intersection of philosophical desire and the pragmatic demands of dealing with people in research contexts. In the case of the cultural studies audience research, this nexus was intensified because the pragmatic demands of researching people were combined with the theoretical problems generated by television as text. Unfortunately, direct engagement with textual theory relevant to the televisual text is not a feature of the research. As was usual for the time, Hall ignored the question in the 'two paradigms' review article. Semiotics was considered capable of unlocking the ideological intentionality of all texts. As a result, an opportunity to recognise the relevance of the early cultural studies audience research as essentially concerned with textual Realpolitik was missed.

Because definitions and delineation of a field have such a strong influence on research design, the absence of attention to problems of 'textuality' in the definition of cultural studies left room for 'textual' experimentation. The same cannot be said for the confusion apparent over related concepts like discourse and ideology. As we will see, the dismissal of the anti-foundational implications of Foucault's archaeologies of knowledge, and the expressed preference for an 'Althusserian' certainty about good and evil, right and wrong, in the early definitions of British cultural studies, reinforced an immovable class-based understanding of the person, which failed to anticipate the fluidity, variability, breadth or scope of the discursive engagements people encounter as part of the contemporary metropolitan experience. Definitional articles like 'two paradigms' now constitute a guide to the contextual development of the research.

A colonising consensus

In 1980, Stuart Hall published a position paper for British cultural studies called 'Cultural studies: two paradigms' (1980b), which explored the development of (British) cultural studies, from its mid-1950s emergence in the work of Hoggart, Williams and Thompson, through its engagement with the European 'structuralisms', to an emerging 'best' approach for cultural studies in the 1980s.

> I have said enough to indicate that, in my view, the line in cultural studies which has attempted to *think forwards* from the best elements in the structuralist and culturalist enterprises, by way of some of the concepts elaborated in Gramsci's work, comes closest to meeting the requirements of a field of study.
>
> (Hall 1980b: 72)

The article offered guidance and advice on how the range of ideas and theories in contention in the field should be approached and understood. In this sense it was strongly prescriptive and is worthy of re-consideration as its 'moment' passes and as new directions develop.

Significantly, American academic traditions were not mentioned in this article. Perhaps they were considered irrelevant for the emergence of what, in Britain, was perceived as the consolidation of the cultural studies tradition. Perhaps they were 'the other' against which this Anglo-European perspective defined itself. Perhaps the change in British identity from imperial power to member of the European community is reflected in the narrowness of the agenda set by the article, which leaves no room to register the intensity of links between European and American scholars. In addition, perhaps the inadmissibility in this article of colonial or feminist perspectives should alert us to the complexity of the changes then shaping early Thatcherite Britain. As immigration from former colonies escalated, and as the British government began to divest the former colonies of any remaining trade or immigration benefits of that status, the implications of re-thinking British identity in the context of membership of the European Community began to be experienced.

In this context, British cultural studies was in imperialising mode; a last attempt perhaps at academic empire building in the New World before the coming of a new European solidarity and a different kind of 'New World Order'. As the development of new academic disciplines began to be restrained in Britain by the impact of Thatcher's economic rationalism on university education, British academics packed their bags and travelled to Australia in the early 1980s and to the United States in the mid to late 1980s (cf. Turner 1993: Introduction). In this context, the new British cultural studies became the academic commodity of the moment for New World academics, like myself. In this context, articles like 'Encoding/decoding' and 'Cultural studies: two paradigms' were ascribed an unexpected, virtually definitional authority. The ideas proposed in these articles became ways of describing what was and what was not included in this last canon. They became part of a disciplining scholarship in relation to which, as Turner has described, so much Australian (and other colonial) academic work was obliged to offer an account of itself.

Where encoding/decoding was an attempt 'to think both the specificity of different practices and the forms of the articulated unity they constitute' (Hall 1980b: 72), the 'two paradigms' article advocated a rationale for accepting or rejecting 'European' ideas. It is important as a work of theoretical appropriation and delineation because, in its reading in the New World, it became a means to temper the nascent enthusiasm for the work of French philosophers like Foucault and Derrida, and to re-assert a British (and interestingly male) dominance in compromise which acknowledged, but ultimately refused, the brilliance of the French perspective.[1] The rejection of Foucault circumvented the need to read French philosophy or to explore its most difficult but compelling insights. The 'two paradigms' article constructed an Anglo-European common ground and identified certain 'alternative rallying points' as out of bounds – rallying points like Lacanian psychoanalysis (and its associated feminist and aesthetic developments), the political economy of the media, and Foucault's anti-foundationalism.

Re-reading the 'two paradigms' article in the 1990s, it seems remarkable that such exclusions were advocated. The 'reasonableness' of the exclusions depended on acceptance of a broader agenda, the study of culture and ideology, as the purpose of cultural studies. In the 1990s this seems a too narrow agenda, especially as it rested on the absolute credibility attributed to Althusser and Gramsci. One can argue that the theoretical directions advocated had run their course by the time Hall was writing and required a development like British cultural studies in and through which to continue. In addition, the exclusions recommended in the 'two paradigms' agenda prematurely closed off the development of the early cultural studies audience research from theoretical insights informed by or critical of Foucault's work, new feminist and literary theory, or insights from other disciplines, like anthropology, archaeology or history.

Culturalism

The key concepts which informed the British cultural studies appropriation of its 'two paradigms' are those which accelerated recognition of the centrality of culture,[2] recognition of the definitional density of the term, and an increasing sophistication in cultural research technique associated with such definition. In popularising the work of Hoggart and Williams, Hall ensured that their insights about cultural process were shared with a new generation of scholars. The perspective challenged traditional ideas of 'communication' as intention and added an expressive dimension to it.

It is 'tempting, but excessive', as Andrew Tolson has commented, to detect something akin to a search for the classic realist novel in the culturalist project, especially those examples that use ethnography and focus on cultural crises (Tolson 1986: 150). It seems certain that in the culturalist project, the prototypical cultural form was the novel. In Williams' work, for example, definitions of culture were developed to assist his project of explaining the significance and history of the novel.[3] A feature of Williams' approach was its interdisciplinarity, combining sociology with literary theory and vice versa – to produce a sociology of culture. Williams identified the community in the text, and analysed literature to provide social commentary – about the organic realities of everyday life, but also to explain the quality of everyday life from the texts it produces. The term 'culturalism' recognised the importance placed on culture and experience as explanations of cultural forms, and on the culturing dimension of social reproduction, as used by Williams and Hoggart. As Williams described it, culturalism is a term used 'to indicate a methodological contrast with structuralism in social analysis' (Williams 1985a: 93). That methodological contrast is most evident in the important role attributed to 'experience' in cultural explanation. Each is an evocation of the lived experiences of the historical subject, rather than information about, or a measure of, the novelist. British cultural studies seized on and developed a sociology of culture informed by a desire to explain the literary text.

In culturalism, then, culture was to be demonstrated in 'experience', just as 'experience' was demonstrated in cultural forms like the novel. From such a perspective, ethnographic observation can be seen to be an essential ingredient in the culturalist enterprise, not just as authentication, but importantly as documentation. Moreover, as Hall noted, Williams actually abolished any distinction between 'culture' and 'not-culture' by his interpretation of experience as 'real material practice-in-general' (Hall 1980b: 63), thereby greatly increasing the range of material relevant to explanation of the forces at work in a novel. Yet perhaps, as Hunter (1993:

144–55) has argued, such a culture–nature dialectic is an unnecessarily expansive generalisation for the less than praiseworthy task of shoring up the position of the cultural critic as omniscient 'intellectual', examining contemporary trends and pronouncing their meaning. In Hall's account, however, culturalism proposed that 'experience was the ground – the terrain of "the lived" – where consciousness and conditions intersected, structuralism insisted that "experience" could not, by definition, be the ground of anything' (1980b: 66). For 'experience' to be meaningful, it has to be lived 'in and through the categories, classifications and frameworks of the culture'. In other words, 'experience' was thought of as the place where culture and nature meet. It was the 'test' of culture – the site where cultural categories, classifications and frameworks were enacted in engagement with nature. Everyday life was, in this narrow sense, a 'natural' phenomenon. Everyday life was 'nature', but its process was 'culture'.

Hall valued the 'culturalist' paradigm for its recognition of the role of 'culture' in historical transformation; that the realm of culture is not cut off from the on-going life and work of a society, as in elitist definitions, but is integrally and vitally connected to it. Such a stance demanded both a contextual approach to cultural production and a commitment to studying the relations of production 'actively, seeing all activities as particular and contemporary forms of human energy' (1980b: 59). Culture then became 'social process', and the study of culture involved grasping 'how the interactions between all these practices and patterns are lived and experienced as a whole, in any particular period' (1980b: 60).

Among the objects of cultural study were included explorations of the 'structure of feeling', the experiential dimension of the structures of relations which form the social totality. In relation to the cultural studies audience research, this emphasis focused on television texts/programmes which are extremely popular, at least in the sense of rating highly and in some senses capturing the public imagination – for example *Crossroads* was studied at the time of a controversy; *Dallas, A Country Practice* and *EastEnders* at the height of their popularity (see Chapter 4). Popularity was treated as a sort of 'crisis of culture', a significant cultural moment, a characteristic of cultural studies again noted by Tolson (1986: 148). The cultural form was always evidence of something else – something other than itself, of the social process which produced it.

A second key understanding was the rejection of the determining base– determined superstructure theory, especially when articulated as economic determinism. The culturalists replaced it with 'the dialectic between social consciousness and social being' (1980b: 63), which accords 'experience' an authenticating position in any cultural analysis. This perspective had underpinned cultural and subcultural research in Britain, and continued to influence the particular way the cultural studies audience research approached television viewers – the predilection for group or individual interviews of a semi- or un-scheduled nature – or in, for example, Hobson's case (see Chapter 4), of sitting observing and discussing with women viewers. In this sense, television viewing was considered a 'way of being', a dimension of everyday life – like tea-time or bedtime – almost as part of the 'un-natural order' of everyday life.

The emphasis on the 'sense of cultural totality', understood as a living evocation of the social formation, lived and demonstrated in social praxis, was yet another key concept of British culturalism. The vision was of culture as perpetual development: as development creating distinctions, residues and differences, then appropriating and re-incorporating the left-overs to reproduce itself (and new 'others') once again. This 'cultural totality' is imagined as a self-perpetuating organism-like vortex, sucking in emerging ideas, and excreting residues in the process of maintaining itself. The residues, in turn, transform themselves into and are experienced as oppositional culture, waiting to be devoured, reappropriated by social formations hungry for domination.

Such consensus on 'cultural totality' is now challenged by multi-cultures, which acknowledge other, often multiple, cultures within nations and social formations. For example, in Australia some indigenous Aboriginal associations are now advocating a separate Aboriginal state within 'Australia' – an ethnically rather than territorially bounded self-governing state within the nation. This example, felt initially as 'shocking' only because it requests formal recognition of de-territorialised self-government, invokes other dreams of freedom, like a separate self-governing feminist or religious state within the nation, and dispels forever the power of 'nation' as a way of imagining cultural totality. It should remind us, too, that the 'cultural totality' referenced by (British) cultural studies was an old, nineteenth-century 'sense of cultural totality', which assumed homologies of structure and the commonality of forms 'underlying the most apparently differentiated areas' (Hall 1980b: 64), only because it also assumed racial and territorial equality and/or unity.[4]

The theory of 'cultural totality' resulted in a sort of schizophrenic ambiguity in the cultural studies audience research. While homologies of structure were sought in production, narrative, and audience readings, only the male researchers imagined the audience as a 'totality', as synonymous with 'nation' – within which Morley, for example, mapped demographic difference and the respective distance from the dominating centre. The women researchers sought to explain women audiences, yet offered no account of the relation of women to the mass audience. So the textual research assumed 'cultural totality' while the 'ethnographic' research tolerated or celebrated cultural diversity.

If culture is seen, as it was by the culturalists, as 'threaded through all social practices, and (as) the sum of their inter-relationship', then a strong case can be made for the appropriateness of using 'ethnographic' methods in

studying culture. If it is recognised that 'cultural totality' is an old dream
from the age of mono-cultures, the case for ethnographic method becomes
even stronger, since quantitative methods are designed to rationalise
difference and diversity while ethnography, for all its faults, assumes
difference, and may even encourage or celebrate it.

Two other 'ideals' of 'culturalism' were noted in 'two paradigms'. Both
depend on the assumption of totality. First, Williams' proposition,
influenced by Goldmann, that the 'categories which simultaneously organise
the empirical consciousness of the group, and the imaginative world of the
writer' are 'not individually but collectively created' (Williams 1971, quoted
in Hall 1980b: 61). Second, E. D. P. Thompson's demonstration that the
'unity' of cultural life is characterised by 'struggle and confrontation
between opposed ways of life', particularly between 'dominant, residual and
emergent cultural practices' (Hall 1980b: 61). These understandings
contributed to a consensus that studying culture meant studying the
'relations between elements in a whole way of life'; that the mental structures
which pattern cultural production are collectively, not individually,
authored; and that a patterning of cultural practices develops over time,
which demonstrates the changing nature of culture and points to the
positioning of people in relation to the on-going life of the culture. All affirm
the privileged, 'authenticating' (ibid.: 63) status accorded to 'lived
experience' in culturalism. 'Talking with, observing, participating then
become accepted methods of apprehending the structures of meaning as
"lived"' – the phenomenological approach described by Willis, which
constituted the ethnographic method of cultural studies (Willis 1980: 94).

The structure of feeling

Another key concept which was highly valued by cultural studies and which
depends on the assumption of 'cultural totality' is the 'structure of feeling'.
The 'structure of feeling' was held to express the relationship of texts to the
culture of a period and to the lived culture, since the 'structure of feeling'
was thought to embrace both the empirical consciousness of the group and
the imaginative world of the writer. In Hall's account, the discussion of
'structure of feeling' must be understood in the context of Williams' theory
of 'culture'. As Hall put it:

> The 'culture' is those patterns of organization, those characteristic forms
> of human energy which can be discovered as revealing themselves – in
> 'unexpected identities and correspondences' as well as in 'discontinuities
> of an unexpected kind' (p. 63) – within or underlying *all* social practices.
> The analysis of culture is, then, 'the attempt to discover the nature of the
> organisation which is the complex of these relationships'. It begins with
> 'the discovery of patterns of a characteristic kind'. One will discover

them, not in the art, production, trading, politics, the raising of families, treated as separate activities, but through 'studying a general organisation in a particular example' (p. 61). Analytically one must study the 'relationships between these patterns'. The purpose is to grasp how the interactions between all these practices and patterns are lived and experienced as a whole, in any particular period. This is its 'structure of feeling' (p. 60).

(Hall 1980b: 60–3)

Clearly Williams' 'structure of feeling' had a stronger connotation of 'sensibility' than of 'feeling' about it. It did not need, as Lovell has suggested, to be complemented by a notion of 'structures of sensibility' (Lovell 1983: 45) because the concept, as explained by Williams, already encompassed this possibility. Williams' concept, even in *Culture and Society*, which was first published in 1958 (Williams 1985b: 100), included 'sympathetic observation' and 'imaginative identification'. In *The Long Revolution* (Williams 1975), first published in 1961, the use of 'the structure of feeling' implied a sensitivity to, a sensibility about, appropriate behaviours and outcomes.

The 'structure of feeling' promised the ability to recover the 'felt sense of the quality of life at a particular place and time' (Williams 1975: 63), a sense of the 'lived culture'. Analysis of 'the structure of feeling' was thought of as another way of knowing a culture. It was a mode of knowing that Williams distinguished from the 'social character' and from the 'pattern of culture'. As he described it, the 'structure of feeling' is

as firm and definite as 'structure' suggests, yet it operates in the most delicate and least tangible parts of our activity. In one sense, this structure of feeling is the culture of a period: it is the particular living results of all the elements in the general organisation. And it is in this respect that the arts of a period, taking these to include characteristic approaches and tones in argument, are of major importance...I do not mean that the structure of feeling, any more than the social character, is possessed in the same way by the many individuals in the community. But I think it is a very deep and very wide possession, in all actual communities, precisely because it is on it that communication depends.

(Williams 1975: 65)

Williams demonstrated his method in his analysis of English writing in the 1840s. He outlined how the 'selective tradition' narrowed the range of literature, newspapers, the documents, the institutional developments, and the social and political history generally considered when explaining the period, and asserted instead the importance of the interrelationships between cultural and social institutions in accounting for a literary period. Williams' method explored the relation between 'the social character' and 'the structure of feeling'. The 'social character' was claimed to be a 'valued system of behaviour and attitudes taught both formally and informally' (Williams 1975: 63). The very notion of 'social character', the 'abstract of a social group', was posited as extremely complex, a generalising abstraction which drew on 'other' established, though not dominant, social characters – the aristocratic and the working class. Once again, precursors of society/the mass audience as a structured whole in which dominant, negotiated and oppositional formations co-exist were in evidence. Williams maintained that it is only through the 'study of relations between them that we enter the reality of the whole life' (ibid.: 80). He considered 'the structure of feeling' to conform to the 'dominant social character' by being most strongly 'evident in the dominant productive group' (ibid.: 80). However, in addition to dealing with 'public ideals', 'the structure of feeling' had also to find some way of dealing with their 'omissions and consequences as lived'. Characteristically, Williams turned to the fiction of the time, and in tracing 'the structure of feeling' embedded there discovered the analytical impossibility of differentiating it from the characters, contexts and situations in which the omissions and consequences of public ideals are lived (ibid.: 84–8). An emphasis on 'structure of feeling' is obvious in several of the audience–text studies (see Ang 1985; Tulloch and Moran 1986) though its centrality was displaced as a mode of cultural explanation by being subjected to the requirement to explain consumption. Structure of feeling became a means to the end of explaining consumption – why the texts were considered pleasurable – rather than a way of understanding culture.

The British culturalist projects of Hoggart, Williams and Thompson were elaborated in the 'two paradigms' article with key concepts from the European structuralisms. Firstly, the emphasis on 'determinate conditions' of cultural production was adopted. Rather than reducing the working of culture always to relations between people, the emphasis on 'determinate conditions' demonstrated the complexity of movement between levels of abstraction rather than the diversity of social practices. Hall pointed out that it is crucial that both halves of the dialectic – 'men make history... on the basis of conditions which are not of their making' – be maintained if 'a naive humanism, with its necessary consequences: a voluntaristic and populist political practice' (Hall 1980b: 67) was to be avoided. In the cultural studies audience research the tendency to slip into populist politics is pervasive, and bears testimony to the tendency of audience research to focus on people rather than conditions, or, perhaps more accurately, to deduce the study of conditions from what men are able to say about them. Epistemological abstraction and the authority of experience are not commensurable and it is interesting that, faced with such a choice, cultural studies researchers continue to choose 'experience'. The demand for an account of diversity in terms acceptable to 'the diverse' compromises and evades commitment to abstraction.

The structuralisms were understood to share with culturalism a recognition of the importance of the 'conception of the whole', the 'necessary complexity of the unity of a structure'. For culturalism that unity was demonstrated in praxis, in human activity as such. For the structuralisms, on the other hand, the importance of stressing not the 'homology of practices' but the 'differences between practices' was a more crucial consideration. Where in culturalism, the 'same contradictions appear, homologously reflected in each [human activity]', demonstrating totality or unity through accumulation as it were, structuralism was thought to facilitate the capacity to 'conceptualise the specificity of different practices... without losing its grip on the ensemble which they constitute' (Hall 1980b: 69). In terms of the cultural studies audience research, the structuralist insight became 'encoding' and 'decoding', the 'determinate moments' of televisual discourse and the emphasis on the lack of identity between them. The beginning of the shift to 'diversity' was registered in this emphasis on diversity, but with a certain insouciance, since in this context 'diversity' was always thought to mean structured diversity – such as gender or class inequality. Structural diversity assumes 'totality'.

In the 1990s, however, diversity can be based on differences valued positively by the oppressed, as occurs in the case of indigenous, ethnic, or religious cultures, which demand greater separation and autonomy from totalising ideals like 'nation'. Such cultures problematise the definition of the boundaries of culture previously assumed to be 'national' as genealogies are ransacked to deliver each personal 'diversity'. National 'totalities' are increasingly mediating agents between international and local allegiances. Nations have become aspects of global diversity in a new 'totality' based on participation in the international consumer society.

A third important aim was to decentre the importance of 'experience' and to place ideology 'at the centre of its conceptual universe'. For Hall, ideology was integral to structuralism, 'without it, the effectivity of "culture" for the reproduction of a particular mode of production cannot be grasped' (1980b: 69). It is hardly surprising that the search for 'ideology' in the range of discursive practices which construct 'televisual discourse' was given high priority by the early audience–text research (see especially Brunsdon and Morley 1978). It is also interesting to notice the sudden displacement of ideology as a central concept in the cultural studies audience research once reception was integrated with production and textual analysis. As will be seen in Chapter 4, 'ideology' is central to Morley's (1980) work, then hardly mentioned (for example, by Hobson), and it is even explicitly avoided by Tulloch and Moran (1986), although it reappears as a quality of the audience in Buckingham. The older culturalist preference for 'experience' over 'discourse' returns like the repressed in the cultural studies audience research, bearing testimony to the preference among British researchers for the 'culturalist' stance, and creating one of the serious shortcomings of the approach as cultural criticism.

Combining the two paradigms

The loss of 'ideology' from the conceptual universe referenced by the audience–text researchers was predictable once the two paradigms of cultural studies were combined. Looking back, it is clear that what began as an attempt by researchers firmly grounded within culturalist traditions to organise the study of television and culture around the concept of ideology would be transformed by the popularity of the medium and its institutional organisation into an explanation of audience participation in the production of the text. What is surprising is that the theoretical harbingers of this shift, evident in Fish (1980), and Barthes (1977) and Foucault (1977), to name a few, were not detected by these predominantly British researchers. It may be that the very qualities which made the cultural studies audience researchers samplers of what might be meant by an 'interpretive community' were the same as those that kept the researchers from recognising the meaning of their own work as applied textual research.

While 'ideology' had been a concern for the culturalist paradigm, it was not its central concern because the 'authenticating power and reference of "experience" imposes a barrier between culturalism and a proper conception of "ideology"' (Hall 1980b: 69). The failure of this blueprint for the study of ideology in the audience (the identification of dominant, negotiated and oppositional decoding positions) signalled a retreat to the culturalist position which has had mixed repercussions in its application in audience research (see section on Morley 1980 in Chapter 4). The study of reception and the mode of reception study necessarily privileged the continued invocation of the 'authenticating power' of experience and marginalised 'ideology' (Hall 1980b: 66). The privileged and authenticating role attributed to experience in the culturalist paradigm was counter-posed against the 'categories, classifications and frameworks of the culture' in European structuralism.

The force of this difference is that for the structuralists 'experience' was conceived, not as an authenticating source but as an effect: not as an effect of the real but as an imaginary relation' (ibid.: 66). From such a structuralist perspective it is obvious that talking to people about their viewing experiences might be expected to confirm their social location, demonstrate the work of their society and culture on them, but not constitute evidence of the institutional conjunctures in which they are placed. Experience can only demonstrate already assumed social relations. The culturalists, by contrast, assumed that by documenting people's experiences, the real relations existing within society would be discovered. In the cultural studies audience research, an assumption of 'research as confirmation' is evident in the suggestion that the audience was already discursively structured, while maintaining the value of actually talking to people about their television experiences. These two accounts of culture and experience are not commensurable and it is not surprising that faced with the demands of real research, the quest for ideology was dropped.

Several other points of divergence between the two paradigms mentioned by Hall are worth noting as a summary of the theoretical and methodological ideas under debate at the time and which affected the practice of cultural studies audience research by reinforcing the preference for culturalist methods:

- the conception of 'men' as bearers of the structures that speak and place them, versus men as active agents in the making of their own history;
- the emphasis on a structural rather than an historical 'logic';
- the pre-occupation with the constitution – in theory – of a non-ideological scientific discourse;
- the privileging of conceptual work and of theory as guaranteed (see Hall 1980b: 66).

The first of these divergences concerned the importance attached to experience. The two paradigms define the historical subject differently. They stress opposite poles of the dialectic mentioned earlier – 'men make history... on the basis of conditions which are not of their making' (Hall 1980b: 67). Where culturalism began with 'men', structuralism began with the 'conditions'. Yet this difference in emphasis suggests, in turn, a difference in definitions of the nature of human agency. For culturalism, the historical subject was a living, breathing, thinking, acting person, an agent acting within an historically defined set of conditions. The historical subject was closer to 'the individual'. For structuralism, the agency of the historical subject was always an example of something else: the historical subject and the behaviour of the historical subject were signs of the social structure, of the culture, of the conflicts of interests legitimated by the social structure, etc. From a British perspective, culturalism was superficially and intuitively more appealing, but possessed its own inconsistency – it held on to individualism while stressing the importance of conditions. For culturalism, agency was action borne of self-interest (as demonstrated by the ease with which Hall accommodated Parkin's views on socio-cultural positioning). For a British researcher, the structuralist perspective must have seemed abstract, bloodless, passionless, and less intuitively appealing because it placed the researcher at one remove from the action. The 'structuralist' researcher was the cultural anthropologist: necessarily observer, voyeur, detached, the product of another culture, the embodiment of the power and knowledge structures which subordinate and enslave the historical subject. By contrast, the 'culturalist' researcher is the ethnographer: Malinowski, Mead, Willis –

in the field, interacting, still detached, still an outsider, but trying hard to belong.

Other divergences followed. For the structuralisms, the logic used to explain the historical subject was located in the social structure rather than in personal and socio-cultural histories, whereas for culturalism the historical subject was believed to be able to account adequately for his or her actions – verbally. The structuralist researcher, as scientist, placed himself beyond the structures which bind the historical subject, so establishing conceptual and theoretical work as beyond question, beyond charges of relativism, and beyond the necessity to conform to the rules of the structures theorised. Such privileging of the conceptual and theoretical work of the researcher suggested an unjustifiable and insupportable confidence in the 'scientificity' of semiotics and other structuralist methods.

The combination of the two seminal paradigms of cultural studies foregrounded the research problems and theoretical concerns of the empirical research effort. The preference for 'ethnographic' methods stemmed from the authenticating position attributed to experience in the culturalist paradigm. The application of discourse analysis to audience research originated from an attempt to define a structuralist method for researching people as audiences, in a way which maintained the notion of an historically-determinate social subject even while invoking theoretical work which obviously 'decentred' the subject. The importance of the 'text'/ television programme as bearer of the meaningful discourse of television was recognised in two different ways: either 'structurally' – the text being read using semiotics; or 'culturally' – the lived experiences of the production personnel and their contributions to the meaning system of the programme being observed and catalogued. In regard to the structures of production and of the televisual message, either structuralist or culturalist strategies are used. The combination of the two paradigms in practice offered two radically different sets of research methods and, as will be demonstrated, researchers tended to choose between them on pragmatic rather than theoretically justified grounds. The challenge offered by the two paradigms was less to circumscribe and supersede the old, than to generate new research initiatives.

The 'alternative rallying points'

Hall completed the 'two paradigms' essay by outlining his objections to three 'alternative rallying points' which strayed from the cultural studies project – Lacanian psychoanalysis, the political economy of culture and the epistemological hiatus posed by the work of Foucault. It is interesting that of these three rallying points (a) Lacanian psychoanalysis has proved its resilience, especially in the work of feminist writers, (b) political economy of culture after almost disappearing from the media studies/cultural studies agenda is now making a significant return in studies of global entertainment industries and information flows, and (c) Foucauldian anti-foundationalism continues to provide a source of renewal and re-evaluation within disciplines related to cultural studies such as anthropology (Clifford and Marcus 1986; Marcus and Fischer 1986) and archaeology (Hodder 1986).

Lacanian psychoanalysis

The problem for British theorists with Lacanian psychoanalysis was its unashamed decentring of 'the subject', which was believed tantamount to 'dismantling the whole of the social processes of particular modes of production and social formations, and reconstituting them exclusively at the level of unconscious psychoanalytic processes' (Hall 1980b: 70). The limitations of a theory based in the study of unconscious processes are obvious, yet Hall's dismissal of the contribution of psychoanalysis (discussed in no other context in the essay) ignored an important contribution to researching people as audiences by feminist researchers. This was the attempt to explain 'the transactions between the episodes of the private history and the public history' (Gilbert Ryle, quoted in Burgin et al. 1986: 1) by creating an imaginary space, 'the space between perception and consciousness' (Burgin et al. 1986: 2). The psychoanalytic work addressed the psycho-dynamics of the relation between women and the fantasy worlds of popular cultural texts (especially those derived from melodrama), pleasure in the text itself, and the pleasure of experiencing positions for engagement structured within the text (Kuhn 1987). It developed a politics of representation. The role of desire in maintaining this power structure is a crucially significant issue for women, one appropriately addressed at a psychoanalytic level, even though the relation between 'women' and 'woman' (see de Lauretis 1984: 5, 6) remains problematic.

Psychoanalytic and feminist preoccupations continue to set the pace in cultural studies, most obviously perhaps in the tendency to choose to study women's genres and in the preoccupation with explaining the television soap opera as melodrama. It is also obvious in the greater importance attached to explanations which address the definition of personal identity.[5] Discussing this sort of work as the displacement of social processes by unconscious psychoanalytic ones suggests a failure to comprehend the possibility that the historical subject may engage in different modes of 'experience' simultaneously, and to even grant the possibility that unconscious, inarticulable complexities may confound the desire and ability to speak or act.

STAFFORDSHIRE
UNIVERSITY
LIBRARY

Political economy of the media

The terms of analysis proposed by a more classical 'political economy' of culture were criticised on the grounds that they:

- compromised the hold on the specificity of the effect of the cultural and ideological dimensions of culture;
- posited the economic level as not only a 'necessary' but as a 'sufficient' explanation of cultural and ideological effects;
- focused on the analysis of the commodity form at the expense of 'the carefully established distinctions between different practices';
- confined its deductions to an epochal level of abstraction – the logic of capital.

Such problems were thought to limit the scope for concrete and conjunctural analysis, and to reduce analysis of cultural forms to the 'logic of capitalism', which would affect the way problems of culture and ideology could be thought (Hall 1980b: 70–1).

In spite of such misgivings, an understanding, not only of the nature but also of the meaning of the participation of cultural goods in the 'financial economy', is crucial for knowledge of broadcasting, mass communication, and the development of audience-oriented criticism. The attempted marginalisation of this approach by cultural studies was justified by assertions that the political economy perspective was irredeemably financially determinist. Yet explanations of the meaning and significance of systems of mass communication, of the discursive environments they sustain, of the influence of the financial sector on the nature and shape of media institutions and commodities, is essential to a political economy of the media. As Mattelart et al. have noted:

> It is not the least of the paradoxes we have come across to note the absence of tools enabling us to reply to these vital questions. The studies of semiologists, linguists and psychoanalysts are mostly useless because they refuse to take us through the new industrial materiality of the production of ideas, knowledge and culture. Studies on the social uses and method of production of goods, however, take this process of industrial concretisation so literally that they end up by totally evacuating the symbolic dimension of culture – keystone to systems of power and individual and collective movements of liberation.
>
> (Mattelart et al. 1984: 111)

The distanciation of political economy from cultural studies reflected the emphasis on textual pleasure, the personal and politically dispersed resistances to popular culture, and the insistence on the polysemic nature of texts. Unfortunately forces in cultural studies, pursuing a politics of populism, pushed the political significance of dispersed resistances to a point where there are as many readings as there are audience members and where televisual discourse is an empty abstraction. In much cultural studies audience research, explaining textual pleasure became another way of talking about not just the consumption of media products but also of media effects. Instead of developing a method for analysing discourses in dialogue, the research left a whole range of audience related yet vitally important media problems outside the cultural studies problematic. As Mattelart et al. (1984) pointed out, an account of the 'symbolic dimension of culture' was then lacking from the political economy of culture. Cultural studies has had little to contribute to issues of international cultural politics, and has tended to resort to an unhelpful abstractionism in the face of the use of the symbolic order to maintain oppression. Understanding that 'for a cultural commodity to be popular . . . it must be able to meet the various interests of the people amongst whom it is popular as well as the interests of its producers' (Fiske 1987a: 310) is a long way from explaining the struggle over meaning, and presents little or no advance over most traditional conservative approaches to audience research. In addition, it was in the interests of an academically imperialising British cultural studies to offer an account of political economy of the media, as Fiske did (1987a), which separated the so-called financial and cultural economies and privileged internationally popular texts. Yet the point that Mattelart and others were making was that the political economy of the media can only be properly explained if the cultural significance of mass-produced media commodities is appreciated. The populist politics of British cultural studies, far from amplifying the voice of ordinary people, marginalised indigenous and ethnic cultural production and attempts to develop cultural power through diversity of production.

Feminism and the political economy of popular culture

Some aspects of the political economy perspective found their way into the cultural studies audience research in spite of the fear of creeping economic determinism. This incorporation occurred because of the overlap between the study of 'relations of production' and that of the economic and political contexts which generate such forms, to include what Radway (1984), for example, included as 'the institutional matrix' in her study of the reading of romance novels. Radway began with an historical overview of the publishing and marketing of romance novels as a context within which the form must be understood. A similar use of political economy combined with psycho-analytic insights ('commerce and femininity') was used by Bowlby (1985) to contextualise her reading of the novels of Dreiser, Gissing and Zola. Both Radway and Bowlby usefully integrated the study of political economy of culture with textual analysis and, in Radway's case, the study of reception as well. These examples of feminist writing are about literature, and in that academic arena the importance of accounting for the production and marketing for women by men of popular books, especially the romance genre, has long been recognised (see Jones 1986). The feminist interest in the political economy of culture is also related to the frustration of attempts to produce and popularise alternative women's genres (Williams 1986; Muir 1988; Boot and Glover 1987). Similarly, research about popular music has almost always stressed the importance of the workings of the music industry for the availability of popular music commodities (Frith 1978; Chambers 1985) though the studies of popular music tend to avoid reception in any form other than chart success.

The two 'simultaneous economies'

In the context of such work, it is interesting to step back and reconsider the position presented by Fiske (1987a), that the 'cultural commodity circulates in different though simultaneous economies' – the financial economy and the cultural economy. In the financial economy, the cultural commodity has a monetary value and in the cultural economy its value is measured in 'meanings, pleasures and social identities' (Fiske 1987a: 311). Fiske used this theory of the dual economy to make several points about reception: that audiences are both commodities[6] (i.e. they are sold to advertisers) and producers[7] (they produce meanings, pleasures and social identities) (ibid.: 312); that popular cultural capital 'consists of the meanings and pleasures available to the subordinate to express and promote their interests' (ibid.: 314); that there are 'resistive, alternative ideologies' which sustain the subordinate classes (ibid.: 314); that 'these resistances are not just oppositions to power but are sources of power in their own right'. Fiske's use of the popular cultural economy is similar to Hebdige's (1979) analysis of the ways punks appropriated the paraphernalia, junk and garbage of the dominant culture and subverted the meaning of such objects to their own ends. Yet Hebdige's analysis went further. It pursued the absolute necessity for the dominant culture of buying back these meanings, of transforming them into new commodities (in the financial economy – torn T-shirts, press reports, the Sex Pistols, dog collars and studded belts, etc.). Following the 'cultural totality' line, Hebdige documented a culture hungry for dominance and control of ideas and commodities. His position avoided the 'two economies' theory and explored instead the links between the financial and cultural realms. This offered greater potential to explore the reproduction of mass culture rather than being limited by the low explanatory power of the 'meanings, pleasures and social identities' litany. The 'two economies' theory is low in explanatory power, and offers little by way of an advance over the needs approach of 'uses and gratifications'. We may all sleep better for knowing that lots of resistance to dominant ideas is going on among the 'subordinate classes', but surely we should also note that that resistance is 'safely' contained, from the perspective of the powers controlling the media.

The containment of resistance is the *raison d'être* for the media as socio-cultural technology.

The fear of anti-foundationalism

The last 'alternate' rallying point within cultural studies was Foucault's approach to the study of discourse. It was with Foucault's 'general epistemological position' that issue was taken, particularly with his epistemological method. For Hall, Foucault 'resolutely suspends judgment', 'adopts so thorough-going a scepticism', so finds determinacy or relationship only in 'contingency' that he must be considered 'deeply committed to the necessary non-correspondence of all practices to one another' (Hall 1980b: 71). Foucault certainly did not invoke ideology to explain the relationship between knowledge and power. In fact, the recognition of the complexity, the 'block' which had previously been named 'ideology', the foundational manifestation of the superstructure, was destroyed by the complexity, detail and historical grounding of Foucault's accounts of discourse. As Morris and Patton pointed out:

> Foucault does not approach the question of power in terms of some fundamental principle from which its manifestations may be deduced (neither the Mode of Production, nor the State, nor the Logos), but in terms of the concrete mechanisms and practices through which power is exercised, and in terms of the play of historical forces which orient that exercise.
>
> (Morris and Patton 1979: 8)

In other words, Foucault's position was unacceptable to Hall because of its relativism and because it posited discourse, not ideology, as the fundamental organising principle of human society. Context and situation were the preferred explanatory principles of both the specificity and articulated unity of culture. Foucault's approach to the analysis of discourse is central to an understanding of how the political can be discovered in the everyday. As will become obvious in the following chapters, the ethnographic work of the cultural studies audience research was seriously weakened by lack of an appropriate and sufficiently versatile orientation to the study of discourse.

The research agenda of early cultural studies audience research

Prescriptive essays like 'two paradigms' offer guidance, a rationale, to researchers. It would be misleading to imply that the essay presented the reasons why particular research decisions were made. The early audience research agenda of the cultural studies integrated and improvised on the conservative agenda outlined in the 'two paradigms' essay, in accordance with the particular theoretical ideas and ideals of each researcher. From the combination of the two paradigms (British culturalism and the European structuralisms), the researchers endorsed the structures of production as the 'determinate moment' in which the 'message' of television was constructed. They equated 'televisual discourse' with 'audience discourse', that is, 'textual' with 'social' discourse (see Kress 1983), while avoiding recognition that their research practice problematised the nature of the television text. They endorsed the use of ethnographic research techniques as the preferred approach for audience research and often for researching the structures of production as well. The 'experiment' drew more widely on the British 'culturalist' tradition, especially on the work of Raymond Williams, and on the subcultures and deviance research of the 1970s, than on the structuralisms. 'Culturalism', after all, justified the empirical stance which produced the research, and appropriated audience research for cultural studies.

NOTES

1 In Australia, especially in the work of Meaghan Morris, Elizabeth Grosz, Terry Threadgold and many other women theorists, the significance of (and preference for) French cultural philosophy was pursued, but largely ignored by male academics unwilling to address the hard issues discussed in feminism and psychoanalysis.
2 For Hunter (1993), this definition of culture was too broad and needs limits so that culture can be something rather than 'everything'; so that it has some content.
3 See for example Williams' (1984) discussion of the ways changes in the nature of the 'knowable community' changed the nature of the work of the novelist.
4 See for example the Brunsden and Morley's (1978) analysis of *Nationwide*, where the nation is the totalising homology, within which consumerism is subsumed.
5 See Ang's (1985) discussion of the foundation of the 'melodramatic imagination'.
6 This idea cannot be attributed to Fiske. It is much older, and was certainly forcefully put by Smythe (1981) in *Dependency Road*.
7 A strong position on reading as production is presented by de Certeau (1984) in the introduction to *The Practice of Everyday Life*.

Chapter 4

The 'new phase' in audience resear[...]

encoding/decoding [handwritten annotation]

INTRODUCTION

In this chapter I examine five examples of television audience research from the 1970s and 1980s. The research was a response to Hall's (1980a) challenge for researchers to address both textual production/structure and audience response when interrogating the hegemonic power of the media. To make it easier to talk about the projects as a group I have given them a name, 'the cultural studies audience experiment', though they are by no means an exhaustive list of studies I would include in other contexts under such a heading. The research projects are the *Nationwide* research, made up of Brunsdon and Morley's (1978) *Everyday Television: 'Nationwide'* and Morley's (1980) *The 'Nationwide' Audience: structure and decoding*; Hobson's (1982) *Crossroads: the drama of a soap opera*; Ang's (1985) *Watching Dallas: soap opera and the melodramatic imagination*; Tulloch and Moran's (1986) *A Country Practice: 'quality soap'*; and Buckingham's (1987) *Public Secrets: EastEnders and its audience.* I have limited the study to these examples because they all specified engagement with one popular television programme[1] and set themselves the task of explaining the programme through what people said about it rather than of explaining people through the way they respond to the programme.[2]

The encoding/decoding project resonated strongly with the ideal of interdisciplinarity celebrated in Barthes' reflection that the 'unease of classification' is the 'point from which it is possible to diagnose a certain mutation' (Barthes 1977: 155). The research of the cultural studies audience experiment provides just such a 'point'. Both John Fiske and David Morley have defined this point as that where sociology and semiotics meet in a globally unifying approach to the study of mass communication. They see the value of the 'experiment' as the provision of insight through an accumulation of research genres. The problem with this view is that textual analysis and audience talk traffic in different languages. Acts of translation are needed – either to transpose each genre into a new common form, or to redefine the objects of research.[3] For this reason the cultural studies audience experiment is more like a paradigm shift than an accumulation. The research assisted, in my view, a profound reorientation in cultural studies. It changed the role that has been pursued until now by both researcher and critic, and spoke from an emerging position generated by the 'epistemological turn' in the social sciences.

Perhaps the most straightforward account of the research – my preferred reading – is as a 'multiple reading' experiment. The research delivered accounts of the texts as read both by the researchers and by others – by production teams, by viewers, or by journalists in newspaper and magazine articles. They pointed to the possibility of a more plural understanding of the television text than Fiske's three variations. The multiple forms of the text, demonstrated in examples of the various genres (academic criticism, viewer discussion, popular press criticism, academic research accounts of viewer discussion, and even of viewer discussion of press reports) were transposed into popular academic criticism. My reading points to the unique contribution of the cultural studies audience experiment as an 'experiment' which addressed the production of discourse as the common element in both production (writing) and viewing (reading), and for better or worse, disregarded the difference between them.

I would like to be able to argue that the researchers, regardless of intention, placed themselves in a relation to the programmes and to the things people said about them as a kind of critic-researcher – a new, and in many respects alien, academic role, and that all discussion about the programme was at last accepted as Text.[4] From such a perspective, television texts can be understood to reverberate, to resonate beyond their own boundaries in the discourses that permeate community and cultural context. The interdisciplinarity required of such research would have to have been achieved by amplification of the role of the critic, since it adds to the skills required of the academic critic those of ethnographer and social semiotician. Interdisciplinarity echoes the post-modernist focus on criticism and transposes a range of 'variations' on a textual theme into a master 'key' called discourse. Such new interdisciplinary criticism would perhaps look so different from its older forms that, initially, misrecognition would be almost inevitable as experimentation by mixing research genres and competing accounts of text occurred. I believe that just such a faltering misrecognition occurred with each of the cultural studies audience research projects described here. By focusing on 'encoding' and 'decoding', the 'determinate moments' of cultural production, rather than on the 'discursive form of the message', Hall's central tenet – the importance of the 'discursive form of the message' – was gradually relinquished (Hall 1980a: 128–9). Each subsequent project moved further away from confronting the challenge of an amplified understanding of the television text. Each borrowed theoretical insights designed to explain problems other than discourse. For example, the 'programme as meaningful discourse' was a significant feature of the

Nationwide research which addressed the circulation of the 'product' in its 'discursive form'. In *Everyday Television* (Brunsdon and Morley 1978), a semiotic framework was used to analyse the 'televisual sign' (ibid.: 131) as ideology, and in *The 'Nationwide' Audience* (Morley 1980) interviews were counted as discourse in order to map the distance of the ideas sustained by the programme from its 'preferred' reading. In this project, the emphasis remained on discourse. Hobson (1982), however, replaced the focus on the circulation of the 'discursive form' of the message with the story of a power struggle between the producers and fans of *Crossroads*. The programme had meaning only as popular television, a terrain contested by television management and various audiences. A populist politics replaced discourse. In the *Dallas* research, the emphasis on discourse was re-instituted, but less as an analysis of the discourses produced by the letter writers than for the power of the text to activate discourses of either 'populism' or 'mass culture'. The pleasure of *Dallas* for women viewers, and the production of an account of that pleasure in the convergence of the 'melodramatic imagination' and 'structures of feeling', outweighed the significance of other discourses evoked by *Dallas*. Tulloch and Moran (1986) substituted the text–as– performance as their unifying concept (in place of the 'discursive form of the message') and Buckingham recuperated the inherent textual unruliness of the television text to a relatively safe literary perspective – that of reader-response criticism.

During the time-scape of the 'experiment' (roughly 1973–1988) the Althusserian search for ideology was displaced by the articulation of textual meaning in other terms – such as pleasure and popularity – most probably to escape the restrictions imposed by the search for ideology (see Hobson 1982: 136; Tulloch and Moran 1986: 11; Ang 1985: 17; Buckingham 1987: 37). Looking at 'the experiment' as a whole, it appears that between 1978 and 1987, 'ideology' was displaced from the text on to the audience. The search for perverse texts was replaced by the documentation of perverse reading in aberrant or ideological decodings. The researchers increasingly adopted textually defined theories of reception, which compromised the more radical and critical challenges offered to such work by sociological and cultural media studies, and placed the research and its objects (popular television programmes and their audiences) within the boundaries of the stable and legitimate interests of high culture and literary theory – despite the populist and feminist rhetoric so prominently featured in the 'experiment'.

The empirical audience research, its so-called ethnographic dimension, was increasingly used only to corroborate or demonstrate the insights of textual (albeit 'reader-response ') theory rather than as constitutive of the text. Yet paradoxically, the ethnography was crucial to the studies as verification or validation of the 'meaning' of the text. Having divested themselves of the concept 'ideology', the research needed an 'ethnography of the audience' to confirm the theories of 'text' adopted from literary theory –

of text as performance or as textual invitations to meaning construction. This ostensibly text-centred research delegated responsibility for textual meaning to the audience. In effect, it treated working-class audiences as equivalent to the natural order – to *tabula rasa* (given class and British culture) where the consequences of popular mass culture accumulate as the cultural flotsam and jetsam littering an otherwise empty landscape.

A greater decentring of the conceptual centrality of the text (as the focus of literary or media analysis) was obvious in subsequent work by both Morley (1986) and Radway (1988). Both writers developed their early work in ways which effectively retained 'discourse' but broke the link with specific texts, and the 'discursive form of the message'. Each foresaw future directions quite differently. For Radway, the break with the specific text was liberating because it was overshadowed by larger umbrellas – text became genre became commercial culture.

> The limitations of our disciplined research practices and our common-sensical interest in communication circuits are increasingly a problem, I have come to believe, because we have had to grapple in recent years with theories of culture, ideology and subjectivity, which ask us to think of social formations and cultural practices in new ways, all of which confound a simple transmission model of cultural communication.
>
> (Radway 1988: 363)

The relation between genre, text and audience addressed in Radway's *Reading the Romance* (1984) was generalised in her later writing to the discursive constitution of subjectivity, the relation between subjectivity and discourse, and so to the 'endlessly shifting, ever-evolving kaleidoscope of daily life and the way in which the media are integrated and implicated within it' (Radway 1988: 366). Radway proposed three sites where the 'confrontation between the popular and the dominant, officially legitimated culture' occurs: the family, the school and the 'leisure worlds' sought out by the individual. Morley (1986), by contrast, later broke with the specificity of the text–audience link in a manner which subjected individual viewers to the power structures of the domestic environment, specifically the power structure of family dynamics. By opting for an interactionist perspective, Morley jettisoned the link to cultural totality which 'the text', for all its obfuscation, had provided. The family or other social groupings constituted either voluntarily (the family, clubs and societies) or compulsorily (the family (for children), school, prison) became the agents of social control and determined the meaning of texts. On the positive side, the audiences envisioned by Morley and Radway were not 'masses' but groups of 'real' people in whom commercial culture lives. For such groups, the relation of the group to the means of cultural production (whether in the form of texts, genres or 'leisure worlds') is just as important as the relations between group members, which may to some degree be defined by the nature of the cultural commodity at the centre of the group's attention.

This, however, is the problem at the centre of an emerging conundrum which concerns the changing basis of social formation in a contemporary media-rich environment. For Morley, an 'old world' writer, the text was not considered essential as a link to the larger culture, because the critical category of social analysis continued to be class. As a result the television audience could be conceptualised independently of the texts of television. For Radway, a 'new world' writer, class is an unconvincing explanation, and the text, at least as a cultural type and as a linking category, as evidence of cultural type, remains an essential component of audience research. In both cases (the audience–text research and the newer reception approaches) the heat was taken off the text, and one must add, off the structures of production and all those involved in it. The heat was also taken off the academic researcher, who no longer had to justify his or her reading of a text. The heat was focused directly and remorselessly on the audience, which was expected to offer satisfactory accounts (through its engagement in 'ethnographic' research) of the meaning of popular cultural texts, as well (presumably) as for their attachment to them. What was overlooked in the return to the audience were the problems inherent in relying on what people are able to articulate (see Eco 1974), as opposed to what they understand and think about. And what was lost in this project was the specificity of address, the meeting of discourses in the interaction of reader and text, which constituted the promise, and the difference from traditional audience research, of the cultural studies audience experiment.

The radical possibility of a shimmering diversification of the global mass audience into overlapping interpretive communities was replaced by notions of audiences helping specific texts to be realised, in their performance/ reading, or by notions of audiences as collecting, adopting and taking home texts, as 'nomadic subjects' engaged in a sort of harmless beachcombing and bricolage of cultural products.[*] Audiences became the conservators of cultural bric-à-brac, the meaningfulness of their activities analytically useful in placing the group within the power structure of the dominant culture, as Hebdige has shown in his analysis of punk 'bricolage' (Hebdige 1979a: 103ff.). Such an approach does not explain the discursive interpellation, either of the text by the audience or of the audience by the text. It does not alone offer an adequate critique of commercial culture, because everyday life is not a museum (however much we like to imagine some domestic environments are) but part of the making of contemporary culture. And instead of addressing the transpositional significance of media commodities, such an approach tends instead to be translated as the exoticism of the everyday.[†]

THE 'NEW PHASE'

In turning to the cultural studies audience experiment, it is necessary to step back from *post hoc* analysis and to remember that the studies included were examples of research which it was hoped would prove to be Hall's 'new phase' in audience research. In response to Hall's challenge, the researchers produced work that changed many of the ways we think about media audiences and audience research today. The studies were the precursors for contemporary research about fans and discursive communities. What follows is, nevertheless, a critical reading of the research, focused on some of the crossroads in the research activity where decisions were made about direction, where destinations were altered, and/or where itineraries were abandoned for safer, already existing, or more comfortable routes to an aesthetic which combines reader views and textual criticism

When research is innovative and challenges received wisdom, as this research did, it merits sustained contemplation and close scrutiny because, in the concerns and issues it pursued, lie clues for new directions. The issues raised by this research include the contested fields of text, audience and discourse. The issues raised by this research address not only the interdisciplinary controversies about text, audience and discourse but also the ways they are combined as research practice and linked to the thorny problem of media politics. This interdisciplinary melting pot continues to complicate the audience research agenda. The value of revisiting the early research in the 1990s lies in reclaiming its insistence that viewers have voices and critical perspectives about popular culture which deserve attention. The 'cultural studies audience experiment' was popular culture research where what the viewer had to say was deemed to count enough to propel researchers into fieldwork engagement with real people. That fieldwork engagement continues to challenge the armchair sophistry of reader-response, reception aesthetics[5] and spectatorship studies where researchers position themselves as the only viewers who count. At a time when questions are being asked about the validity of fieldwork as method, when the rights of researchers to speak for communities and constituencies who participate in research have become problematic, and when the goal of giving ordinary viewers a voice in critical reflection on cultural production appears in jeopardy, it is once again time to examine audience research practice and to define a revised trajectory based on the lessons learned from the past. It is crucial that researchers who value the ideals of audience research as cultural critique examine in detail the theoretical foundations of their practice.

THE *NATIONWIDE* RESEARCH AS ACADEMIC DISCOURSE

The *Nationwide* research had two components: the textual analysis carried out by Brunsdon and Morley, *Everyday Television: 'Nationwide'* (1978) and the empirical audience research carried out by David Morley alone, *The 'Nationwide' Audience: structure and decoding* (1980). As text, the television programme *Nationwide* was imagined as a multiple text, simultaneously the sum of all episodes of *Nationwide*, a BBC week-nightly current affairs television magazine programme, and yet 'characteristically' or typically represented by any one episode. Morley sought a research strategy which would allow him to map a third *Nationwide* – the *Nationwide* viewers construct in discussing, thinking about and evaluating a popular television programme. His aim was to allocate due weight to both the 'text' and the 'audience' rather than to imagine the audience as 'spectators' only or as consumers/receivers only. The 'audience' he interviewed consisted of students co-opted for the research while attending evening college or other further educational classes.

The *Nationwide* project began with a close reading of a selection of episodes of the programme. Brunsdon and Morley's (1978) aim was to reveal the ideological biases of the programme and, perhaps more importantly, to unveil the production practices which allowed the programme to exert its sway over the hearts and minds of ordinary Britons. They wanted to discover how the audience was implicated in accepting and even perpetuating the ideas and meanings given privileged status within the programme, even when those ideas were based in obviously utopian fantasies about the nature of life in Britain at the time. The possibility of resistance or transformation of the programme's ideology was carried through into Morley's audience study.

The discursive themes of *Nationwide*

Brunsdon and Morley examined the language used by members of the production team and analysed how the programme talked about itself as well as how it talked to its audience. They demonstrated that the 'direct address' of *Nationwide* was focused on a narrow range of themes: the world of home and leisure; people's problems; the image of England; national and political news. A small number of themes were reiterated continually, mostly themes which linked British nationhood to ideals about political constituency. National mythology was shown to have been co-opted as programme mythology which promulgated the idea that the relationship between the programme and its audience was natural and ideal, a good example of what an ideal social democracy should be.

As national television, the programme was evaluated by Brunsdon and Morley as having created a discursive forum for the dominant ideologies of nationalism, individualism, consumerism and patriarchy, for particular and committed views of national unity based on the individual, patriarchal domination of the household, and on a commitment to home ownership and consumerism. They identified these recurrent ideological themes as referencing four distinct social institutions: the nation, the self, the family and the economy. Brunsdon and Morley's determination to pin down a 'preferred reading' in terms of an overall national political orientation in the programme led to a variety of institutions and discourses, implicated in the programme's discursive diversity being judged as 'dominant ideology'. The significance of this institutional diversity for the later audience-based study of the programme's discourses was not explored, though hypothetically it could have suggested not only that the programme sought to promote dominant ideas across a range of institutional commitments, but that Morley's attempt to politically classify what people say about the programme according to a unified political stance would prove misguided. Political stance, in regard to discourses of national politics and identity, will not necessarily correspond to political stance in regard to 'family' or 'self'. An ardent left-wing radical can hold extreme chauvinist (dominant ideological) views about the role of women in the household and in society. The audience interviews Morley reproduced in *The Nationwide Audience* (1980) showed people swinging from radicalism to conservatism, doggedly insisting on the veracity of personal judgements, and at times being unrepentantly self-contradictory, depending on the issue being discussed, but Morley interpreted such variability as resistance – as a permanent personal, class-based position rather than as a teetering high wire performance. Instead of focusing on such acts of balancing and juggling as the purpose of his audience research, Morley sacrificed its potential as an exploration of the variability of interpretation to a demographic vision of class determination and sociological classification.

Audience discourse

Ideology is a central concept in the *Nationwide* research and the analysis of discourse in both *Everyday Television: 'Nationwide'* and *The 'Nationwide' Audience* is oriented to revealing it. As already described, the ideology of *Nationwide* centred on the myths of individualism, nationalism, the family, patriarchy and the economy. The subsequent study of audience discourse was organised rather differently by Morley. First, he pursued Hall's (1980a) suggestion that the audience is already discursively structured into decoding positions which reflect political stance: viz. dominant, negotiated and oppositional decoding positions. Secondly, he attempted to verify these decoding positions empirically, by group interviews about episodes of *Nationwide*. Thirdly, he attempted to combine insights from both culturalist and structuralist paradigms in this enterprise. In particular, this involved accommodating the structuralist idea that the historical subject is a crossroads where things happen (Lévi-Strauss 1978: 4), with the culturalist emphasis on the authenticating role of experience. What is interesting is the form that this struggle between position and experience, structuralism and culturalism takes in Morley's work.

Among the projects in the cultural studies audience experiment, Morley's work alone focused on the theoretical problems of discourse. Since this was the first research to look for textual discourse in the audience, and since the only prototypes were traditional audience research, it is not surprising that the ideals expressed in Morley's theoretical writing about audience and discourse were not realised in the empirical research. The position from which he began was that the audience is structured discursively prior to encountering the television text, and that this structuring accounts for the variability of interpretation and for discrepancies between production intentions and audience readings (or as Hall puts it, 'selective perception') (Hall 1980a: 135). Secondly, he believed that audience discussion would be structured according to three hypothetical positions from which decodings of a televisual discourse might be constructed – the 'dominant–hegemonic position' which subsumed the 'professional code' (ibid.: 136); the 'negotiated code' – 'containing a mixture of adaptive and oppositional elements' (ibid.: 137); and the 'oppositional code' with which 'it is possible for a viewer perfectly to understand both the literal and the connotative inflection given by a discourse but to decode the message in a globally contrary way' (ibid.: 137 8).

A problem with what is expected of a 'decoding' becomes apparent here. The statement of the difference between 'decoding' and 'understanding' is reminiscent of Hall's distinction between the message and its meaning. Morley suggested that it is possible to 'understand' the message, but to ascribe it a meaning (to 'decode' it) according to other criteria (i.e. according to discursive positioning). The difference between 'understanding' and 'decoding' resides in the ascription of political significance. What Morley found was that 'social position in no way correlates with decodings' since three sets of groups, the apprentices, the trades union officials and the black further-education students, who all share according to Morley's evaluation 'a common class position' produced decodings that were dominant, negotiated and oppositional respectively (Morley 1980: 137). Morley's attempts to explain these unexpected findings tend to be unconvincing. He commented, for example, that the 'cynical response' and 'defensive stance' of the apprentices resulted from their desire to appear 'worldly-wise', returning them by default to an 'acceptance of *Nationwide*'s formulations' (ibid.. 138–9), that they rejected the programme's 'mode of address or articulation' but 'still inhabit the same "populist" ideological problematic of the programme' (ibid.: 139). This second explanation is even more unsatisfactory as Morley suddenly described the previously 'dominant ideology' of the programme as the '"populist" ideological problematic of the programme'. Clearly what Morley had discovered is that the audience did not read the programme in the same way as the researchers, and that his research strategy could not accommodate the complexity of the research task he had undertaken. This is not to suggest that the research project was ill-conceived but that it demonstrated the difficulty and dimensions of the problem of researching discourse and the interaction between people and television texts to be of a more complex nature than had previously been imagined – an extremely significant finding.

The belief of the *Nationwide* researchers in 'ideology' and in the importance of finding a way to use discourse analysis for media audience research, enabled them to theorise a link between the particular comments of audience members, the social formation, and television as a medium of mass communication. The *Nationwide* research confirmed the value of the analysis of social discourse as a form of audience research. However, the researcher's expectation that the programme would be decoded politically, in accordance with dominant, negotiated or oppositional positioning in discourse, failed to anticipate the breadth of the discursive agenda addressed by either the programme or its viewers.

Homage to ethnography

The question of the 'ethnographic' credentials of Morley's work remains. Morley did not claim the status of ethnography for his work; it has been attributed to it by others. Morley claimed it as a development of the qualitative methods used in the interpretive 'paradigm' of audience research. In addition, Morley's work differed markedly from that used in subcultural analysis. Because a modification of mass audience theory underpinned it, there was no attempt at historical analysis of those involved in the research, no structural or semiotic analysis of the constituency of the interview groups, and no phenomenological analysis of the situation entered by the researcher.[6] Nevertheless, Morley's research did generate a feeling for what Eco (1974) termed the 'transcultural' project, which was revealed as the differences in the meaning of television viewing for researcher and researched became clear. As 'ethnographic' research, even in this limited sense, the *Nationwide* research demonstrated the necessity for strategies of audience–text discourse analysis to bridge the gap between researcher and researched, and to clarify the power/knowledge struggle in which each is implicated.

Nationwide and the discursive agenda in popular culture research

Morley's work was a significant intervention in the study of popular culture. It focused on a popular evening television news magazine programme but emphasised how a variety of audience groups interpreted it. In so doing, the *Nationwide* research extended the terms of the popular culture debate. To the evaluation of the programme (its status, quality, production values, etc.) was added the characteristics and quality of its reception as socio-cultural research. The *Nationwide* research opened the way for researchers to move beyond the 'active versus passive' debate, beyond either psychological or social effects on people, and to thoroughly question the political basis of audience participation in popular cultural activities, especially through discourse analysis. The emphasis was less on changes in people caused by the media, and more on the question of cultural participation and its meaning in a mass-media environment. Morley's *Nationwide* research was a first step towards a new type of textual exploration which presupposed and engaged with 'an average reader resulting from a merely intuitive sociological speculation' (Eco 1979: 8). Following Eco, the *closed* structure of the TV news magazine text would presuppose an un-schooled or unruly audience. Its imagined spectator would be ill-defined, leaving the reader's project open to occupation and influence by other powerful discourses, like nationalism or racism. The *Nationwide* research began the process of breaking down the typification associated with the television audience and of replacing it with structured categories of viewers. It began the analysis of differences within the mass, based on class structure and political affiliation. It opened the way, as we will see, for identifying other discourses which structure the interaction of people with texts.

CROSSROADS[7] AND CRISIS RESEARCH

Hobson presented her research, *Crossroads: the drama of a soap opera* (1982), as an examination of the 'production of popular television programmes and the understanding or appeal of those programmes for their audience' (Hobson 1982: 10). This statement foregrounds the importance Hobson attached to structures of production and reception, and especially to the significance of those structures for women viewers. Hobson's narrative however – the story she tells of her research – concerned a crisis which developed between television management and the regular *Crossroads* audience. Aided and abetted by the daily press interest in and exploitation of the ATV management decision to dismiss actor Noele Gordon and Meg Mortimer – the key character Gordon played – from the programme, the crisis became a research opportunity which meshed with Hobson's long-term audience study. The management decision meant the audience would have to re-shape its Gestalt of the programme, and re-define the nature of the hierarchy of relationships which existed within the dramatic world of the soap opera. The struggle Hobson created was about paternalism towards the mass audience and protestations from that audience about the exclusion from, and the expropriation of, their power to determine the narrative direction of the commercial television production, *Crossroads*.

Context: the domestic situation

Hobson confined her analysis of the audience of *Crossroads* to the women who viewed and discussed the programme with her. Her conclusions can be

STAFFORDSHIRE
UNIVERSITY
LIBRARY

grouped into three categories: findings about the relationship between the audience and the text, findings about the reasons for viewing, and findings about women's performances as members of the television audience for *Crossroads*. Hobson's research was less conservative as sociology than Morley's. For example, Hobson felt no need to mention how many women participated in her study, though she did mention that the research took place over a long period of time. She described her interviewees as active and involved viewers who combined information from their own life experiences and knowledge of both the genre and the programme to interpret and evaluate the stories and characters in *Crossroads*. She noted that their critical attention was particularly engaged, as in so many audience studies of popular cultural texts, with assessing the 'realism' of the programme. Like most critics of the programme, this audience was aware of the programme's technical difficulties and short-comings, but refused to allow such matters to interfere with their viewing pleasure. Their reasons for viewing reflected their interest in the soap opera genre and the particular ways *Crossroads* measured up as an example of the genre.

The context of reception

Hobson's interest in the everyday domestic environment as a context for the relationship between audience and programme led her to stress the 'importance of the television audience and the need for their perspective to be considered in relation to the programmes which they wish to watch' (1982: 138). She took upon herself the role of advocate for the audience. She pointed out that the audience builds up an understanding of the themes of television, and of a particular programme, over a long period of time, and that the meaning of a programme for its audience should be expected to be qualitatively different from that of its meaning for television executives or production staff, both in terms of the themes of the programme and the meaning of the programme as a fixture in the domestic environment. She noted that family structure and daily patterns affected the nature and quality of viewing because women put the family first. Most of the women interviewed felt that ideally they would have liked to stop and watch the programme, but that the time at which it was scheduled worked against that luxury.

Crossroads as multiple text

In her analysis of what the women viewers said, Hobson treated the broadcast programme as a material object, though when talking about the meaning of the programme she claimed its meaning depended on what the viewers made of it. From her audience perspective, the materiality or concreteness of the programme was considered inherent in its demand for attention and time which allowed the programme to intrude into the domestic realm, to disrupt family routines, to insert itself as part of domestic conversation, to offer models of an idealised domestic scenario. The text–audience relationship here is a negotiation not so much of meanings, but of time and commitment. Hobson argued that this commitment of audience to programme justified the right of the audience to have its wishes consulted in decisions about programme development and change.

Hobson's analysis of the collection of letters written to the *Birmingham Evening Mail* to protest about the sacking of Noele Gordon from the programme served a dual purpose. In the examples included, the letter writers besought the programme makers to take their opinions and wishes into consideration. They revealed awareness of their comparative powerlessness by using their age and pensioner status to petition the powerful. They disclosed the companionship offered to them by the programme (particularly in the case of aged viewers and those physically more restricted and confined to the domestic sphere than other social groups). Like prayers, the letters spoke of a desire to change the existing mass-media power balance.[8] The inclusion of the interests of the weak and powerless reinforced the demand – inherent in this research – that the audience should be given the right to determine programme stories. By painting a picture of the *Crossroads* audience as comprised of housewives, the aged and the infirm, Hobson exploited traditional ideas about the vulnerability of the mass audience. The treatment of the letter writers also extended Hobson's rather covert and contradictory argument about the materiality of the text, since the mass audience is usually imagined to accept uncritically the programmes offered to it. The argument for the vulnerability of the mass audience which Hobson marshalled to sustain her populist stand on viewer access to influence over programmes, stories and characters presupposed the materiality of the texts over which the struggle was being waged.

When Hobson discussed the programme or its meaning, she reverted to a sender–receiver model in which only the contexts of production (here, the 'sender's' intentions) and the contexts of reception (here, the viewer's wishes) were addressed. The programme, as text, slipped out of focus as Hobson used the more 'ethnographically' accessible aspects of the encoding/decoding model and ignored the possibilities for combining the two paradigms of cultural studies. Compared to Morley's work (1980), the *Crossroads* study reverted to 'culturalism' and repudiated the semiotic project. Hobson uncritically and unquestioningly embraced all approaches to understanding the programme, no matter how contradictory. She pre-empted ideology by focusing on a particular power struggle between the producers and the audience, a struggle not over textual meaning, but over production decision-making. Her decision not to evaluate and analyse the use of 'domestic' themes, concepts and values in *Crossroads* in effect replaced criticism of the politics of patriarchy with a 'false' political struggle, the struggle to control the text. For the right to exercise power in a patriarchal and ageist society, Hobson substituted the right to determine the fate of a character.

Making *Crossroads*

Hobson presented the programme as a product of the structures of production, and as testimony to the creativity and calibre of the members of the production team, emphasising particularly the work of the producer, the director and the performers. Yet she also claimed that 'to try to say what *Crossroads* means to its audience is impossible for there is no single *Crossroads*, there are as many different *Crossroads* as there are viewers' (1982: 136). In this statement she contradicts her own explanations of the pleasure supplied by the programme – the pleasure experienced because the programme reflects the life experiences in which the viewers are engaged. Buckingham took this statement to imply that Hobson believed viewers of *Crossroads* and other soap operas are 'free to choose from an infinite variety of different readings' (Buckingham 1987: 35). However Hobson slipped out of the theoretical dilemma posed by this definition of text by going on to assert that the viewers are and should be, in her view, the only critics who count (Hobson 1982: 136). She traded off a discussion of the meaning of *Crossroads* as a signifying system, for a discussion of textual control. Where, as we will see, Buckingham traced a pattern of reception from textual structure to the readings by the audience, Hobson pursued a quite different project, a populist project on behalf of the *Crossroads* audience. Even though she claimed there were 'as many different *Crossroads* as there are viewers', Hobson could not avoid her own estimation of what the programme meant. For Hobson, what the text meant was of less consequence than the fact that it did have a meaning for its viewers, and that the programme mattered to them. She argued that the involvement of the audience with the programme justified their rights to greater recognition in the production process, both in terms of lobbying for improved production standards and for consultation over major changes to the *Crossroads* community.

Research design and the *Crossroads* project

Hobson paid little attention to the implications of the different theories of text and discourse fielded in her study. While she reported what the producer, director, writers, etc. 'intended' the programme to mean, and what the audience liked or disliked about the programme, she asked the housewives interviewed not what the programme meant but why they liked watching it, and she analysed letters from viewers about why they liked watching it and did not want it changed. She avoided the topic of ideology, and talked instead about *Crossroads* in terms of its themes, such as the nature and problems of family life. In terms of research design, the shift from meaning to liking is highly significant. The research actually addressed different questions and different aims in its various phases. Such slippage of research focus is instructive. On the one hand, it demonstrates that, even in this most well-intentioned research, viewers were in fact denied their choice of critical positions because they were still understood as receiving not creating the programme. On the other hand, the researcher's intuitive change of focus, her need to ask questions she felt her interviewees could understand and respond to, points to a type of theorisation frequently omitted from encoding/decoding perspectives – the systemic implications of mass broadcasting as a cultural phenomenon.

A crisis of crossed cultures

Throughout the letters and interviews, the theme of the disparagement of *Crossroads* appears and re-appears. In the final chapter of her book, Hobson located this disparagement in a crisis of crossed cultures. The culture of television professionals ('this programme offends my professional tastes') colliding with that of the constituency they had fostered, the culture of the users of the programme ('this programme entertains me'). As a low budget production, *Crossroads* provided opportunities for young and less experienced professionals to gain experience and establish a reputation, but allowed them very little room to demonstrate their skills. Audience appreciation was shown to be held in very low esteem by television critics and professionals alike in evaluating the work of television professionals. Other aesthetic standards prevailed.

Hobson provided clear documentation of just how little power is exercised by audiences – this in my view is the value of her project. Yet she presented the confrontation between ATV and the *Crossroads* audience as one in which the outcry from the audience won over the producer. The threat that the central character was to die was modified to her simply moving on, but still out of *Crossroads*. A solution, available from the beginning of the furore, was presented as a strategy devised to soften the blow to the audience. The loss of a character from the televisual world was supposedly softened for the audience by at least an imaginary immortality. The researcher endorsed sentiment over power, and became implicated in the exercise of network power. Hobson colluded with the channel in suggesting that the imaginary power of the audience to demand the television it wanted was maintained; that the value system of the programme – its support for social consensus – prevailed, rather than admitting that the channel won the battle and terminated the actress's contract. All the letters entreating that 'Meg should stay' were conveniently ignored, by Hobson as well as the production staff. Hobson avoided voicing even a suspicion that the production staff may have agreed to minor script changes in order to maintain their power over the programme as a whole unchallenged. Obviously the production company can tolerate/accommodate audience intervention at the level of sentiment but not at the level of story or what they consider commerce – cancelling/not cancelling a performer's contract. Hobson's story of the power play which followed the dismissal of a performer/character provides a useful example of the limit of audience power. It is perhaps extraordinary that even such a minor concession was granted. It is an example of Young's (1985) description of the ways in which the privately-owned media and the state collude in silencing criticism by transforming criticism into 'mass opinion' which in reality is an aggregation of private interests, wants and needs.

The feminist agenda of the *Crossroads* research

The lack of interest in ideology and/or discourse in Hobson's work draws attention to the difficulty experienced as academics by women researchers who worked at the Centre for Contemporary Cultural Studies in the mid-1970s to early 1980s (see Hobson 1980, 1981; McRobbie and McCabe 1981). It is situated at the beginnings of the division of feminist theory from the dominant masculinist traditions. The women researchers were establishing and justifying a feminist approach to cultural sociology while confronted by a vibrant masculinist agenda (Hall and Jefferson 1975). They pursued culturalist, Marxist, and feminist ends – yet their work at this time remained frozen in a reactive posturing or gesturing towards the work of the 'lads'. The feminist research pursued the aims and ideals of subcultural research, but omitted or limited historical or semiotic analysis of the subsystem. Instead, the work produced a level of analysis characteristic of the consciousness-raising groups popular with feminists in the 1970s and 1980s. In other words, this feminist research attempted to replace masculine modes of research (which resulted in patriarchal or chauvinist analysis) with research grounded in the values and beliefs of feminist communities, and tried to extend the 'community' rules of such groups (rules of loyalty and recognition which redressed the neglect of patriarchy) to a research agenda which endorsed and valued women's popular cultural forms. Yet, in just the ways that consciousness-raising groups were reacting to patriarchy's oppression of women, the cultural studies feminist research was reacting against a research agenda grounded in masculine interests and concerns.[9] The inadequacy of existing social theory to account for women's experience motivated a 'return to experience and the subjective plane both to record and to substantiate this reality as a firm critique of available theory and to find materials towards the preliminary construction of alternative and more adequate theories' (Grimshaw et al. 1980: 75). This feminist politics is evident in Hobson's work, especially in the status she accords to empirical methods, and also perhaps in the avoidance of Marxist and structuralist theories popular at the time this work was undertaken.

Hobson justified her atheoretical stance on the basis of recovering the specificity of women's experience, as 'the return to the subjective'. The problem is that this 'privileging of the personal' was originally motivated by a concern with structural determination, which could be explained only if the method used permitted some bridging of the gap between the personal and the political. In culturalism this gap was often bridged by tracing homologies of structure and by the recuperation of 'experience' through ethnography. Hobson provided no homology of structure, no tacit equation for the subjection of production personnel to the commercial ethic of the production company, or for the subjection of women as audiences (worth only low budget programming) to men as audiences (worth high budget programming), or for the economic and social subjection of women to men in the family.

Aesthetics and popular culture

Hobson grounded her discussion of popular culture in the professed likes and dislikes of the women interviewed. Rather than produce a reading critical of *Crossroads*, she tried to justify the production of the programme as praiseworthy cultural work on the basis of the pleasure it gave its viewers and the creativity 'against the odds' of its production teams. In seeking an aesthetic, Hobson avoided criteria such as authenticity and uniqueness of the cultural form (for example, Adorno 1945; Benjamin 1979), or the creative vision of the 'author', or tradition or style (see Lovell 1972: 331). It is as though the critical disdain with which the genre is usually treated forced her to take up an overtly populist position – 'the viewers are the critics. Or at least, the only ones who should count' (Hobson 1982: 136). Hobson seems here to have accepted the rationale that if a programme is popular it is beyond criticism, an argument which if extended to other instances of 'popularity', such as the popularity of pornography among men, is more than a little worrying. While this view works well as an endorsement of the ratings system, it fails fundamentally as a means of regulating the availability of programmes on broadcast television.

Wolff (1981: 115) has stressed that reception aesthetics not only prioritises the role of the reader/viewer, but also recognises that role as both 'creative' and 'situated'. In focusing on women viewers, Hobson stressed their situation and even their situational creativity, but not their textual creativity. By situating women's viewing in the home, Hobson was able to demonstrate that the 'meanings and pleasures that women find in soap operas... are inevitably inflected by their situation in the politics of the family, and part of the pleasure in viewing them lies in their felt defiance of masculine or parental control' (Fiske 1987a: 76). The struggle over textual meaning as part of the discursive struggle between social formations, is replaced by examples of what it is easier for women to articulate, the domestic meaning of specific acts of viewing. Hobson's lack of a theory of the text, her refusal to analyse the details of textual meaning (whether constructed by production personnel, herself as critic, or the audience) defines her work as outside the ambit of reception aesthetics.

The emphasis on the viewing situation in Hobson's work led Fiske (1987a: 72), for example, to describe it not only as television 'ethnography', but also as demonstrating a sort of covert revolt by housewives against patriarchy.[10] While Hobson appeared to develop a version of reception which can be described as popular, it is a popular reception in which consumption and production mediate each other by presenting observations and interviews from contexts of both production and reception. She presented only a very limited analysis of the 'creativity' of the viewer or the interpretive work in which the viewer engaged. Yet as Fiske points out, the value of viewing for the audience consists in 'the programme and the watching of it (for the two are inseparable)' (Fiske 1987: 75). Viewing necessarily involves the creation of meanings, necessarily calls on discursive activity. The notion of televisual discourse, central to Hall's encoding/decoding model, was displaced in Hobson's analysis by the latent meanings evoked by the existence/availability of the programme in a particular viewing situation. For Hobson, the meanings evoked in the audience by a television programme then are meanings which predate television and the programme, and can by definition demonstrate only the dynamics or power structures of the family. There is no possibility, using a currently accepted culturalist method (for example, Hobson 1982, Morley 1986 or Gray 1987) of discovering anything other than the co-optation of particular sorts of programmes to the maintenance of the power structure within the household. The problem here is that in accepting the existence of a text only as it is expressed in discussion by the audience, the hermeneutic specificity of the research exercise is compromised. If there is no 'textual meaning', there is no ideology and no structural relation between audience and text to be explained. And the aesthetic pretensions of the work disappear.

DALLAS – TALES OF PLEASURE AND PAIN

Dallas was a US drama produced between 1978 and 1991 and broadcast by the CBS network (Brooks and Marsh 1992: 199–203). The programme was, of course, set in Dallas, Texas, and the focus of the drama was the oil magnate J. R. Ewing and the problems he faced and created for his family and business associates in Texas and throughout the world. In the early 1980s, the time of Ien Ang's research, the drama had achieved international fame. The relationship between J. R. and his frequently estranged and alcoholic wife, Sue Ellen, and the contrast between the characters of Sue

Ellen and her sister-in-law, Pamela, provided a site for Ang's exploration of the pleasures for women viewers of this drama.

In *Watching Dallas: soap opera and the melodramatic imagination* (1985), Ien Ang presented 'a framework within which *Dallas* could be taken seriously' (ibid.: vii) and where issues 'concerning pleasure and its vicissitudes, its relation to ideology and cultural politics' (ibid.: viii) could be discussed. The framework for the analysis of *Dallas* consisted of a combination of emphasis on 'how' the programme produces pleasure and on how it is read by viewers. Somewhere along this hypothetical axis, Ang believed the 'meaning' of *Dallas* would be found. The choice of this focus necessarily obscured others which might have been pursued – foci such as the socio-political meaning of *Dallas* or the cultural significance of the programme as another example of the imperialising intrusion of American culture throughout the world.

Ang addressed the notoriety which surrounded the programme in the 1980s, especially the difference between viewers' opinions and the climate of dismissive opinion, which she called the 'ideology of mass culture'. She recognised the programme as a cultural artefact, but chose to focus her analysis on the qualities of the programme which produced emotional satisfaction for viewers. Viewers were portrayed as having to guard their furtive pleasure in the programme from the ravages of cultural spoil-sports the critics who refused to acknowledge the cultural validity of viewer preferences. In this sense, Ang followed the populist course charted for feminist audience research by Hobson by including an audience research component in the project, but took advantage of the developing body of feminist criticism which focused on women's textual pleasures.

The research drew on theoretical insights from two quite distinct media studies agendas – agendas of the political economy of the media and feminist criticism. Ang positioned what she had to say about the pleasure of *Dallas* between these two academic discourses, and used letters from viewers of *Dallas* to inform and test out her ideas. Some controversial aspects of the research included the sampling, the way the information disclosed in the letters was used, and the preference for explanations of the pleasure of *Dallas* which stressed emotions rather than cognition or socio-cultural knowledge, yet made minimal use of contemporary psychoanalytic theories of textual pleasure. The most important shift in Ang's research was from the focus on the 'meaning' of the programme as popular culture to a focus on the 'pleasures' experienced in viewing the programme – particularly feminine pleasures.[11]

The viewers

Ang's respondents were a small, self-selected sample of *Dallas* viewers who professed themselves to be fans, or at least regular viewers of the programme, and who responded to an advertisement Ang placed in a women's magazine asking viewers who liked the programme to write to her explaining why. This approach to the selection of research participants privileged women, since the *Viva* readers were mostly women. The audience research data took the textual form of letters rather than observation, interviews, questionnaires or surveys. The letters were used to interrogate and evaluate academic writing about popular culture, and to 'introduce the interested Dutch reader to theoretical perspectives on television and television serials' (Ang 1985: vii). The inclusion of material from the letters was used to legitimate a pedagogic purpose. In many respects this pedagogic purpose dominated *Watching Dallas* because the audience for Ang's book was seen not only as the academic community, but also as 'the interested Dutch reader'. Considerable sacrifices to this vision of the 'ideal readers' appear to have been made throughout the book – sacrifices which compromised the rigour of the analysis and the scope of the speculation. The education undertaken was an introduction to the 'perspectives which stem mainly from Anglo-Saxon media and cultural studies'. In other words, Ang solicited information from the audience and then used that information to teach them about British cultural studies – an academic perspective which valued popular texts. This re-education was justified as a means to counteract the unjustifiable denigration of popular culture which Ang judged to be a feature of European critical analysis. Ang named this judgemental position the 'ideology of mass culture'.

The ideology of mass culture

The 'ideology of mass culture' was deduced by Ang from the letters written by the respondents who disliked *Dallas*. What was most striking about the negative letters was the sense of assurance and certainty with which the writers dismissed the programme. Where fans of *Dallas* were silenced by the emotional nature of their interaction with the programme, those who hated it were loquacious and vehement in their rationalising judgement. Ang therefore questioned 'whether it is really so logical to connect the experience of displeasure, which must in the first instance be an emotional reaction to watching *Dallas*, so directly with a rationalistic evaluation of it as a cultural product'.

For Ang, the 'ideology of mass culture' was a 'more successful' discourse than others in determining the social image of TV programmes like *Dallas*. She claimed it combined an 'official' European 'aversion to American television series' with an elaborate and well-articulated academic theory which acts as a justification for this aversion. Ang suggested that the 'official aversion' was considered to be motivated by a sense of 'threat to one's own, national culture and as an undermining of high-principled cultural values in general' (Ang 1985: 93). She objected to the suggested link between the economic conditions of production and the aesthetic and narrative structures of television programmes, which she described as 'crude economic determinism'. Her concern about the ideology was with the ways it affected the viewing and enjoyment of television, particularly American television series. The irony of Ang's approach was that she attempted to take up Hall's (1980a) formulation of the audience as 'already structured in discourse', but did so, not in relation to dominant, negotiated or oppositional decoding positions, but in relation to a position about mass culture which suited her analytical purposes. Those viewers who were critical of *Dallas* were positioned within the ideology of mass culture; those who enjoyed it were not.

Ang identified one other discursive position, the ideology of populism, which was contrasted with the ideology of mass culture. 'The ideology of populism' was a pluralist concept, at the core of which lay a rationality 'summed up in the well-known saying: "There's no accounting for taste"' (Ang 1985: 113). Ang considered this 'ideology' as the complete opposite to the ideology of mass culture, and as offering a position which could be 'forcefully employed against its codes'. It was used infrequently by the letter writers because it is anti-intellectual or practical, where the ideology of mass culture is theoretical, trying to convince people that 'mass culture is bad' (ibid.: 114). In a re-working of Bernstein's elaborated and restricted codes (Bernstein 1971), Ang accounted for the power of the 'ideology of mass culture' by referring to it as an 'elaborated code'. By contrast the 'ideology of populism' was presented as a 'restricted code', possessing a more limited vocabulary and grammar than its counterpart, which meant it was unable to counteract the power of the 'ideology of mass culture' to spoil women's pleasure.

Use-value and pleasure

The discussion of the ideology of mass culture was part of Ang's strategy to present the programme *Dallas* as an object worthy of academic consideration, as a way of counteracting the programme's bad press. She argued that *Dallas* was 'explicitly offered to the public as an object for pleasurable consumption' and that its inherent 'promise of pleasure [was] the use-value by which the industry trie[d] to seduce viewers to watch' (Ang 1985: 19). Applying the concept 'use-value' to a commodity such as a television programme is hazardous. To claim that only the use-value of the programme is relevant to its audience ignores the programme's existence and development within a system of exchange, of market relations, and of commercial broadcasting logic. It is the same as arguing that the value of gold is determined by its use-value rather than by its exchange-value, when both use and exchange combine and interact to define the cultural meaning and value of a commodity like gold. Clearly it is not the 'promise of pleasure' that makes a television programme popular and worthy of research interest, but the value of the cultural meanings, and the manner in which, the programme brings them into play. To understand the pleasure of *Dallas* for women viewers, inadequately approached through her ideological devices, Ang introduced two additional theoretical constructs – the melodramatic imagination and the tragic structure of feeling.

Melodramatic imagination and tragic structure of feeling

Ang defined the melodramatic imagination as 'a psychological strategy to overcome the material meaninglessness of everyday existence', 'a refusal, or inability, to accept insignificant everyday life as banal and meaningless', and 'born of vague, inarticulate dissatisfaction with existence here and now' (Ang 1985: 79). The melodramatic imagination was therefore a property or quality of people, one which was possessed differentially and which 'appear[ed] to express a mainly rather passive, fatalistic and individualistic reaction to a vague feeling of powerlessness and unease' (ibid.: 82). Ang linked the 'melodramatic imagination' to a related construct she called the 'tragic structure of feeling', which in turn was produced from the 'formal structure' of *Dallas* as a prime time soap opera. Her argument was that only when the ways in which *Dallas* developed these psychological propensities is understood will the meaning of the text become clear. The generic structure of *Dallas* was identified as playing upon, or referencing metaphorically, both the tragic structure of feeling and the melodramatic imagination which inform the logical and meaning-making principles some viewers used to order and understand their daily lives.

In describing the tragic structure of feeling and the melodramatic imagination, Ang's pedagogic purpose again imposed itself on her analysis. Explaining these concepts provided the rationale for a lengthy, educative description of the textual structure of *Dallas*. Similarly, the melodramatic nature of soap opera and the nature of melodrama itself were outlined for the reader of *Watching Dallas*. Ang followed these 'lessons' about the nature of soap opera and melodrama with a discussion of family tragedy in *Dallas*. She pointed out that soap opera conflicts are always family related and, in particular, address the problem of reconciling personal development with family harmony. The ideology of the family in *Dallas*, she claimed, suggested that family unity is essential as a condition for living and that family unity matters more than personal happiness. Ang hypothesised that this ideology operated as the reality principle against which the impossibility of desire could be acted out. The combination in the programme of soap opera and melodrama conventions, and their focus on the tragedy of the impossibility of personal desire, formed the basis for the programme's development of the tragic structure of feeling. The feelings referenced by the tragic structure of feeling and the type of imagination described as 'melodramatic', were held to produce by interaction experiences of pleasure in the viewer.

The relation proposed by Ang to operate between viewer and programme was a psychological relation. The value of this 'psychology' for Ang was that it explained that a programme like *Dallas* both cultivates and exploits the melodramatic imagination or tragic structure of feeling possessed as defining characteristics by the community of regular viewers. This viewing psychology, in turn, became a precondition for full appreciation of the genre, just as knowing how to play the piano enhances the quality of the classical piano listening experience. Ang's vision of the interaction between viewer and programme set up a sort of self-sustaining eco-system, capable of maintaining its own audience community and predisposing them to receptiveness to other similar programmes. Ang's insight is important because it recognised the discursive foundation which informs the genre. It explained the inability of viewers to account for the pleasure they experienced in the programme. Learning how to read the programme was inextricably linked to the pleasure of reading it.

Discourse in the *Dallas* research

The enigma of the ways discourse was analysed in *Watching Dallas* stemmed from the fact that Ang did not clearly specify the distinction between discourse and text, discourse and ideology, nor discourse and dialogue. For example, Ang identified statements in the written responses (such as 'mass culture is bad' and 'there's no accounting for people's tastes') and called them the ideology of mass culture and the ideology of populism, respectively. Instead of teasing out the range of positioning evident in the writers' responses, she generalised them as for or against *Dallas*, and therefore as positioned by one of her hypothetical ideologies or the other. This approach was similar to Hall's only in its acceptance of the audience as 'already discursively structured'. In this case the structuring imagined – though admittedly tentatively linked to discourses of nation – was of gender and popular culture preferences. Ang's 'discourses' of mass culture and populism were not linked to class or income but to the structuring aspects of global culture. In Hall and Morley, prior discursive structuring was believed to be determined by political stance (dominant, negotiated or oppositional), associated with class positioning within the social formation and expressed ideologically in the audience reading of the programme. In Ang's research the political stance was replaced by one based in orientation to popular culture (for or against *Dallas*) which was again expressed 'ideologically', in that disliking *Dallas* was considered ideological, where liking it was not.

The complexity of the diverse subject positionings enacted by each viewer were lost in the over-simplification brought about by the unnecessary layer of analysis introduced through the ideology of mass culture, the tragic structure of feeling and the melodramatic imagination. The complex interweaving of themes based in discourses of gender, nation, religion, family, and television were reduced to the voice of the ideologies of mass culture or populism. As an analysis of gender and television this completely undermined the relationship between discourse and power at the heart of the feminist project. The force of Ang's analysis was to set up *Dallas* and its female characters as icons, but as Young points out 'contemporary feminists should be searching not for icons but for inroads to the cultural terrain that constitutes the "popular" and to the systems of power that shape and define the female subject' (Young 1988: 188).

Ang's position was based in the 'feminist potential' of the 'pleasure' of *Dallas*. In turn, the pleasure of *Dallas* was equated with the pleasure of 'all other forms of popular culture for women', which Ang argued, 'must no longer be simply condemned: we must recognise that they have a positive value in women's lives' (Ang 1985: 131), so that they can be placed within a 'feminist plan of action' (ibid.: 132). Once again, a position of feminist populism was asserted. The desire to value the feminine was counterposed against a recognition that the object of this feminine pleasure was that which perpetuates the domination of women, the spectacle of patriarchy in operation. The necessity for a feminist appropriation of feminine pleasures demands an understanding of the nature of those feminine pleasures, which is what Ang tried to demonstrate. The problem with the research lay in the choice of perspective from which to analyse pleasure. As Tompkins has pointed out, theories of the text which foreground pleasure and identity in this way tend to emphasise 'individual consciousness in favour of systems of intelligibility that operate through individuals' (Tompkins 1980: xix), such as theories of discourse. An unresolved tension between discourse and individual (emotional) consciousness created an ambiguity in the *Dallas* project. Where pleasure is personal, discourse is social. Ang's emphasis on pleasure displaced the analysis from the social to the personal, from what is publicly displayed (the text) to what is privately experienced (pleasure). She then read back from accounts of the pleasure experienced by her respondents to reconstitute the text as a system of pleasure only, and on the way undercut the point of discourse analysis.

READING *A COUNTRY PRACTICE* – TEXT AS PERFORMANCE

Moran (1993: 130) has described *A Country Practice* as an Australian 'country serial', following the position of its executive producer, but the programme was widely regarded in both the community and the press as a soap opera, which in the context of Australian conventions was less melodramatic than US soaps and less realist than similar British programmes. The programme's community of characters consisted of the employees of a small country hospital and general medical practice in a fictional town called Wandin Valley. The programme's stories dealt with the medical and social problems experienced in the town. Like *Dallas, A Country*

Practice was prime-time viewing, and for over thirteen years it attracted a family audience for the Seven Network in Australia. More recently it has been broadcast in Europe. Its production was eventually discontinued because its loyal but dwindling audience did not rate highly on the demographics advertisers desired.

Tulloch and Moran's (1986) *A Country Practice: 'quality soap'* shared with Ien Ang's (1985) *Watching Dallas*, a pedagogic purpose – a commitment to educating the readers of the book about the meaning of their interests in popular culture. Education involves reform and change. It involves beginning with one set of skills and knowledge and ending with another, and most importantly knowing when and how to use those skills. *A Country Practice: 'quality soap'* offered its readers more knowledge about television production and the preoccupations and concerns of those who make programmes but, paradoxically, less of an insight into viewing as a popular leisure activity.

Tulloch and Moran focused on the construction of the broadcast programme by analysing the multiplicity of qualitatively distinct performances layered into that structure. By attempting to piece together the various *A Country Practice* texts disclosed in the discussions with production personnel and audiences, the aim was to better understand the text/message. By examining the diversity within the overall pattern of meaning attributed to the programme by the variety of people involved in its production, Tulloch and Moran believed that the meaning of the programme as text would be revealed. Even more insistently than with the other projects in the cultural studies audience experiment, the problem faced was of reconstituting the whole from the parts, because as Williams has pointed out:

> The relationship between the making of a work of art and its reception is always active, and subject to conventions, which in themselves are forms of (changing) social organisation and relationship, and this is radically different from the production and consumption of an object.... This makes the case of notation, in arts like drama and literature and music, only a special case of a wider truth. What this can show us here about the practice of analysis is that we have to break from the common procedure of isolating the object and then discovering its components. On the contrary we have to discover the nature of a practice and then its conditions.
>
> (Williams 1980b: 47)

Williams advocated an opposite strategy from that followed by Tulloch and Moran. His view was that it was necessary to know the 'nature of a practice' before the conditions of its production can make sense. The *A Country Practice* research suffered from the assumption that the 'nature of the practice' was somehow already known, when this was precisely the question that needed to be answered by the audience. Instead, the performance of the text by audience was added to the sum of production knowledge already gathered. The use of ethnography enabled the researchers to reassert the old Marxist literary emphasis on texts as cultural critique while appearing to describe other 'objects'. In this way the dimensions of cultural criticism remained the same – the evaluation of the quality of the text as object.

In *A Country Practice: 'quality soap'*, Tulloch and Moran sought a way to incorporate 'authorial intention' and its implications for the construction of meaning into a reception-oriented theory of the text. By extending the status of 'audience' to everyone involved in the production, distribution and reception of *A Country Practice*, Tulloch and Moran could talk about the programme as text while holding on to the importance of reception as the determinant of its meaning. They attempted to create an equivalence among the various 'voices' they invited to describe and evaluate the programme, which included specialist or professional audiences who literally write, script, direct, edit and produce the programme. Including such distinctions among audiences introduced a new agenda for the discussion of media power as a stumbling block for the cultural studies audience experiment.

Like Hobson and Ang, Tulloch and Moran examined the popularity and pleasure of the programme. The way that the programme was made, promoted and sold; the knowledge, cultural competences, and social and textual skills that the audience brought to the viewing experience, and what the audience found when viewing the programme (1986: 9–10) were all addressed. The nature of the pleasures inherent in the programme (Ang 1985), was replaced by the 'main environments in which the pleasures of *A Country Practice* [were] formed' (Tulloch and Moran 1986: 10). To the understanding that pleasure is a property of the text they added a sophistication – the idea that pleasure is associated with the complexity and quality of the performance of the text (ibid.: 11). The difference between actors or scriptwriters as audiences of *A Country Practice* and the broadcast audience was considered one of genus. In regard to meaning, they suggested that the text neither contains a single meaning nor supports a multiplicity of meanings, but that meaning is 'contested and re-made' in each instance of its performance by both production personnel and the broadcast audience (ibid.: 11). The problem with this approach was the ease with which performance could be reduced to the quality control exercised by the production house.

Tulloch and Moran treated their television 'text as performance' as a development of the theatrical 'performance text' described by Elam (1980: 3). The performance text Elam described is 'that produced in the theatre' and it is contrasted to the dramatic text which is 'composed for the theatre'. The 'performance text' is the 'dramatic text' performed. It is ephemeral and transitory. Elam described it as a 'macro-sign' in which meaning is constituted by the total effect of the performance. In the 'performance text', all the contributory elements are unified into a textual whole. Yet this 'textual whole' does not work as a single sign but as a 'network of semiotic units belonging to different co-operative systems' (see Elam 1980: 7). The spectator of the 'performance text' is understood as an integral part of this network, completing the performance text by subjecting it to a 'new codification' based in his or her positioning in relation to that text, and communicating these personal meanings to other spectators. 'Spectator–spectator communication' becomes part of the 'text' and significantly, part of its pleasure.

The similarity of the theatrical 'performance text' to the notion of the broadcast television 'text as performance' is obvious. Television production involves the integration of a large number of different co-operative systems, more than for a theatrical performance in that post-production inevitably alters and integrates the foregoing performances changing them, again, in the process. Like the dramatic performance text, the television programme as performance is dense with semiotic possibilities. This is not the same as suggesting that the text is polysemic. The notion of the semiotic thickness or density of performance texts refers to the clutter of the traces of the contributory systems involved in their construction. Like the performance text, the television programme as performance is heterogeneous in that its contributory systems operate discontinuously, both spatially and temporally. Auditory, visual and verbal cues appear and disappear during the performance, and much of the audience's pleasure in the text derives from 'the continual effort to discover the principles at work' in the unfolding of the text (Elam 1980: 44–6, 92–7).

Tulloch and Moran claimed a continuity between 'those who write and those who watch the show' (1986: 11) within the notion of 'performance'. All are part of the larger unity – the performed text. The difference between 'performances' is theorised as one of kind not quality, since everyone is 'reading' the text in terms of their own understanding of it. Yet the book they produced (*A Country Practice: 'quality soap'*) is constructed around a distinction between 'making the programme' and 'finding an audience' which suggests that the researchers imagined a completeness to the text prior to its reading. In regard to the television programme as performance, one set of performances of the text finished at the point where each episode was delivered to the television channel for broadcast. This break or discontinuity between production and distribution/reception, the 'completeness' of the episode in the can, is the point at which the analogy between the performed theatre text and the television programme as performance breaks down. At this point, the nature and meaning of broadcast television as distinct from other cultural production was denied and 'media power' was interpreted as the power to have the final say on the production of the text or the meaning of the text (ibid.: 11).

In *Finding the Audience*, Tulloch and Moran (1986: Part 2) sought diverse accounts of the programme – from television programming executives about their scheduling decisions, discussions with stars and the programme's publicist, letters from fans, interviews with tertiary students asked to watch and discuss the programme, discussions with high school students who completed a questionnaire and had previously watched a particular episode, and discussions with the producers about the future of the programme. All competed in a cacophonous roar demonstrating above all else that the notion of what an audience is changes, depending on who is talking and in what relationship they stand to the programme. The voices are jumbled in the confusion of a class-based 'culture of the masses' where sympathy (from the researcher) is assumed to ensure acceptance (from the researched). The inadequacy of the theorisation of discursive formations – inadequately conceived in Hall's early essay, unresolved in Morley (1980), evaded by a commitment to populist feminism in Hobson (1982), obfuscated by feminist theory and inadequate sampling in Ang (1985), returned like the repressed to haunt the pages of *A Country Practice: 'quality soap'* where at last the problem can be named.

The under-theorisation of audience is more recognisable in the *A Country Practice* research because of the attempt to unify the different reading of the programme as performance. Tulloch and Moran emphasised that they focused 'not on one product, *A Country Practice*, but on a variety of *A Country Practice* texts, each being "read" and "performed" in terms of the cultural experience of its audiences' (1986: 10). This is similar to Eco's suggestion that what is indispensable to studies of reception is 'a geographic map of these cultures and of the various systems of rules and subrules they follow' (Eco 1974: 60). But then Eco had anticipated that 'the semiotics of the future' would develop the 'metalinguistic tools' to unify the classes of linguistic and non-linguistic systems (Eco 1974: 55) – a project that has proved more intransigent than he apparently imagined. For example, the continuity and difference between the performance of *A Country Practice* by its script editors and its performance by a boy from a suburban high school still cannot be articulated. The explanatory grid across which these 'performances' could be mapped was never adequately described – though at least it was imagined by Tulloch and Moran. What they imagined perhaps was Morley's mapping of the relation between the dominant ideology of *Nationwide* and the groups who participated in his research – a mapping of programme ideology and audience demographics. Yet without ideology and understanding the text as a series of performances, the *A Country Practice* research lacked both a terrain on which to map its audiences and a theory of what was being mapped. A little later, the audience was to be understood as a geography of dispersed communities – a solution which demonstrated more awareness of the problem of understanding the 'culture of the masses', but which threatened to seduce us into believing that 'difference in decoding (Fiske 1987b: 316–19) rather than competence in 'transcoding' implies power over a text.

EASTENDERS – READER-RESPONSE AND CRITICISM

In *Public Secrets: 'EastEnders' and its audience* (Buckingham 1987), the relationship between a popular television programme and its audience was examined from four perspectives – the structures of the organisation sponsoring its production, the structures of the text, the structures of the marketplace (structures of its public reception) and the structures of the audience. The 'determinate moments' of encoding (in this case the institutional structures of production), of distribution (press coverage, promotion and commodity licensing) and of decoding (the empirical audience research) were all faithfully addressed, yet the attention to discourse and meaning was more marginalised in this research than in any of the other projects.

Buckingham introduced a major change in the direction that research in the cultural studies audience experiment had been heading. Instead of looking for the ways in which the meaning of the programme was structured in ideology, Buckingham changed tack to pursue the ways the programme encouraged 'viewers to produce meaning in certain ways and not others' (1987. 37). This change signalled a relinquishment of the more familiar popular culture commitment to media politics. Instead, Buckingham described in detail the things that audiences 'do' with texts while refraining from comment on the political significance of those activities. Once again the analytical agenda was primarily textual. Textual analysis provided the platform from which the activities of audiences were to be interpreted. Buckingham demonstrated, for example, how the audience may be positioned in complicity, ignorance or relative omniscience in relation to the unfolding of the text, and that this positioning affected the pleasure of viewing. He introduced psychoanalytic, semiotic and reader-response theories to interrogate the interpretive possibilities of the text, but in Barthes terminology, he appears to have understood text as work rather than as Text (Barthes 1977). Using this approach Buckingham was able to demonstrate the complexity of the soap opera and the basis of its appeal, so that, in his words, 'if one cannot say what *EastEnders* "means" to its audience, one can at least say a good deal about how it works' (Buckingham 1987: 36).

Buckingham's analysis began by examining the assumptions that the programme made about the existing knowledge of the audience – knowledge of story, plot and the world beyond. Next, he analysed how the programme encouraged its viewers to go beyond the information given, to generate hypotheses and inferences, and to make predictions about what would happen next. Third, he examined the extent to which the programme permitted or encouraged diversity of interpretation (1987: 37 ff.). In other words, 'positioning' was deduced from the formal qualities of the text, rather than by the struggles in discourse in which it was grounded. His fourth strategy involved talking with viewers, mostly school children, to assess the extent to which they took advantage of the positioning offered to them by the programme. His theory of the audience was one of constrained reception. There is no sense in Buckingham's research that the programme might have been better if the audience had had more opportunities to influence the production of the story. The realities of textual production he charted are of progressive exclusion of the audience from the structures of production, followed by a sort of approving celebration of the broadcast programme.

Instead of analysing the political activity of the audience, or its role in condoning the hegemonic practices of the media and in reproducing the *status quo*, Buckingham targeted cognitive and formal audience activities. The terms of analysis were abstract and theoretical, and extended the concept of 'activity' not only beyond the behaviourist bottom line of switching the TV on and switching it off, but also beyond the cognitive processes of perception and knowing. What was felt to be perceived and known was demonstrated to be linked to the text and accessible through formal textual analysis, informed by an understanding and sympathetic, rather than derogatory, orientation to the audience. Buckingham argued that such processes made it possible for viewers to discuss the programme without narrowly determining the meanings they would make. On the negative side, this type of analysis did not provide a good indication of the discursive significance, and therefore cultural power, of the programme.

EastEnders – an a-political text?

Buckingham's discussion of the politics of *EastEnders* collapsed together concepts of discourse, ideology and commonsense knowledge. He proposed that a text 'cannot be seen to "contain" an ideology which it simply imposes on its viewers – even a "hidden" ideology which viewers are not consciously aware of, but which can be recovered from the text by means of analysis' (1987: 86). Discourse was treated as a sort of background pool of knowledge which informed viewers' textual work. It was of secondary importance to textual analysis. The notion of 'commonsense knowledge' was adopted as an account of discourse, at least the type of discourse identified as relevant for *EastEnders*. This treatment of discourse was rather like culturalist definitions of ideology and mirrored Brunsdon and Morley's (1978: 87–92) discussion of how the *Nationwide* discourse was grounded in commonsense, where commonsense was understood as an ideological form of knowledge. Buckingham suggested that discourses may 'provide norms or stereotypes of what constitutes good or acceptable behaviour'; that they are not 'necessarily as rigid or as consistent as this', not 'primarily bodies of attitudes or beliefs' but 'means of generating knowledge', 'ways of understanding the world', ways of presenting 'what is known' and 'what it means to know' (ibid.: 87). The distance this definition of discourse has travelled from Hall's (1980a) terminology is demonstrated in its application.

Buckingham's exploration of the ideology of *EastEnders* began with a rather patchy account of changes in family and community in London's East End since the 1950s. He described the ways the programme reflected these changes and he referenced the structural conflicts affecting life in Britain in the 1980s. This useful social context was then substituted for an examination of the discourse of the programme. Rather than demonstrate how the political nature of the discourses produced by such changes privileged certain themes and ideas over others, Buckingham suggested that changed local conditions had miraculously produced the programme's discursive position. While the programme foregrounded socio-cultural change in space (the East End) and time (since the 1950s), it also presented a version of the significance of these events for people in the 1980s. It constructed that time and space around the contemporary dilemmas in which the scriptwriters and production team were themselves implicated. By defining *EastEnders* as a-political, as merely reflecting society rather than as actively contributing to its culture, Buckingham ignored the space for public debate created by popular television. Looking at the ways discourses about sex, gender and self, or even of 'community', were raised in the programme would have offered an alternative to the labelling of audience knowledge and cultural competence as ideological. In this respect, Buckingham generalised from the admittedly ideological and highly committed interest in the programme by lobby groups like the religious Festival of Light to the mass audience, and stereotyped mass audience ideas, too, as ideological. Yet, by allocating so much power to the text he refrained from considering why this programme attracted such passion from public lobby groups, apart from registering it as another indication of the disdain for popular culture and the mass audience which characterises such groups.

This definition of active viewing is far from new. It characterises cognitive developmental, symbolic interactionist and 'uses and gratifications' approaches (see, for example, Noble 1975; Wartella 1979; Palmer 1986). Where the 'uses and gratifications' approach traced an almost infinite diversity of uses for television based on physical, social or emotional needs, Buckingham stressed the importance of interpretative activity. He advocated mapping its diversity across gender, age, race, and other major socio-cultural distinctions among children. This again was not new, having been part of the agenda of much interpretive work about children and television, especially that carried out under the auspices of the Prix Jeunesse since the early 1970s. What is new in Buckingham's approach is the definition of the viewer's role as a sort of apologist for the text. The work that children perform in viewing television was taken to have been evident in the ways they took up, interacted with, resisted, acquiesced to, or opposed the possibilities for creating meaning offered by the text. From this perspective, different texts could be assumed to offer their viewers different sorts of invitations, so the relationship between a programme/text and the people who usually view it, is crucial for understanding its meaning. Buckingham's 'active' audience was not conceptually more active than those researched by other approaches, but was active in different ways and to different ends.

In Buckingham's work, the transformation of the cultural studies audience experiment from an appropriation of traditional audience research to a complex variety of reader-response criticism was achieved. The transformation was wrought at a cost, however. If the text is believed to be ideology free, to offer only interpretive possibilities, then production does not culminate in meaningful discourse but in interpretive possibilities. An active audience is needed to transform the text into meaningful discourse. Yet the theory does not provide a way of evaluating the nature, relevance, or political implications of these interpretive possibilities, especially if there are few conventions associated with interpretation (as is the case with popular cultural texts). The text is understood as 'finished in its unfinishedness' (Jauss 1982: 212–13). Its significance is always pending. It holds back from providing meaningful interpretive possibilities for real viewers to proclaim its meaning,[12] and takes it chances in the hurly burly of discursive entanglement.

At this point, it seems to me crucial to reconsider the qualities of popular culture as an interpretive system, and the value of applying literary criticism to its analysis. Eco (1979) and Fish (1980) have pointed out that the reader of literary criticism operates within a more constrained environment of policed (by the academic community) conventions than the reader of popular fiction. It does not necessarily follow from this that texts are non-ideological. Quite the opposite! It means that we have to look again, and more carefully, at how popular culture texts constrain the relatively undisciplined reading of mass audiences. In demonstrating the ways mass audience readings are patterned by the text, Buckingham strategically changed the thrust of the cultural studies audience experiment. His understanding of text – the text supposedly without meaning, without ideology – has the power to pattern, to orchestrate discourse. But the point of such orchestration – the text's discursive commitment – does not appear in Buckingham's analysis. And it may be, as Ien Ang implied, that popular culture texts specifically invite stereotypically sexist, racist or emotional (psychological) responses through the invocation of polarising cultural triggers like the 'ideology of mass culture'. Popular culture texts do not operate in a terrain of educated, abstract, and restrained debate, but in one of intense competition for the crown of being considered 'commonsense'.

NOTES

1 Janice Radway's (1984) *Reading the Romance: women, patriarchy and popular literature* was not included because its focus is the popular culture genre – the romance novel – not a television programme. Radway's work has been important to my analysis because of the standard and quality of her research. It became, in many respects, an ideal against which the television studies are evaluated.

2 Walkerdine's (1986) 'Video Replay: families films and fantasy', a study of a family watching Rocky 2 on video, was not included because the text was a film not a TV programme, and because audience research was conceived as part of a study of six-year-old girls rather than of the cultural meaning of the programme. Walkerdine's imaginative research provided considerable inspiration for the critical analysis of the five studies included.

Hodge and Tripp's (1986) *Children and Television: a semiotic approach*, was not included for a similar reason. The work was conceived as a response to effects research and sought to produce a counter discourse on children and television rather than to explain a particular text – though this is done as part of the process of arriving at a different destination.

3 What I mean by 'redefining' objects of research is discussed in Chapter 7.

4 For terminology, see Barthes (1977).

5 See Jauss (1982: 144) for an example of the critic presenting himself as the typical reader for want of skills and opportunity for the 'overdue empirical research'.

6 See Cohen (1980: 83) for a statement of the importance of these three steps in the ethnography of subcultures.

7 The programme known as 'Crossroads' in the UK was an early evening British soap opera set in a motel situated at a crossroads. It should not be confused with the mid-fifties US 'dramatic anthology' of the same name which featured 'dramatizations of the experiences of clergymen' (Brooks and Marsh 1992: 195).

8 Most letter writers did not argue, however, for the retention of the character on the basis of a sense of community. The audience of the letters is a constituency, 'principally a clientele: people who use (and perhaps buy) your services because you and others belonging to your guild are certified experts' (Said 1983: 152). Once this is recognised it is obvious that what shocks the reader about the TV network's treatment of its clientele is the obfuscation and deception. The loyalty and commitment of the letter writers was rewarded with disdain as the network pursued its control over the means of cultural production.

9 For example, researchers like McRobbie (1981) and Hobson (1980, 1981) explicitly addressed the absence of girls from the studies of youth subcultures, as well as the derogatory terms used by the male researcher to describe girls when their presence was acknowledged (see McRobbie 1981). The researchers attempted to prove the importance of researching girls' culture, and that the ideas of women researchers about how they should be studied were legitimate academic work. This alternative feminist research agenda provided the rationale for Hobson's study of housewives and the mass media (Hobson 1980). Housewives select and enjoy an alternative set of programmes from their husbands. Their media interests 'reinforce the sexual division of spheres of interest', both within the home and in 'the masculine world of work and politics' (Hobson 1980: 114). The issue of the division within the home of the power to control media equipment (the TV set, the remote control device) according to gender, and to define a hierarchy of programmes within the home, has since also been taken up by Morley (1986) and Gray (1987). As Hobson put it, 'part of the

ethnographic project for feminists has been to give a voice to the personal experience of women and girls who are studied in the research' (Grimshaw, Hobson and Willis 1980: 76). This affirmation of neglected voices in feminist research, the attention to the importance of women's interests, also created a crisis of legitimation in women's research. Rather than risk the insights or problems of the structuralist paradigm, especially in regard to discourse and discourse analysis, researchers looked back to older empirical methods. Such research was adequate 'to give a voice' to women's interests, and to document the involvement and particular characteristics of women's experiences under capitalism.

10   Other researchers, for example Morley (1986) and Gray (1987) have also documented resistant and alternative patterns of viewing among women, where the women arrange video viewing together in the absence of men and children. These situations and practices are suggested as constituting a popular feminist culture – except that the researchers never disclose the numbers or social class of the women involved. The practice is identified but its extent is never fully discussed, therefore its status as 'popular' is questionable. The notion of a covert and hidden feminine culture, hidden from the family and among the domestic routines which constitute family life, yet which somehow sustains a resistance to patriarchy, needs careful scrutiny. A hidden culture which somehow subverts the power structures of everyday life, manifesting itself in rituals of resistance such as alternative viewing practices, is likely to be practised, as Victor Turner (1977: 49) points out, by women most deeply committed to the 'traditional scenario'. Such rituals are equally likely to justify and legitimise patriarchy as to question it. In fact, their very existence confirms the women's commitment to the *status quo*. Participation in such 'resistant' activities, framed by the time schedule of domestic commitment and bounded by the length of the videotape or television programme, maintains the value placed on the sanctity of the domestic realm, especially as so much of the material viewed can be described as myths of origin, myths which 'explain' how a home comes to be established and/or maintained. An alternative culture is not always 'oppositional'; it may have its own different, though equally valid, reasons for accepting the 'dominant' ideology.

11   Ang received forty-two letters in reply to an advertisement she placed in the Dutch women's magazine *Viva*. The text of the advertisement ran

> I like watching the TV serial Dallas, but often get odd reactions to it. Would anyone like to write and tell me why you like watching it too, or dislike it? I should like to assimilate these reactions in my university thesis. Please write to . . .

(Ang 1985)

12   The point is crucial since Jauss's distinction defines the polar limits of audience activity. The Popperian position allocates the audience the task of interpretation as completion, while Lukacs's position points to a more improvisatory role for the audience. The text appears complete but is in fact a question mark until it is enacted/performed/lived. This is how Jauss puts it:

> At this point the dialogue diverges into two diametrically opposed definitions of the work of art, Lukács's formulation, 'unfinished in its finishedness', and Popper's, 'finished in its unfinishedness'. Popper dissolves the initial distinction from within: the work of art, is, in its unfinishedness, *finished*, since 'art makes the penultimate the ultimate', which is to say that 'through art, we take from nature that which it takes from us through the fact of our being alive: eternity.' For Popper art is acosmic, it is 'the human formulation of things'; the work of

art is finished in its unfinishedness, since it first achieves closure – be it in itself open or not – at the moment of the receiver's participation: 'the ultimate conclusion of any given work of art is the receiver.' On the other hand, Lukács maintains his differentiation by giving it a transcendental justification. The work of art is *unfinished* in its finishedness because 'it brings the temporal into relation with the timeless', which can also mean that 'the question is our absolute', since it presupposes the 'great answer' to which man is yoked without knowing it. Thus, the new theory of the open work brings the hermeneutics of art to a crossroads: the work of art, which for Popper opens out to the receiver, points aesthetics in the direction of dialogicity of aesthetic communication; the work of art that, for Lukács, opens out into the 'transcendental', reclaims for aesthetics the Platonic reassurance of a timeless perfection that in its monologic truth, leaves nothing for the receiver but the role of contemplative understanding.

(Jauss 1989: 212–13)

Chapter 5

Critical transposition

But reading is translation within the same language, and criticism is a free version of the poem or, to be more precise, a transposition. For the critic, the poem is the starting point towards another text, his own, while the translator, in another language and with different characters, must compose a poem analogous to the original. The second phase of the translator's activity is parallel to the poet's, with this essential difference: as he writes, the poet does not know where his poem will lead him; as he translates, the translator knows that his completed effort must reproduce the poem he has before him. The two phases of translation, therefore, are an inverted parallel of poetic creation.

(Paz 1992: 159)

TRANSLATION AND TRANSPOSITION IN AN AUDIENCE RESEARCH CONTEXT

The above quotation from Octavio Paz is useful for the perspective it offers, by analogy, on the relation between the performance of audience and audience research as an act of textual criticism. In my view, Paz's understanding of the relation between translation and transposition can be usefully transposed to an understanding of the relation between the practice of audience research and the performance of audience. From such a perspective, the activity of audience research becomes a more equal mixture of social science and criticism, a process of translation followed by transposition. Likewise, the performance of audience is defined as a two-step procedure which mirrors criticism, as a combination of textual translation and poetic improvisation. The similarity to semiotic analysis is evident, with both translation and transposition being necessary for a satisfactory act of translation – an act always striving to achieve the impossible goal of perfection.

From an analytical perspective, at least three linked texts are created in audience research (and each of these may take on multiple guises): the broadcast text; the audience performance as text, and the audience researcher's version of the audience text. Similarly, at least three transpositions occur: the producer/production team transpose documented experience into its broadcast form; the audience transposes the broadcast text into life experiences; and the audience researcher transposes the performance of audience into academic discourse. Like the transposition involved in criticism, audience research can be a process of critical transposition – a means by which the performance of the research participant is transposed into a different genre. As the poem is transposed to a genre of writing called criticism, so the texts people make in audience (cultural meanings), are available for transposition into the genre of writing called audience research. If such a perspective is adopted, some of the definitional problems associated with the concept of audience are solved. Instead of developing proliferating typologies of audience – the audience as consumer, community, constituent, receiver, couch potato, target, the child audience, the female audience, the aged audience, DINKS, etc. – it is possible to concentrate on the performance of 'audience' as memories, reflections, conversations, impersonations, improvisations, even interior decoration or personality can become expressions of audience. Social class, gender and ethnicity remain frameworks within which the performance of audience is articulated – shaping and privileging the modes adopted in the enactment of audience, but not explaining the process. The creative activities which express relations of audience are, in this view, the enactment of textual meaning. The shift, I suggest, is from imagining that we can recover the meaning of audience by watching people watching television, reading a book or listening to the radio, to recognising that the performance of audience exceeds the time-space of engagement and overflows unpredictably into the process of living. Both the observation and the interpretive work are required for audience research. In my view, too often literal translation alone (often as quotation) has been considered sufficient as audience research.

Audience research as collaboration

In order to gain access to the elusive, improvisatory dimension of audience, collaborative interaction between researcher and the researched is required. There can be no access to the meaning of audience unless research participants decide to share information about their experiences and performances of audience with the researcher. The viewer/reader engages with a text/programme and integrates that engagement with the negotiation of a life-path. The researcher addresses the negotiation as the performance of an audience relation and uses this engagement in turn to explain the audience relation, to transpose the reported experiences and performances into a new text, a text of criticism, a text which locates those activities not only within the academy, but also within a broader understanding of mass communication as contemporary international culture.

Translation does not occur in a vacuum – the translation itself mediates between groups who, for a variety of reasons, wish to understand each other better exploit their relationship, or sometimes simply to better ch other. To engage in audience research is therefore to enter into of powerful media discourses which lie outside the academy, sometimes co-opting academic research and at other times ignoring it. As translation, academic research is a mediation among interest blocks – government, industry, the media, academic colleagues and viewers themselves. The media are frequently the least acknowledged but more influential participants in the process of audience definition. They broker these relations (Nightingale 1993a). As a result, the discursive power struggle generated by audience research should be one of its most important products.

The promise of the early research

In my view the research in the cultural studies audience experiment was moving towards such an understanding of the multi-level processes of translation/transposition involved in this type of analysis. This is most evident in the research about *Nationwide* by Morley (1980: Chapter 6) where some time is spent exploring how audience readings conform to the encoding/decoding model. But other of the projects stopped short of recognising the transpositional aspects of audience. In Hobson (1982), in Tulloch and Moran (1986), and to a lesser extent in Buckingham (1987), the audience was considered the final repository for the text, the place from which the text shone back in appropriated form, evidence of the meaning of the message. Yet, since each of the projects asserted its belief in the activity of the audience, the manner in which this reflective evidence was accepted seems strange.

The polysemic text

The three textual levels I mentioned above (the broadcast text; the performed text; and the researcher's text) are not analytical categories that the researchers of the cultural studies experiment worked with, though at least three other different understandings of 'text' were used, frequently interchangeably and contradictorily. The first of these, the notion of the text as an independent entity 'possessing' meaning and pushing a series of ideological positions through its polysemic structure, is demonstrated in Brunsdon and Morley (1978). They sought, in their preferred reading of *Nationwide*, a statement of its overall ideological position. Their corresponding notion of audience was one which proposed that groups of people are already discursively structured by the social formation and thus sensitive to the political innuendo of *Nationwide*'s message. In other words, the broadcast audience was understood, not as aggregates of individuals, but as people defined and constructed by their positioning within the social formation and by their relations with other people similarly located. The broadcast audience was thought to be what Annette Kuhn has described as the 'social audience' (Kuhn 1987). People live, not as masses, but in patterns of communal interaction with other people, and Morley argued that it was on the basis of those communal interactions that people understand television programmes. This led Morley to engage in considerable interpretive work concerning the relation between the mode of address – that is, the nature of the interviewees' talk about the topic of a programme segment – and the acceptance or resistance of the position taken in the item. On the other hand, the statements made by research participants were also quoted verbatim into the research text (*The 'Nationwide' Audience: structure and decoding*, Morley 1980) and thus retained the literal dimension of the translation process.

The negotiated text

The second notion of text – the text as a negotiation, or mutual facilitation, between audience and text was used in *A Country Practice* research. This definition embraced the audience in either the performance of the text or in the discursive environment created around the text by the Press and particular interest groups. Audiences were considered an integral feature of the text, as were its production team or the marketing and distribution executives who defined its form. Such audiences were considered not 'interpretive communities' so much as performing communities. They were bound in service to the text, competent to speak about it because they regularly watched it and had acquired sufficient mastery of its themes, characters, plots and modes of representation to 'read' it. They spoke a language, forged in the moments of viewing the programme, informed by their reading of it. Such audiences exist somewhere between the 'spectator' of film theory and the social audience. On the one hand the audience is a product of the text itself, while on the other, textual activity is determined by social positioning. The problem with both these positions is that they cannot explain the meaning either of the text or of what audiences say about the text. The theory supplies no evaluative position for the researcher other than benign acceptance. By definition, all that is said, whether by production team, audience or distribution personnel, is a manifestation of the text.

The unfinished text

A third theory of text, traces of which appear in all the research except *Nationwide*, proposes that the meaning of the text exists only as reading. What a text means was understood as always in process, always evolving in the talk or writing which surrounds it. The presence of ideas about text as reading in the cultural studies audience experiment seems to be linked to the

STAFFORDSHIRE
UNIVERSITY
LIBRARY

cultural studies interest in populist politics, yet it parallels understandings developed more eloquently as reader-in-the-text (Suleiman and Crosman 1980) and reader-response criticism (Tompkins 1980). I would argue that the focus on popular culture points to the embryonic presence within the experiment of a theory of text which is even more radical than reader-response.

In the work of Stanley Fish (1980), reader-response criticism assumed an interpretive community where everyone was educated in criticism. Some homogeneity rather than heterogeneity within the community was assumed. By pointing to the diversity, and to the unruly reading of the mass audience, the cultural studies audience experiment extended this theory. The understanding of what was possible, theoretically, if such an understanding of media audiences was pursued was much too radical for the early 1980s, and it appeared to work against another research aim: to provide unity in an account of popular television. For example, in the *Crossroads* research, Hobson tried to allow her audience to interpret and evaluate the programme. She refused (as researcher) to offer an account of the programme, except as the edited amalgamation of discussion and research which became the book itself. By concentrating on what the production staff said they were trying to achieve and on how the audience appropriated that production – a naive matching of authorial intention and viewer perception – Hobson avoided looking at the poetics of audience action and reduced their activity instead to mimetic action. The viewing process in which the audience was engaged became, in the terms outlined at the beginning of this chapter, translation rather than transposition.

Hobson preferred to generalise the audience as a unity, as a constituency, made up of groups of people who shared common interests and standing within the social formation (the dependent: women, aged men, and the social security recipient). She assumed that the television programme should be evaluated on the basis of its ability to meet the needs of its constituency. This idealised hallucination of a world in which audiences really get the television they want – rather than the television others want them to have, of a world where television and its texts provide a simple reflection of the world as it really is, of a world where texts are subordinated to audience wishes for fair and just representation, demonstrates the populist basis of this view of text and the reasons why its similarities to reader-response are so marked: both assume a homogeneity of reading practice. As constituents, this community was considered to possess the right to have its voice heard – a right disputed, evaded or ignored by the channel representatives (Hobson 1982). The perspective was informed by concern for the alienated and abrogated rights of the mass audience and was developed to explain the popularity of mass media commodities. In Tulloch and Moran (1986) and Buckingham (1987), the voice allocated to the audience – the reasons they are most frequently recorded as giving to explain their attachment to a programme – describe either representation or the perceived 'realism' of the programme. In other words, a project of analysing the audience translation of the programme was undertaken.

The problem of what is said and what remains unspoken

Slippage between these three text–audience definitions resulted in considerable ambiguity within the studies, especially around the problem of textual meaning. With the exception of *Everyday Television* (Brunsdon and Morley 1978), all of the studies tried to find ways to avoid reading the text while inevitably having to do so. Buckingham, for example, tried to substitute description of *EastEnders* (of its textual structure and conformity to generic conventions) for its meaning, yet he inevitably produced his own reading of the programme in so 'describing' it. What he really refrained from was a description of the text's ideological implications. Statement of this meaning was sought from the audience. The empirical project of the audience which characterised the cultural studies audience experiment produced great confusion over textual meaning and placed too much emphasis on the value and significance of what people can say about the text. The problem of relying on what people can say is both complex and difficult, and in most of this research Eco's (1974) warning about the short-sightedness of inferring that what is *said* by the audience is in any direct way an indication of what is understood remains unheeded.

Secondly, relying on what people say about a television programme to evaluate it is also a problem. Not only may there be a gap between what is said and what is understood, but a reliance on what is said suggests an underlying definition of the historical subject as someone who is in possession of a 'reality', a reality of which an account can be given; it also suggests that the account will be based in a definition (shared with the researcher) about what constitutes an account; and assumes some shared agreement about what constitutes rational (and irrational) behaviour. In other words, it suggests both a shared culture and an awareness of one's position within that culture. In all five studies discussed in this book, the researcher takes what is said at face value, rather than accept what is said as another text that requires 'reading' (except for Ang (1985) – in the specific instance of people who do not like *Dallas*). In such circumstances, the assumption that researcher and audience share a culture is essential. Yet in most cases, class, gender and education (not to mention age and ethnicity) differentiate researcher from audience.

Researcher identification with the research participant

In the denial of difference between researcher and audience that this unfounded assumption supports, there is a tendency to lose sight of the significance of Lévi-Strauss's understanding of the historical subject as a 'crossroads'. This failure to understand the historical subject as a 'crossroads' (Lévi-Strauss 1978: 4) leads to a tendency to emphasise the uniqueness of individual action, rather than to search for ways of detecting the traces of culturally-authored action and discourse in what is said or done. Reliance on the things people said as a measure of the text compromised the audience–text studies by deflecting analysis away from discourse, and on to the particularities, the content only, of what was said. This ignores a possibility (encountered with my own research) which I consider extremely important – that when talking about television, the viewer may have a motivated agenda in which the researcher is implicated or which the researcher even activates. Talking about television encourages viewers to explain themselves. It opens up the dimension of 'reception' in which the viewer is most active – the realm of transposition[1] where simultaneously people find their own life discussed in textual form and incorporate television commentary on that life into their everyday operational strategies and tactics.

Vagaries of discourse

The relationship between discourse, ideology, and message was not clearly articulated for the cultural studies audience experiment. As a result, 'message as meaningful discourse' and 'message as ideology' were used interchangeably. While the conceptualisation of audiences as communities, in all its variety, is well suited to the analytical opportunities presented by discourse analysis, this option was in general ignored. The link, of course, is the conceptual inseparability of language, discourse and community. Just as text and audience are symbiotically linked, so too are community, discourse and language. This continuum locates discourse as the Janus-like middle term between community and language – the location identified by Kress (1983: 3) when describing its two faces – the social and the linguistic. Kress suggested that both faces are 'significant for an understanding of the media'. In Kress's definition:

> Discourses are organisations of meanings which are prefigured in, determined by, and existent in social and material structures and processes. Discourse represents the mode in which ideology finds its discursive expression. Discourse in its turn has its material realisation in the linguistic unit of text, that is, in complete units of organised linguistic features and processes. Hence from both a sociological and from a linguistic point of view it is desirable to replace the vague term message (as in 'media messages') with discourse on the one hand – when one considers the question of organised meaning from a social point of view –

and with text on the other, when one considers the question of
organisation of meaning from the point of view of language.

(Kress 1983: 3)

This distinction is not present in the cultural studies audience experiment.
Where material structures and processes of TV institutions were counted as
message production, social structures and processes were not. The
researchers refrained from tracing discourse from its textual materialisation
into its social forms. These realms were kept separate, as evident in this
statement by Morley:

> If we raise the question of audience interpretation of messages, we are
> already rejecting the assumption that the media are institutions whose
> messages automatically have an effect on us as their audience. As against
> that assumption I am raising to the central place in my analysis the
> question of how we make sense of the sense of the world that the media
> offer to us. This is to pose our activity in our sitting-rooms, watching the
> television, as an active process of decoding or interpretation, not simply a
> passive process of 'reception' or 'consumption' of messages.

(Morley 1992: 76)

Morley reiterates a recurrent theme – that interpretive approaches to
audience research are incompatible with effects research. I disagree with his
view. The very existence of the broadcast media assumes an audience already
structured in the discourses needed to engage with it. They are predicated on
the expectation and anticipation of effects – not necessarily the feared direct
behavioural effects but the particular interpretive effect Morley characterises
as interpretation. In this quotation, Morley characterises interpretive
audience activity as 'making sense of the sense of the world that the media
offer to us' – interpretation is confused with rational information processing.
Morley's position assumes that the viewer is aware of the sense of the text
'the media' intends and possesses the skills required to evaluate that
meaning. Audience activity is reduced to a kind of meta-commentary –
comments about the media's comments about the world. Earlier in this work
(ibid.: 75), Morley had reaffirmed his preference for the sender–message–
receiver model of what he calls 'communications' and the semiotics–
sociology media analysis proposed by Fiske. His preferred audience–text
research strategy can be represented diagrammatically in the following way:

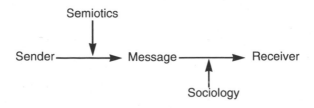

Where Kress recommended the replacement of message by both text and discourse, Morley prefers to treat message as text only, and to conceive of audiences as 'active' only in making decisions about what to do with the text as delivered, in other words, they may accept, amend or reject the message.

In the above extract, Morley appears to repudiate the innovative aspects of the *Nationwide* research, and to dismiss approaches to research in which consumption and reception are held to be mutually interactive. Creative processes of at least equal significance to cultural production are ignored and audience performance is limited to a rather narrow range of conscious cognitive activities which demonstrate a degree of comprehension. The possibility of other types of performance than judgemental comment, particularly in playful appropriations or improvisations where intuition may replace reasoned argument, are not explored.

The inseparable divide reactivated by Morley between text and audience perpetuates the power relation set in place by what de Certeau has described as the 'scriptural economy' (de Certeau 1984: Chapter X). The rupture of production from consumption, of writing from reading, of commercial or public independent institution from constituency, not only supports the aspirations to power of those who produce texts, but it also focuses the interests of that dominant power on limiting what is recognised as reading to a smaller repertoire than might otherwise have been addressed: to only the activities judged relevant for analysis of consumption and the evaluation of institutional performance. The project of reappropriating to reading a broader range of activities is described by de Certeau as 'justifying the reader's impertinence' (de Certeau 1984: 176). In de Certeau's words:

> Barthes distinguished three types of reading: the one that stops at the pleasure afforded by words, the one that rushes on to the end and 'faints with expectation', and the one that cultivates the desire to write: erotic, hunting, and initiatory modes of reading. There are others, in dreams, battle, autodidacticism, etc., that we cannot consider here. In any event, the reader's increased autonomy does not protect him, for the media extend their power over his imagination, that is, over everything he lets emerge from himself into the nets of the text – his fears, his dreams, his fantasised and lacking authorities. This is what the powers work on that make out of 'facts' and 'figures' a rhetoric whose target is precisely this surrendered intimacy.
>
> (de Certeau 1984: 176)

When we grasp the impertinent audacity that has the courage to take meanings and play with them, a much larger repertoire of activities can be defined as 'interpretation'. The temptation is to imagine that the larger repertoire of what counts as audience is impossible to apprehend in research practice.

In the cultural studies audience experiment, the researchers borrowed social science convention and recognised only letters and interview excerpts as their accounts of audience. Even the methodological problem of identifying the different analytic strategies required for (and the differing rules which govern) monologic (i.e. written) as opposed to dialogic (i.e. conversational) language use, was ignored in preference for direct quotation. In only Morley's research was there a concerted effort to account for what was spoken about, 'to discover who does the speaking, the positions and viewpoints from which they speak, the institutions which prompt people to speak about it and which store and distribute the things that are said' (Foucault 1979: 11). Obviously the cultural studies audience experiment did not address these issues. The difference between linguistic and social discourse was not recognised, nor was the problem of who is speaking consistently addressed, what interests were represented by that speaking, and what institutions prompted the speaking. The difficulty of discourse analysis, and a lack of methodological skills appropriate to it, precipitated a retreat to less problematic approaches to what audiences say about television. The discourse of the text was ignored altogether and an unwarranted identity assumed between researchers and their interviewees. This unjustifiable assumption permitted the researchers to speak on behalf of the audience, and to give not a second thought to worrying about expropriating their voices.

The approach taken to the analysis of 'social discourse' by culturalist researchers like Willis (1977) emphasised the constructedness of the social subject. As cultural products, people 'speak' their culture, 'speak' their experiences, 'speak' the forces that have formed them. From such a perspective, the expression of personal wants and needs also constitutes a speaking of the culture. The meaning of such speaking is located not in the nature of the individual, but in the commercially dominated culture which has formed and continuously reforms them. The work of the researcher is crucial in 'reading' what is said against the backdrop of cultural difference between researcher and researched. The analytical retreat to 'sender–message–receiver' models by the cultural studies audience researchers (when faced with the problem of interpreting interview material from the audience for instance) constitutes a break not only with a discourse-based theory of communication but also with the understanding of the relationship between the historical subject and the culture in which he or she is formed. Rather than attempt to identify the ways in which the culture is speaking through their interviewees, the researchers again and again stop at the point at which the diversity of what is said appears to defy interpretation. For example, Hobson retreated to the 'sender–message–receiver' model involved noting the interpretive action of the audience on the text, which was considered the same as the cognitive and emotional reactions of the audience to *Crossroads*:

However, my research with the audience has revealed that their interest is not simply in finding out how others will cope with a situation and learning from the messages of the programme, but, critically, also involves their own feelings and thoughts about how situations should be coped with. Communication is by no means a one-way process and the contribution which the audience makes to *Crossroads* is as important as the messages which the programme-makers put into the programme. In this sense, what the *Crossroads* audience has revealed is that there can be as many interpretations of a programme as the individual viewers bring to it. There is no overall intrinsic message or meaning in the work, but it comes alive and communicates when the viewers add their own interpretations and understanding to the programme.

(Hobson 1982: 170)

According to Hobson, programme makers put messages into the programme, and audiences make meanings about the programme, but no explanation of either set of messages is advanced. The analytical work of the researcher in constituting the text (Barthes 1977: 154–64) is also denied. This quotation demonstrates the difference in analytical approach from Morley (1980), for example, in that there is no attempt in Hobson's research to interpret the wider social or political significance (beyond family interaction patterns that is) of what is said by her interviewees or by the programme. In Tulloch and Moran's study of *A Country Practice*, whatever the audience or the programme-makers say about the programme is an example only of the difference in 'performance' of the text. Buckingham (1987: 154–7) concentrated on balancing the audience and text halves of the communication equation, but his focus on children as 'active producers of meaning' (ibid.: 156) again affirmed the regression to a 'sender–message–receiver' position and limited the focus of his research to establishing activity on the part of children. The discursive significance of audience activity, beyond pointing back to the diversity of the audience, tends to be ignored.

Ang (1985), by contrast, tried to account for the discourse of her interviewees by positing two 'ideologies' (the ideologies of mass culture and populism) which operate independently of institutional or social basis simply to spoil or justify (respectively) the pleasure people find in texts like *Dallas*. She ignored who her interviewees were, what institutional interests (other than the two ideologies) may have been present in what they said, and identified only a theme or pattern of response which overlooked the 'social' nature of discourse. While Ang does not regress to a 'sender–message–receiver' model of communication, her work introduced another confounding analytical problem associated with the lack of clarity about the definitions of discourse used in the cultural studies audience experiment.

It is implied in the 'Encoding/decoding' essay (Hall 1980a) that the value of a discursive model of communication is political, that the purpose of media analysis is political. This 'political' aspect is even envisaged more specifically as 'national'. Yet in Ang's work, a theme is introduced which is characteristic of feminist politics but is, in some senses, antithetical to the political thrust of the encoding/decoding model. That theme is the theme of 'identity'. For feminist theorists like Ang and Radway, identity is a political issue, and the pleasures of media texts like *Dallas* demonstrate not only what women like, but also the ways in which women construct their identities around such texts. One could say that they also inevitably suggest the equal relevance of personal and political explanations of textual pleasure. The particularism of personal explanations undermines the social and political relevance of discourse analysis, unless the politics of that pleasure is demonstrated. In the *Dallas* research, situated as it was midway between new left radical feminist populism and Lacanian psychoanalytic theories of feminine identity, the politics of pleasure took second place to particularist explanation. In this sense, the *Dallas* research shared a preference for particularist explanations of the audience more reminiscent of psychological and social psychological research than of discourse analysis.

The treatment of discourse in the cultural studies audience experiment is instructive. What could, and probably should have been, the beginning of a new type of media research which refused the division both of audience from text, of writing from reading, gradually changed over the ten to twelve years of the experiment into an approach which effaced the audience. For example, viewers proved less important for the *EastEnders* research than they had been for the *Nationwide* research. Instead of uniting audience and text in the same project, discourse came to be identified as a sign of the ideology in the audience. Such disappearances and absences demonstrate both the shared commonality of purpose in the cultural studies audience experiment and the experimental nature of the research – the lack of consensus about how it should be done or what, in essence, it should be about.

This slippage – from a position full of radical potential to a sort of minor elaboration on more or less acceptable ideas from the reader-response fringes of literary theory – occurred for two reasons. Firstly, the understanding of what was meant by discourse in the early 1980s was much more limited than it is today. The sophistication of writing about Voloshinov and Pêcheaux in Morley's work, for instance, was simply not matched by a comparable sophistication in research practice. Foucault's work provided one of the few models available, but really was not appropriate as the type of research for a major confrontation with the empiricist methods and empirical rationality of mainstream audience research. It was important that the research practice advocated be recognised as a contender to replace traditional communication models of the media. For researchers unused to the more technically sophisticated and more micro-level analysis of fields like psycholinguistics, linguistics and social semiotics, there were few discourse-research models available.

The second reason for the slippage was, in my view, related to the narrowness of definition of what was taken into account as audience activity. As already mentioned, the cultural studies audience experiment appeared unable to imagine audience action beyond the limited spheres addressed by most mainstream audience research. The result was a tendency to concentrate only on the translating work undertaken by the audience – on the translating work audiences do in order to repeat the text. This under-conceptualisation diminished both 'text' and 'audience'. The text became linked to its denotation and the audience was understood as possessed by ideologies which twisted their ability to explain that denotation. The possibility that the audience might engage in criticism of a poetic or 'transpositional' type was either not considered or perhaps, if it was, no one at that stage knew what to do about it.

NOTE

1 I have in mind here Nightingale (1992) and (1996). In the 1992 research about groups watching football on TV, and in the 1994 research about Japanese and Australian viewers, the viewers were encouraged to identify programmes they remembered and to discuss their memories of viewing. In such contexts, viewers actively created their own stories of television and the significance of their favourite programmes. Viewers actively engaged in complex modes of articulation with discourses of gender and nation.

Chapter 6

Cultural translation

The intellectual nature of a story is exhausted with its text, but the functional, cultural, and pragmatic aspect of any native tale is manifested as much in its enactment, embodiment, and contextual relations as in the text. It is easier to write down the story than to observe the diffuse, complex ways in which it enters into life, or to study its function by the observation of the vast social and cultural realities into which it enters. And this is the reason why we have so many texts and why we know so little about the very nature of myth

(Malinowski 1954: 111)

Malinowski, the ethnographer who played such a significant role in the establishment of British ethnography, demonstrates in this statement an interest in issues which, thirty years later, continue to preoccupy cultural studies researchers. The text, as work, has a finite quality: a beginning and an end, an existence as spoken or written word, as television or computer program. But there is another text, just as important but infinitely more elusive. It is the text which lives in the community of its users and which 'enters into life'. This is the text that I believe the cultural studies audience experiment tried to capture. The experiment failed to anticipate the difficulty of the task undertaken, and could not resist the allure of the 'intellectual nature' of texts. The 'experiment' addressed the difficult task of accounting for the ways in which particular popular television programmes enter into the broad 'social and cultural realities' in which they are produced and used. In this sense they represent a functionalist incursion into the structuralist territory of the text. They followed the inclination of the ethnographer. As with the above statement by Malinowski, the fascination of the experiment resides in its tantalising promise: a promise to extend cultural analysis into the fields of policy making (about children and television, about media education, etc.); to extend the range of cultural criticism beyond a preoccupation with texts, and into the world of industrial capital, commercial culture and national and international politics. Yet, paradoxically, this promise was undone by the concentration on consumption in the research we have examined, and by the populist ethic of cultural studies (McGuigan 1992).

Consumption

Consumption figured in the cultural studies audience experiment both as a justification for the decision to study popular cultural texts, and as the problem to be explained. This circular argument – that high consumption makes popular culture worth studying, and that the reason for studying popular culture is its high consumption – robbed the research of its 'critical' edge and blocked the more traditional cultural studies critique based in authenticity. In addition, it replaced the critical media studies emphasis on political economy with a justification grounded in populist acceptance. The manner of such distanciation of consumption within the research agendas obscured opportunities for the development of criticism based on ideas or discourses generated by consumption and consumerism.

The research demonstrated, in its own right, a complex conflict within cultural studies between competing theories, ideas and explanations about popular cultural phenomena. The conflict concerned whether mass culture is thought of as inherently good or bad – whether its institutional origins mark it as the ideas of the ruling classes, or whether its popularity and bad reputation identify its celebration as resistance to the ruling classes. Each of the studies, except for Morley (1980), explicitly proclaimed its commitment to the vindication of the popular text, affirming the latter view, and avoided the discomfort of knowledge about control of media production. The commitment to materialist aesthetics meant that the high ratings achieved by some television programmes, and the pleasure viewers claimed to experience when viewing them, were accepted as an indication of the value of the text. The discursive commitment of the popular text was overlooked in the rush to rescue it as an authentic example of popular taste.

One cannot help but ask why the popular text needed so much vindication – why was the issue not settled in 1982 by Hobson or in 1985 by Ang? The answer is undoubtedly linked in part to the newness of such texts as objects of serious academic scrutiny. Each researcher felt obliged to justify their choice of a popular television programme as academic research. The lack of resolution of the worth of the popular text persisted because of an incommensurability between the two paradigms of cultural studies – not between areas of gross disagreement, but between those areas where both British and European theorists had developed perspectives and a language which were almost, but not quite, identical. In particular, the incommensurability arose from the lack of consensus about three ideas: the relation between the historical, and therefore social, 'subject' and 'culture'; the importance attached to 'experience' in cultural explanation; and the relation between discourse and ideology.

Many British theorists were not particularly sensitive to the difference of European ideas from their own. As a result they could read and write eloquently about 'the subject', using European sources, while doggedly retaining individualism – the 'individual' chose solidarity with community, and chose oppositional ideas rather than submit to the dominant ideas of the ruling classes. In doing so, the British position differed dramatically from, for example, that of Lévi-Strauss (1978), who considered the person a 'crossroads' – an intersection where ideas meet – rather than as one who predates culture as a separate entity free to decide among ideas. Again, the British perspective failed to register that they placed a qualitatively different value on experience as cultural explanation, and so overlooked the difference between the documentation of experience as authentication and the authority of direct quotation. By including an audience research agenda in the cultural studies project, in what is really documentarist rather than 'ethnographic' research, the cultural studies audience experiment was suddenly open to methodological demands and criticism from social scientists. Functionalist and empiricist psychological and social research traditions seldom question the theoretical basis of their research methods, or identify as relevant the basic tenets of a cultural agenda. By contrast, the cultural studies audience experiment addressed the audience–text nexus and produced data and stories – information easily misread as belonging to other research paradigms, especially symbolic interactionism, which lack comparable theories of text, culture or subjectivity. In such a context, some means of identifying and celebrating the difference of 'cultural' audience research was, and remains, essential. Cultural studies audience research should examine and question the meaning of the methods it shares with social science approaches. The break with the traditional paradigms could also have been clearly spelled out. Instead, a spurious commonality was claimed which included acceptance of the sender–message–receiver model, of the 'individual' as research 'object', and of 'consumption' as the rationale for research.

Attention to the specificity and appropriateness of research method was most noticeably absent from the explanation and maintenance of a critical perspective when researching the contexts of production. As noted earlier, the cultural studies audience experiment demonstrated that production teams, production companies and the Press adhere strongly to a belief in the mass audience. The 'mass audience' is the accepted way of thinking about audiences in the television industry. It provides the rationale for reliance on, and self-evaluation by, television ratings (see Hartley 1987). The community concepts implicit in cultural studies research seem irrational in industry terms. In the *Crossroads*, *A Country Practice* and *EastEnders* research, attempts were made to analyse the discursive significance of the decision-making of production personnel. In each case the researchers seemed uncritical, almost unctuous, in their acceptance of the insights, explanations and power of the television professionals. While this acceptance can be linked to reliance on the hospitality and generosity of such personnel, and to the less than powerful professional status of academics in the world of television production, it results in the researcher being compromised. In the

Crossroads research the audience was 'explained' by the television professionals in terms of the accepted model of democratic process: the people demonstrated the strength of their feelings, and the company bowed to their wishes. Hobson, in the end, echoed their view of the audience – and seemed to affirm that populist and consensus democracy reigns in television land. In the *A Country Practice* research, a sort of identity – a relation of homology – was postulated between readings generated in production, distribution and reception. No one seriously questioned the logic of assumptions made about the nature of the broadcast audience. In the *EastEnders* research, by contrast, the audience seemed completely cut off from the production personnel. The form of Buckingham's analysis was linear, like the sender–message–receiver model. While the audience was envisaged as a 'community' in the researcher's interactions with them, it was positioned in a linear relation of reception to the text. In all three cases an ambiguity about the nature of the audience is obvious. The ambiguity arose because the theories of audience which inform professional television practice (theories of the mass audience) sit uneasily, in a state of incommensurability, alongside attempts to utilise theories of audience as community – community in the 'ethnographic' sense used to justify the empirical research, and community in the textually defined sense which licenses discursive unity/community.

Ethnography

In the mid-1980s the research tactics used in the cultural studies audience experiment were characterised as 'ethnographic' by Fiske (1987a), presumably, in order to distinguish the research from the social and psychological functionalism of 'uses and gratifications' research which, at times, it superficially resembled. The use of the term 'ethnographic' is paradoxical, and in my view confuses ethnography and documentarism. The best 'ethnographic' practice in the five studies we have examined was production research, not audience research, yet it is of the 'audience research' that the term is held to be characteristic. Hobson's observation and description of the production of *Crossroads* and Tulloch and Moran's methodical pursuit of each aspect of the production process of *A Country Practice* are exemplary, if not politically insightful. Both Tulloch and Moran brought rich personal histories as television researchers to the observation and analysis of the production teams and production values pursued in *A Country Practice*, yet this expertise was not transferred to the context of audience research. The audience research was in all cases minimally documented and lacking in descriptive acuity. Authenticating experiences were reported, but the discomforts and disorientation, the paranoia and insecurity that the field work presumably engendered[1] (and how the researcher dealt with these problems) were omitted. Theories of text and discourse were not clearly articulated as research practice, resulting in often platitudinous extrapolation from letters or records of interview. Their research activities resemble much more closely the reporting activities of journalists than the field accounts of ethnographers. In particular, one is reminded of the pioneering work of Henry Mayhew,[2] the first British journalist to document the need for social reform by collecting the oral histories of nineteenth-century street urchins.

The cultural studies audience experiment relied disproportionately on the authenticating quality of its 'ethnographic' data. This reliance exemplifies what Rosaldo has described as 'the false ethnographic authority of polyphony' (1986: 82). Even though the researchers' voices and those of their interviewees were at times equally heard,[3] there is little sensitivity to the power relations or cultural differences in operation at the time of observation or interview. The pattern of quotation is like a dance – the researcher leads and the researched follow. And this precisely is Rosaldo's point. The researched dance to the researcher's tune, using all their intelligence and physical ability to take advantage of a chance for representation in the wider context of a research report or a book. In the context of contemporary media research, the motivation to take part in research may be less, the inequality of a research contract in which access is freely given may be better understood, and the potential loss of privacy or the lived consequences of misrepresentation may be more immediately experienced. In fact, as mentioned in the examination of both *Crossroads* and *EastEnders*, it was openly denied that such factors could influence the research. The quality of the relationship between researcher and interviewee was claimed to overcome such methodological problems and the good relations which the researcher experienced were assumed to be shared by the interviewees. The marked contrast with the paranoia experienced by Walkerdine (1986) during her observation of a working-class British family should be registered. The pervasive component of research practice best understood as 'translation' – the interpretation of viewer utterances in the language of the research report – was ignored.

Translation is crucial and inescapable in cultural research, whether as reading (Paz 1992) or as a variety of linguistic interpretation. Research participants translate their experiences into explanations for the researcher. Researchers translate the recounted experiences into research reports and narratives of other sorts for their colleagues in the research community or for the general public. Jakobsen (1992: 145) mentions three types of translation: rewording (intralingual); translation proper, as of foreign languages (interlingual); and transmutation (intersemiotic). In the type of research we have been looking at, interlingual translation is perhaps the only type we can disregard; though this cannot be assumed, especially if jargon and argot affect the language in which the research is conducted. Research participant's words do not speak for themselves; innuendo and allusion, the languages of glance, touch, laughter, intonation must all be accounted for. The research process assumes that a real interaction, the research interview or discussion, will be re-presented as writing, as documentation, a report or an academic article. The necessity for translation was a sub-text of Walkerdine's (1986) despair at her non-acceptance as working class by a working-class family. For the family, Walkerdine's working-class childhood was eclipsed by an adulthood in which she had moved into what was perceived as a different class – middle class. Whether differences are real or imagined, transitory or continuing, the necessity for translation remains. Everyday realities, the particularities of the mundane, require transmutation into representation – as generic types or equivalences of everyday realities – which conform to the patterns or representation demanded by the academic community or by policy makers. Rather than accept the inevitability of translation, the cultural studies audience experiment denied it in the mistaken belief that accurate, unedited quotation would compensate for the researcher's control of the final written report. The lesson that the cultural studies audience experiment has taught us is that the pursuit of cultural research always possesses a translative dimension. Translation and its pursuit cannot be denied or overlooked. It is the process which should be the focus of our activity.

From triangulation to multi-focus research

Triangulation was an established strategy for community research, to be advocated when 'the nature of the problem under investigation demands a multi-method approach'. For Gorden:

> Community studies must triangulate information from public records, personal documents, newspapers, direct interviews with the focal persons, participant-observation, and pure observation merely to obtain the many types of information needed to cover the complex phenomenon we call a community. Experimental studies, naturalistic communities studies, and statistical surveys can be fruitfully combined in many instances.
>
> (Gorden 1987: 12)

Even though aspects of triangulation can be detected in the cultural studies audience experiment, the research shifted its focus over time from a unitary concern with community to what I will call a multi-focus orientation to popular texts, most evident in the *EastEnders* research. The central focus, for example, in the *Nationwide* studies was the ideology of the programme and its reflection in the verbal discourses of the audience, understood as an interlocking diversity of communities. This centrality of focus gave way in the subsequent studies to research strategies better described as multi-focal. In the *EastEnders* research the focus changed with each section of the book. The research was about the interests and plans the BBC and the production personnel had for the programme; then about the textual pleasure of *EastEnders*; next the vested interests of the Press, the corporate sector and sectional lobby groups in the programme and its audience; and finally about audience interpretation of the programme. The most crucial changes in focus were from explaining the popularity of the programme to justifying the interpretive 'work' of the audience and providing background information for teaching about the programme in schools. In the *Dallas* research the focus held more firmly to the 'pleasure' of *Dallas*, yet in this case the empirical research was slight (consisting of only forty-two letters, which are not analysed in their own right) coupled with quotations from the letters and analysis of the programme using theoretical exegesis and description of current trends in feminism. The coherence of the multiple foci was tenuous, fluctuating between explaining the processes by which *Dallas* was experienced as 'pleasure', justifying feminine and feminist interest in the programme, and teaching about it. The multiple foci of the research permitted it to be simultaneously popular culture research, empirical audience research, and teaching material. It is interesting that in all the studies (except Morley's once again), the ethnographic initiative was not the central research strategy but used only to validate production and textual initiatives. In this regard, the description of the studies as 'ethnographic' is even more puzzling, since their central concern remained with the status and meaning of the text.

The ethnographic convention

Since description of the studies as 'ethnographic' cannot be completely justified by the research methods used, other reasons must be sought, because describing these studies as 'ethnographic' may serve another purpose. As I pointed out in the last chapter, the term has acquired conventional status within cultural studies as the way of referring to the empirical audience research undertaken within the field. Accordingly, the term is used not to classify the research as belonging to, or even as having any links with, ethnography, but to signify the allegiance of the research to another academic field – British cultural studies. In the British cultural studies context, the term 'ethnographic' gives the work connotations which include cultural, community-based, empirical, and phenomenal, all of which terms were pursued in the cultural studies audience experiment. The term 'ethnographic' became a way of talking about research which possesses these characteristics. Invoking these characteristics also signalled the difference of the research from 'cultural' research with other characteristics, such as textual studies and perhaps even psychoanalytic studies. The term 'ethnographic' legitimated the research, denoted its cultural, phenomenal and empirical methods, and even signified its emphasis on 'community'.

The problem is that the term 'ethnography' has other lives. It has a life within the discipline of anthropology and a life within the research traditions of symbolic interactionism, both of which affected the ways in which the cultural studies audience experiment was enacted and evaluated. These other lives of the term 'ethnographic', reference both historical and theoretical links with the past of cultural studies, with its past triumphs as well as its failures. The other lives of 'ethnographic' also suggest possibilities for an 'ethnographic' future in cultural studies, especially since the discipline of anthropology is currently appropriating many of the theoretical insights from literary studies which 'met' in cultural studies in the 1970s (see Clifford and Marcus 1986).

Using 'ethnographic' to reference the 'cultural studies' past

The second reason for using the term 'ethnographic' may have been motivated, therefore, by desires to retain something, be something, achieve something it had not yet achieved. The case for the use of the term as an attempt to 'retain' something from the past of cultural studies is obvious. During the 1970s, British cultural studies was characterised by an intense interest in subcultures and deviance, and drew on research methods from both anthropology and symbolic interactionism to pursue its ends. Often the term 'ethnography' was used to refer to symbolic interactionist methods (see Pearson and Twohig 1975; Roberts 1975; Willis 1980; Grimshaw et al. 1980), as it is still by symbolic interactionists (see Wartella 1987). But at least two other heritages are referenced in the cultural studies use of 'ethnography' as a legitimating method – heritages which eventually shook the phenomenal centrality of the symbolic interactionist underpinnings of cultural studies, as cultural studies researchers such as Willis had always argued they must (Willis 1980 and Grimshaw et al. 1980) – and led to the ascendancy of literary and structuralist approaches instead.

I have discussed the meeting of the two paradigms of cultural studies in Chapter 3, and here I want merely to draw attention to a slightly different issue. The struggle within cultural studies, the struggle between the two paradigms, characterised as a struggle between culturalism and structuralism by Hall, has now been played out on the terrain of almost all of the social sciences. In anthropology the exploration of the implications for ethnographic practice of 'textual criticism, cultural history, semiotics, hermeneutic philosophy, and psychoanalysis' (Clifford 1986: 4) – the 'epistemological turn' in anthropology – has led to significant soul-searching. But similar processes have been registered in archaeology (Hodder 1986) and history. In each case, what began as a critique of practice, ends in a more rigorous concentration on texts, a revaluation of hermeneutic social science practices, and a greater tolerance of relativism.

The cultural studies audience experiment pre-dated the 'epistemological turn' in anthropology, and so was unable to take advantage of the revision and re-evaluation of method precipitated. For this reason, the 'ethnographic' method employed in the cultural studies audience experiment demonstrated few of the sensitivities in ethnographic research which have since come to signal enlightened practice – particularly sensitivity to negotiation, the sharing of research goals, and the presentation of research outcomes with research participants. The 'ethnographic' tradition of cultural studies had traditionally focused on how the media exploited subcultural groups or appropriated and neutralised their resistance to the dominant culture. This tradition was diametrically opposed to positivist 'administrative' audience research (Gitlin 1978), which presumed the purpose of audience research to be the management or commercially viable delivery of audiences. The hiatus between the phenomenological orientation of subcultural research and the administrative orientation of mainstream audience research promised to be remedied by the 'encoding/decoding' model. Using the term 'ethnographic' asserted a desired continuity between the cultural studies audience experiment and the earlier subcultural research. That desired continuity was for a quality of research which would allow the particular cultural experiences of broadcast television viewers to be understood in the context of communication in capitalist society. In other words, it would allow experience to be read in the superstructural organisation of society, available as representation in its textual production.

The work of Paul Willis (1977, 1978) was widely regarded as the model for the cultural studies ethnographic method. In the mid-1980s, Willis's work was cited as the direction for British cultural studies reception research (Morley and Silverstone 1988), for symbolic interactionist 'cultural' research (Traudt and Lont 1987: 144, 159) and as challenging the anthropological tradition of ethnography to undertake broader and more critical research appropriate to the conditions of the modern world order in the re-evaluation of anthropology (Marcus 1986). What Willis's work offered, as Marcus pointed out, was a demonstration that the cultural (in Willis's case, capitalist society) defines the particular (school non-conformity and labour conformity). Willis achieved this, not by a positivist attempt to prove Marxist theory through his observations, but by invoking Marxist theory as given. As Marcus again has pointed out, Willis's purpose was achieved by the exploration of 'the cultural meanings of the production of Labor and commodity fetishism' which 'provides textual means for bringing the larger order into the space of ethnography' (Marcus 1986: 173). Willis's adherence to the notion of cultural totality, to the structuralist project of reading the culture in its forms – the legacy of Raymond Williams – is seen by Marcus as a positive achievement for anthropology emerging from Willis's work. As Marcus put it:

> Nonetheless, Willis does pose the challenge for the anthropological tradition of ethnography, underlain perhaps by an unattainable ideal of

holism not to be taken literally, to apply ethnography to projects of broader purpose and theoretical significance, like his own. This entails the writing of mixed genre texts, similar to those envisioned by Raymond Williams for social realism, in which ethnographic representation and authority would be a variably salient component.

(Marcus 1986: 188)

If, however, a continuity is assumed between the 'ethnographic' practice of Willis and the multi-focus research of the cultural studies audience experiment, the crucial differences between them could be overlooked. Willis's aim was to demonstrate the working of social process, to explain cultural reproduction through the interlocking of education and the labour process. This type of broad social aim is missing from the cultural studies audience experiment, which concentrated on several more limited aims, such as explaining the popularity of the text, teaching about British cultural studies, or demonstrating its pleasures. The cultural studies audience experiment used its 'ethnographic' data to achieve textually defined aims rather than to explain social process.

Secondly, Willis's ethnographic method did not address the problem of reading complex cultural forms like popular television programmes. Reading the significance of the signs of a subculture (dress, argot, behaviour, rituals, etc.) is qualitatively different from reading television and from reading people's reading of television. The direct communal authorship of the signs of a subculture is qualitatively different from the highly institutionalised, conventionalised, and commercially motivated production of television. The relationship of community to cultural form combines appropriation and authorship so that processes like 'bricolage' are articulated in extremely complex ways. The professionalisation of television production and the complexity of the text as appropriated object, suggest that a case can be made for the application of textual skills of reading to socio-cultural analysis.

The similarities and differences between cultural studies and anthropological traditions of ethnography offer a position from which positive directions for future work might be contemplated. I have drawn attention to:

- the limitations of the 'ethnographic' practice used in the cultural studies audience experiment;
- the tendency to regress to particularistic explanations characteristic of symbolic interactionism, which uses similar methods but lacks the strong Marxist understanding of the cultural totality as an explanatory frame for its observations;
- the lack of a uniting focus in the cultural studies audience experiment which resulted in variability and compromise in the role of the researcher;
- the problem of the 'visualism' of the cultural studies ethnographic tradition which affects not only the choice of research participants (always classified

as working class) and the relation suggested between researcher and researched (always and necessarily voyeuristic).

Nevertheless, the cultural studies audience experiment represented an innovation in cultural research practice. It generated first attempts at mixed-genre writing, at finding a way to integrate audience discourse and observational data with qualitatively different observations and materials about television texts, production, distribution and industries. The criticism of the cultural studies ethnographic tradition from anthropology offers the possibility for improving cultural studies ethnographic practice by diagnosing the problems inherent in the approach as currently practiced, and clearly defining a strong research focus even if it means advocating the possibly 'unattainable ideal of holism'.

Popular writing

The 'epistemological turn' in anthropology facilitated the identification and critical evaluation of the popular writing based on fieldwork experiences (Pratt 1986). This concern about the writing of ethnography in anthropology poses a last challenge to the cultural studies audience experiment – the challenge of popular writing. Like media studies, anthropology has a strong tradition of producing both popular and academic writing. As Pratt (1986) has pointed out, these traditions feed off each other. Sometimes both academic and popular accounts are written by the one researcher, sometimes the popular writing borrows authority from the parent discipline, and sometimes there is an unacknowledged reliance on the popular writings within academic practice. More importantly perhaps, unacknowledged reliance on the themes and imagery of popular writing can point to the explanations and rationalisations the researcher used to justify their role.

The cultural studies audience experiment produced a genre of popular academic writing about the mass media, a genre of writing which aspired to be both academic and popular. It was written for diverse audiences rather than for a specific reading community and constitutes an example of a genre of academic writing which has become more prevalent in the 1980s. The popularity of the programme studied, and the possibility of reader identification with both the act of viewing and the description of viewing practices, offered an ideal opportunity, for both academic and publisher, to increase the number of sales beyond the limitations of small and dispersed academic communities.

The dynamic of the dual ethnographic literature compared personal, impressionistic accounts with the formal, objective, disciplined classification of 'scientific anthropology'. The 'combining of personal narrative and objectified account' was a characteristic of the travel writing from which 'ethnography has traditionally distinguished itself' (Pratt 1986: 33). Unlike the personal narratives of anthropology, the popular writing of cultural studies tends not to be a site for personal disclosure (though David Buckingham's account of *EastEnders* would not be possible without the considerable personal viewing commitment to the programme which is demonstrated), but for a simplified academic writing. The books try to limit or control the use of jargon and special languages in order to engage a broader audience. The piecemeal and incomplete nature of the research design, the subjugation of academic purpose to either teaching (Tulloch and Moran, Ang, Buckingham) or to telling a story (Hobson, and, to a lesser degree, Buckingham), and the loyalty developed to the production personnel during the course of the research, all place the writing in a compromised position as far as ideals of academic writing are concerned. The popular writing style can be understood when the populist politics of the research is remembered. Like ethnographic writing, the popular writing of cultural studies can be linked to older styles of writing about television and film, most often licensed by the makers of the film or product (such as Neil Sinyard's *The Best of Disney* (1988) or Stephen Cox's *The Addams Chronicles* (1991)) and against which academic media studies defines itself. This borrowing from institutionally licensed and sycophantic genres was not primarily to congratulate either audience or industry, but to bring about broader social change. By aiming to teach non-academic readers what their expectations of the media and media industries should be, a more vigorous popular criticism of the media was perhaps anticipated. As popular writing about popular culture, these books undertook a 'populist' role. They attempted to justify popular programmes against the derogatory criticism by the Press and policy makers to rescue the audience from accusations of passivity and mindlessness. As a result they trod a thin line between propaganda and congratulation of the programme and its production staff, and 'acceptable' academic distance and criticism.

Popular culture

As pointed out earlier, the 'encoding/decoding' model proposed a discourse-based theory of communication. Its implied theory of audience approximated most closely the community analogy. The assumed basis for interaction in such a community varies from the real to the imaginary, from interactions based in everyday encounters, to interactions based in imagined membership of a community which never meets or 'actually' interacts, but which experiences itself through mediated accounts and loose forms of voluntary association. Such communities are perhaps better described as 'discursive formations', because the sharing of a language and patterns of explanation, as well as commitment to a particular institution or regime which controls and maintains the discourse, may well exhaust the range of communal action and activity sustained. Janice Radway (1988) has suggested the term 'nomadic subjects' for the wandering, migratory and transitory nature of the affiliations the members of such 'communities' sustain.

As explanations of the audiences of popular television, the cultural studies audience experiment focused attention on the power of a particular television programme to create a discursive environment which attracts nomadic subjects and encourages them to participate in an imaginary (as opposed to an 'imagined') community. Such imaginary communities are differentiated, not simple and unitary. Communal differentiation allows the inclusion of production teams, the textual community of characters or personalities, and the audience within its imagined parameters. Such imaginary communities also suggest a commitment to the institution 'television' or (given the degree of cross-media referencing in popular culture) even the entertainment industries.

Pleasure and fantasy

The emphasis on pleasure and fantasy in the cultural studies audience experiment was linked to the New Left feminist political strategy of recuperating women's leisure interests and enjoyment, and of defining a feminist political strategy based on a knowledge of what women like and why. This was most obvious in the feminist commitment of the *Crossroads* and *Dallas* research, but it was appropriated by the *A Country Practice* and *EastEnders* research, where it was split off from the feminist agenda and (most importantly) politics. The *Crossroads* and *Dallas* studies explained the pleasure the programmes offered their women audiences, but chose different means of doing so. Hobson concentrated on women as a 'social' audience while Ang tried to find a balance between the 'spectator' (the textually-defined audience) and the 'social audience' (see Kuhn 1987 for terminology). Both drew on Modleski's accounts of women as television spectators and of the pleasure of soap opera, which explain pleasure in ego-psychology (rather than psychoanalytic) terms. The pleasure of the text was located, not in the ambiguity and exploitation, ecstasy and pain, of the drama of the development of sexual identity and gendering, but was occasioned by the cognitive and conscious processes of 'recognition' and 'identification'. For example, Ang's account of 'fantasising' captures the cognitive level of her analysis:

> producing and consuming fantasies allows for a play with reality, which can be felt as 'liberating' because it is fictional, not real. In the play of fantasy we can adopt positions and 'try out' those positions, without having to worry about their 'reality value'.
>
> (Ang 1985: 130)

Fantasy is completely under the control of the ego in this account, demonstrating none of the psychodynamic complexity of, for example, Walkerdine's account of her observation of a family watching *Rocky II* (Walkerdine 1986).

Neither Hobson nor Ang specifically referenced Lacanian (or even Freudian) psychoanalysis. Neither was able, as a result, to offer an explanation of the links between discourse and pleasure. The accounts of pleasure offered are 'social' in Hobson's research, and 'emotional' in Ang's work. The accounts of the audience produced are of women as housewives, wives, and mothers in Hobson's work, and of women striving to consciously evaluate different role models in Ang's. The pleasure of viewing was situated in terms of these activities and conscious deliberations. However, situating 'pleasure' in this way led to a tendency to particularist analysis rather than to a search for cultural trends. Situating the experience of both pleasure and fantasy at the level of cognitive processes produced a particularly limited account of these phenomena.

While only Ang discussed 'fantasy', her treatment invoked a feminist politics which cautioned against attempts to reform women's pleasures on the basis that fantasy and politics are relatively independent realms of activity.

> Must we see an imaginary identification with the tragic and masochistic positions of Sue Ellen or Pamela as a form of 'oppression in ourselves', a patriarchal 'remnant' that unfortunately women still have to hark back to because feminism has not yet developed any effective alternatives? Or can such fantasmatic scenarios have a meaning for women which is relatively independent of their political attitudes?
>
> (Ang 1985: 133)

For Ang, the pleasure of politics was a pleasure compromised by 'a feeling of discomfort'. It was compromised because 'here and now we must be able to enjoy life – if only to survive' (Ang 1985: 135–6). Fiction and fantasy may function by making life in the present pleasurable, or at least livable, but this need not by any means exclude radical political activity or consciousness. It does not follow that feminists must not persevere in trying to produce new fantasies and in fighting for a place for them. Where cultural consumption is concerned, no fixed standard exists for gauging the 'progressiveness' of a fantasy. The personal may be political, but the personal and the political do not always go hand in hand.

What happened in the cultural studies audience experiment, as demonstrated particularly in these extracts from Ang's work, was that the rejection of ideology as a useful analytical concept resulted in an hiatus between the personal and the political which was explained as a simple non-correspondence. Not only were popular television programmes absolved of 'ideology', but they were also designated 'a-political'. Mass communication became a system of positive pleasure, a realm of fantastic possibilities to help the beleaguered masses get through the day – and the political implications of this explanation were not questioned.

Yet surely such 'benevolent' pleasure demands interrogation, both in terms of what is known about the history of popular culture and the development of commodity aesthetics, since popular culture can be not only a source of pleasure but also a way of engaging in political activity. The separation of pleasure and fantasy from politics confirms the tendency within capitalism to justify the analytical separation of feeling from thought (see Heller 1979). It negates the demonstration by Marxist feminism of the psychoanalytic implications of the structuring of the unconscious in language. It obstructs the identification of the nature of the power relations of late capitalism and more specifically of the gender dimensions of that power struggle in the quest for control of the means of cultural production.

Textual ownership

The understanding of popular texts cannot be separated from the contexts of ownership and the bestowal of the rights and privileges of enjoying them (legal concerns like copyright and regulation of licences and the right to levy charges for access to services provided). Ownership frames access to a text and defines the parameters of its enjoyment. Malinowski claimed that among the Trobriand Islanders at the turn of the century, the folk tale was subject to private ownership.

> Every story is 'owned' by a member of the community. Each story, though known by many, may be recited only by the 'owner'. He may, however, present it to someone else by teaching that person and authorizing him to retell it. But not all the 'owners' know how to thrill and to raise a hearty laugh, which is one of the main ends of such stories.
>
> (Malinowski 1954: 102, 104)

Malinowski asserted that the equal value of text and context was demonstrated by the lending and borrowing of these tales. Not only the text, but the context, the 'whole nature of the performance' (its quality and timing), and its 'private ownership', contributed to its meaning. The ownership of the stories defined the relation of the community to the story, the grounds on which its enjoyment was predicated and to whom the rights of defining the text belonged. In other words, in the case of Trobriand folk stories, the convention of private ownership conveyed the right to control both the performance and the text. The private ownership of Trobriand folk tales contrasts markedly with the ways legends and myths were told. Malinowski suggested that legends were kept alive by those with vested interests in asserting their personal links with the great deeds recounted, and that myth, through its association with ritual and ceremony, belonged to the whole community, in the sense that the whole community had vested interests in the telling of the myths. Malinowski drew attention, in this discussion, to the importance of recognising the conditions of access to folk culture, and the ways in which that access affects its hearing.

In the cultural studies audience experiment, the ownership of the television programme was addressed in ways which, borrowing Malinowski's classification, equate the communal ownership of myth with the private ownership of folk tales, so that the crucial implications of the private ownership of commercial culture were denied. The point I am making here is not that Trobriand patterns of ownership of folk tales, legends and myths are the same as those in Western society (they obviously are not), but that Malinowski's proposition that the nature of ownership matters, is one which is very salient to the study and to the critique of popular culture. The ownership of texts is one determinant of the context of viewing and of the definitions of situation which frame the construction of textual meaning. If ownership of stories mattered in small societies even before contact with mass production of cultural commodities and the commodity aesthetics of capitalism, then how much more important must ownership be in societies such as our own in which stories (even our folk stories) are or become institutionally owned and controlled, and where access to re-telling has become a commercial transaction subject to copyright laws and exploitation agreements.

Indeed, historical studies of popular culture have demonstrated that the interest of the intelligentsia in popular cultural forms has often precipitated its 'reforms' (Burke 1978; Zipes 1979). Reformist idealism was also present in the cultural studies audience experiment. While the studies attempted to redress the denigration of popular television texts and the disparagement of their audiences, they resulted in research which incorporated programmes and their audiences into the discursive structures of institutions, particularly educational institutions, which had previously mostly ignored them. While this process can be seen as extending the discourses of, for example, literary studies or the secondary education curriculum, it also appropriated the programmes and their audiences for the disciplining attention of those institutions, by defining how they 'should' be studied.

The cultural studies audience experiment suggested that popular television programmes belong to their audiences, in spite of the complex institutional structures they observed in operation in the production of the programmes, and in spite of the demonstration of institutional power they witnessed in their scheduling and marketing. In other words, the cultural studies audience experiment conflated the power to decode with ownership of the text. This misunderstanding can only have been possible because, as discussed earlier, the sender–message–receiver model separated the processes of mass communication in such a way that the broadcast or published programme could be understood as in some way at the disposal of 'the receiver'. This conflation had the effect of creating an over-estimation of the power of media audiences to control mass communication, and an over-valuation of the significance of the 'resistance' some audiences demonstrate in their textual reading (see Fiske 1987a). It deflected attention from the ways in which stories are made to serve institutional interests over audience interests, as well as from the ways audiences are coerced through publicity and public relations. It replaced criticism of the programme as text with the social discourse of the audience. The lack of a strong perspective from which to address the implications of the structures of television production and the commodification of television programmes, coupled with the 'ethnographic' approach to that study, limited the scope of the analysis of popular culture possible using the 'encoding/decoding' model.

The cultural studies audience experiment permits a retrospective exploration of the application of implicit concepts of community to empirical audience research. The theories of community used possessed diverse theoretical heritages. The audience as an 'interpretive community' was borrowed (with mixed success and many misunderstandings) from literary theory. The audience as 'discursive formation' was borrowed from discourse analysis, and even though it is a founding concept of the 'encoding/decoding' model, its potential was never fully explored in the research. Among the many reasons for this is the difficulty of developing research methods capable of sustaining commensurate analysis of both textual and social discourse. While borrowing from the 'halcyon' past of British cultural studies has produced interesting and potentially fruitful challenges for future research, an analysis of the cultural studies audience experiment demonstrates that the project must be brought up to date by incorporating the insights and challenges of the 'epistemological turn' in anthropology. The value of mixed genre or multi-focus research (a characteristic, as discussed, of the cultural studies audience experiment) suggests the potential for better and more directed application than the experiment was able to deliver. The most encouraging aspect of the cultural studies audience experiment was the potential openness to new develop-ments, both theoretical and methodological, within textual analysis, discourse analysis, ethnography and popular culture, while its most worrying aspect was the tight rope walked, the teetering toe-hold maintained on the conceptual strengths of the cultural studies position, with its ever-present danger of falling back into the conceptual mire of the audience 'mass'.

Reflection

In this book I have examined the five research studies of my so-called cultural studies audience experiment in such great detail because the research constituted a project which I believed held the key to the development of a critical orientation to audio-visual media which would embrace audience perspectives and discourses. The process of critical

STAFFORDSHIRE
UNIVERSITY
LIBRARY

analysis led me to become more and more convinced that the directions originally explored by this research instead offer clues for the development of a more radically different type of audience research than the academic community has so far known. In the process of writing this book, I came to realise that my vision for the research was not shared by those who undertook it – a realisation consolidated by the different directions since pursued by the authors of the original research.

In spite of this, I found myself increasingly convinced that within multi-genre research lie new directions for media research. By identifying the points where the research faltered, I encountered ideas for defining directions for future work to demonstrate a stronger critique of commercial culture which includes the audience. There is no turning back: reverting to a critique of texts in the high culture tradition offers no adequate basis for a cultural critique of a world in which commercial culture is the dominant mode; where the institutions of commercial production of cultural texts provide the cultural forms which shape our understandings of what stories are, what television is.

All theory represents a leap in the dark. All innovative research is a compromise between what the theory suggests and what has been done in the past. I believe it is possible for cultural studies research to do better than it has, that it is possible to transcend the faltering beginning that was 'the cultural studies audience experiment' and to produce cultural research that offers a critique of modern television culture, points to a new era in policy making, and to a new rationale for popular media.

Some new directions have already emerged. The emphasis on fans in the analysis of television culture in the late 1980s (see Fiske 1987a; Brown 1990; Seiter et al. 1988) quickly reproduced itself in more in-depth 'fan-omenology' (Lewis 1992; Jenkins 1993) and in a preoccupation with impersonation as a cultural motif. The emphasis on fans usefully drew attention to the new phenomenology of the audience in cultural studies. To the measurable, assessable, and manageable audience as object of commercial research was added the personal obsession and commitment to communitas that characterises the fan (Fiske 1993). The fan/viewer remains atomised and alienated even if elaborated historically and socio-logically. They remain the target for renewed managerial activity to contain the quixotic preoccupations which become pretexts for the development of new and commercially exploitable fan communities. The preoccupation with such exotic audiences temporarily deflected the growing necessity for new research strategies to explain the more pervasive form of audience–text performance, which I call improvisation (Nightingale 1994a, b).

Improvisation includes greater variety of performance based on experimentation and 'intextuation' (de Certeau 1984). In experimentation textual motifs other than character become important. In experimentation motifs which explore patterns of cultural engagement, style, ideals and values are subjected to the test of everyday relevance or usefulness. And the process that de Certeau has called 'intextuation' is equally important because it demonstrates the symbiosis of the body of the viewer with the body of the text (television programme in this case) as cultural sites. It allows us to understand that the television programme holds within its structure signs of the history and the culture which produced it. The body of the viewer, too, is a cultural site which, in very different ways, reproduces signs of a personal history of engagement with that (same) history and culture. The personal history of viewing is an integral component of this latter engagement, written in the body in many and diverse ways. The text and the life/body resonate, and resonation produces overtones which have inter-textual repercussions with other texts, other lives, other bodies. For these reasons a concept-like intextuation draws our attention to the fact that treating the audience as a phenomenon is counter-productive for cultural research practice because it obstructs our vision of the relation between audience and text. In the next chapter I explore the implications of recognising the relational nature of audience–text and begin to consider how this complex interface might be researched.

NOTES

1 Such feelings characterise fieldwork in my experience, that of my students, and that of other researchers (e.g. Walkerdine 1986). They contribute to the disinclination to undertake fieldwork. Even if you are licensed by a reputable institution, parents look at you askance if you ask to spend hours just watching and talking to their children. The glamour of street corner life vanishes rapidly. Constant surveillance engenders paranoia. The insistent demand for a report on your observations to date breeds insecurity.
2 An account of Mayhew's work in the nineteenth century is provided by Bennett (1981). Mayhew was a journalist who pioneered the oral history as a research method to document the life histories and experiences of London street gangs.
3 The research accounts provided by Morley (1980) are again the best documented material, and provide a most interesting discussion across the research data as the researcher acts as commentator on the interaction between interviewer and interviewees.

The reader, according to his personal taste, invests this subject-matter with a concrete or abstract interpretation, sees it as pragmatic or imaginary, imagines what he sees and sees what he imagines. Here too literature and publicity are distinguished only by the different way in which each is laid out on the page to attract the eye of the reader, the rhetoric of advertisements being often more literary (and better written) than the reading matter, which adopts the methods of publicity and fills the same metaphorical function of making insignificance 'fascinating' and translating everyday life into make-believe so that the face of the consumer lights up with a smile of satisfaction.

(Lefebvre 1971: 86)

In Chapters 5 and 6, I discussed audience–text research as translation, emphasising the cultural criticism and transpositioning inherent in it. As translation, research re-produces a process already undertaken by the viewer, and so accentuates certain of the more exotic types of cultural engagement, like impersonation and improvisation. It reaches beyond the traditional analogies for audiences – like 'the masses' or 'communities' – and shifts the analytical dimension of audience research on to a new plane where it is but part of the complex pattern of cultural process. In the arbitrariness of the traditional analogies, we discovered the shifty character of 'audience' – sometimes defined as an object, sometimes as a relation, but always represented – knowable only through the power of the analogies we use to describe it and to generate information about it. As objects of research, relations are like the shady deals shifty characters set up. They force us seriously to question the ethics, values, power structures and processes which produce research and knowledge, especially since the deals researchers strike with viewers often integrate a reconstruction or reflection of the deals suggested to viewers by the media themselves as 'accurate' descriptions of the nature of viewing.

Powerless before publicity

Some of the most popular television programmes offer themselves as analogies for the viewer's relationship with the media. The prospect of audience-generated criticism of television places such metaphorical reflection on the research agenda in a new way. For example, in my view the television genre which has most directly addresses the viewer–television relation is the situation comedy. In this genre, everyday life is the setting for comic interactions which parody the paternalistic power structures of the relation between viewer and television. The transition from modernism to post-modernism and the changing nature of social and cultural being can be traced in the development of early examples of the genre from *I Love Lucy* and *Father Knows Best* in the 1950s and 1960s to *Roseanne* and *Married... with Children* in the 1980s and 1990s.

For example, what I call the *Father Knows Best*[1] model of the viewer–television relation is based in the capitalist hegemonic logic that 'he' who controls the purse strings controls the way we make sense of the world. *Father Knows Best* was a panegyric to paternal power which legitimated not only the existing power structure of the 1950s domestic environment, but also the approach to television management that produced ratings and commodity audiences. The manner in which this programme type is nearing exhaustion as both genre and rationale for the relation between the television industry and its audiences is evident in the recently popular parody of *Father Knows Best* – *Married... with Children*.[2] In the words of the old Frank Sinatra song used as the theme for *Married... With Children*, 'love and marriage go together like a horse and carriage' and 'this I tell you, brother, you can't have one without the other!'[3] This symbiotic relationship is cultural, entirely unnatural. Horses never needed carriages and carriages can be pulled by other vehicles, humans, and all sorts of animals other than horses. The ensemble had been replaced by the self-contained unit of the automobile almost fifty years before the song was written. Yet as late as the mid-1950s, repeated over and over in hit pop songs and radio or television serials, this statement was taken as commonsense. It was commonsense as gender politics before the sexual revolution of the 1960s, before the contraceptive pill, before the revival of feminism and before gay politics all demanded recognition of alternative forms of family.

Even though the words of its theme song are signalled as a quaint and dated view of marriage, *Married... with Children* has testified to the continuation of a deeper commitment to the old-fashioned family values that hide behind the contemporary debâcle family life has become. The programme's domestic relationships would be nonsensical without the ties that bind. Peggy and Al, Kelly and Bud belong inexorably to and with each other. They have created each other in fictional reality and continue in their dramatic world to prefer each other week after week. But they are also creatures of the consumer society. Their 'everyday' life explores remorselessly the 'rationality' that this social location generates in logics of neighbourhood and community, and sometimes in the icons and institutions of consumer culture. Al, jaded practitioner of the archetypal occupation of the mid-twentieth century – 'the salesman' – is an anachronistic reminder of post-World War II commercial expansion designed to get women out of the workforce and soldiers back into commercial employment. Peg also oozes anachronism. She fills the place but performs few of the functions of the salesman's consort, 'the housewife'. Consuming, buying, the only house-wifely chores which directly benefit manufacturers and shopping centres, have outstripped commercially redundant housewifely chores like childcare, housework and domestic crafts.

The programme is a reminder that broadcast television proliferated in a moment of post-war commercial opportunity. That historical moment has now passed, yet its moment of opportunity seized has become the carriage and the burden of the television viewer. Just as the carriage signified the domestication of the horse, and marriage presumed the domestication of women and the threat of domesticated men, broadcast television presumed the domestication and compliant acquiescence of viewers and sought to harness them for its commercial ends. In this context, Kelly and Bud, progeny of Peggy and Al's perfect match, do not so much exist as 'operate'. They survive using television logic – a logic which replaces a recognised social relation, self–everyday life, with a narrower but parallel relation – viewer–television. The fictional Bundy family performs viewer–television as though it were self–everyday life.

Married. . . with Children presents its viewers with more than a perverse *fin de siècle* representation of what the nuclear family has become in the 1990s. What is added to the classic 'father knows best' genre by this programme is an account of television and consumerism. In *Married. . . with Children*, paternal wisdom has been replaced by television logic: and an alternative system of knowing and coping, and ultimately a more equally accessible way of keeping in touch with trends and the outside world, 'television' engulfed the whole family. It occupies a central place on the hearth, where it provides the television spectator with a 'prime viewing' situation (the television-eye view) for witnessing the excesses of Bundy domestic madness as news, sitcom or sport. The programme wickedly discloses a shift in real domestic power – not from father to mother (as in *Roseanne*) but to a power structure where father (or whoever now watches the least television) is as vulnerable as the rest of the family to the commercial imperatives of fashion and shopping and the political clout of publicity. And remorselessly the programme documents a hypothetical destruction of critical intellectual faculties, directly related to the rationality of television consumerism. In the dramatic world of the programme, publicity has conquered the common systems of sense, atrophied intelligence, and promoted sleaze instead of sexuality.

Our understanding of the symbiotic relation between text and audience operates on a similar logic. Those who produce, license, distribute or manufacture media commodities often deny their dependence on the interpretive communities which generate the demand for their work. Such denial reflects their commitment to the patriarchal power they have wrenched from 'the father' to control audiences. In terms of the visual image, the last vestiges of that power remain embodied perhaps in the Brians, Jims or Walters all over the world who front national news and tell us about it. This power relation is now very old-fashioned. Television displaced the 1950s model of domestic power – patriarchal power – with its own commodity-dominated logic, and destroyed the power structure on which its credibility had been based. As a result, the rationale on which broadcast television now rests its credibility, the unquestioning belief in Western imperialism/power, is also threatened.

Everyday life and the critique of modernism

In work devoted to exploring the category of the person, Stephen Lukes (1985: 300) suggested that he could not envisage the end of the individualism, which he saw in evolutionary terms as the height of modernity. Yet this ideal is now openly parodied on commercial television. Perhaps we have reached the time where individualism is too expensive for consumerism. In this context, Foucault's vision and faltering first steps now suggest a bold new beginning. In *The Order of Things*, Foucault (1970: 367ff.) proposed that the foundational disciplines of the human sciences – history, ethnology and psychoanalysis – share an ideology which has selected 'man' as the object of their research. In Foucault's account, 'man' was invented towards the end of the eighteenth century as the pre-eminent object of social research. Just as this preoccupation began, Foucault proposed that it could also end. He mused that, as the result of some unforeseeable change to the arrangements which today prefigure 'man', 'one can certainly wager that man would be erased, like a face drawn in the sand at the edge of the sea' (ibid: 387) as the rationale for the human sciences.

> The epistemological field traversed by the human sciences was not laid down in advance; no philosophy, no political or moral option, no empirical science of any kind, no observation of the human body, no analysis of sensation, imagination, or the passions, had ever encountered, in the seventeenth or eighteenth century, anything like man; for man did not exist (any more than life, or language, or labour); and the human sciences did not appear when, as a result of some pressing rationalism, some unresolved scientific problem, some practical concern, it was decided to include man (willy-nilly, and with greater or lesser degree of success) among the objects of science – among which it has perhaps not been proved even yet that it is absolutely possible to class him; they

appeared when man constituted himself in Western culture as both that which must be conceived of and that which is to be known.

(Foucault 1970: 344–5)

In his later work, Foucault advocated a science of technologies – technologies of production, of sign systems, of power and of the self, in all of which man is implicated, observed and studied, without being the reason for the research. Foucault's research centred on technologies of domination (power) and the self, and such preoccupation led him to select research objects on the basis of their centrality to social administration and 'governmentality' (Foucault 1988: 18, 19). Foucault's technicity presupposed still a mechanistic effectivity in the production of identities, yet understood technologies not as the work of 'man' but as alternative objects of research. If 'man' is considered the 'object' of research, then the researcher is bound to objectify and co-opt. If, however, people are understood as relevant to the research as part of a broader and complex patterning of cultural activity, and that is the so-called object of research, the situation changes, as does the role of the researcher. In such contexts, the researcher is released from the expectation to give an account of other people and can therefore explore other aspects of the ways in which people are implicated in the patterns of culture. Instead of being expected to explain why people like particular types of texts or how they are manipulated, the people and the text can be seen to be together part of a more complex cultural situation.

This critique of man as the object of study, which is also the basis of my critique of cultural studies audience research, assumed its current shape in the many theories of self and everyday life produced since World War II. From the British tradition we are most familiar with the accounts by Raymond Williams (1985b) and Richard Hoggart (1973a, b), but other writers in both America and Europe, explored aspects of the relation between the particular and the generic which are relevant to discussion of what we should do with the audience in cultural studies research. The relation is a way of linking the particular (people as audiences) with the generic (the cultural imaginary) without having recourse to the intervention of universal laws based on generalisation. Relational explanation is based on operation, on the way things work together and affect each other, rather than on causation. The relation between self and everyday life is then the macro version of audience–text, and suggests the importance of considering the ways everyday life has been given a texture by being written and made into an object of study in its own right.

From occupation to symbiosis...

Interest in the theoretical significance of the relation between self and everyday life accelerated with the post-war expansion of television. Self–

everyday life is the larger relation where what is studied as audience–text finds its rationale. In work, like Goffman's, the focus on everyday life seemed to be invented to explain social science's dedication to the individual. Goffman's (1959) theorisation of everyday life as dramaturgy was presented to explain the 'self' rather than 'everyday life', yet the work makes extremely interesting re-reading *post*-de Certeau because it demonstrated the impossibility of 'self' without everyday life. On reflection, Goffman can be seen to have established a case for investigating the more complex objects of study which span the gulf between the particular and the generic. Goffman proposed that everyday life is both the theatre and the stage where the situations in which we are implicated are enacted. Everyday life needs a 'self', an actor to make it recognisable as a phenomenon, but the actor's performance itself designates the space it requires as theatrical. The actor's performance makes the space of everyday life 'theatre', just as its presentation in a space designated 'stage' creates the performance of the actors as 'theatre'.

The concept 'theatre' transcends the relation actor–stage, yet it was the 'theatre' which Goffman imagined in structural/functionalist terms as pre-given – as a habitable, occupiable site; as a location without a history. Such an assumption stems from the acts of occupation, expropriation and exploitation on which the dominant Anglo-cultures of the New World were founded, for in such cultures acts of trespass have appeared completely licensed by technological sophistication.[4] *The Presentation of Self in Everyday Life* was premised on acceptance of the analogy between self–everyday life and actor–stage and spelled out a theory of everyday life as the scaffolding for a theory of the self. The focus was on the actor and the self as characters, as opposed to the actor as a body or some other sign. Both the theatre and the play were under-theorised in Goffman's work and the necessity for scriptwiter, promoter or producer denied. Self–everyday life seems to have been envisaged as some sort of minimalist extempore theatre.

Goffman's method was extremely interesting for the time when it was written. He treated fictional and ethnographic writing, academic journal articles, published and unpublished theses, equally as sources of support for his ideas. In ways that a post-modernist would envy, he made no distinction or differentiation between these genres of writing as sources for his observations. A quotation from a novel could be used as documentation for his 'ethnographic' observations, and vice versa. The main theoretical concepts embraced by the dramaturgic approach included: 'impression management', 'role distance', 'interaction rituals' and 'saving face'. In the 1970s, symbolic interactionist critics of Goffman expressed concern at his preference for 'provocative insight' over 'empirically testable proposition' and at the way his style failed to set limits to generalisation. In these respects, Goffman's work skirted around the psychologistic appropriation of symbolic interaction, which was a feature of its general application in the 1960s and 1970s.

Perhaps more importantly, Meltzer, Petras and Reynolds expressed concern at Goffman's 'significant reconstruction of the image of human beings offered in symbolic interaction' (1975: 71). Instead of the usual 'holistic' notion of the 'self' proposed in symbolic interactionism, Goffman appeared to celebrate the I–me split with his determined exploration of impression management, unauthentic self-presentations, insincerity and hypocrisy. He proposed impression management as the most significant human motivation, both socially and personally. Goffman's work suggested a sociology of the main chance, of consumerism. Meltzer, Petras and Reynolds rightly lay the blame for this 'aberration', as well as for the appeal of the dramaturgic approach, on mass society: 'We can point to mass society, with its mass production, mass marketing and mass manipulation of tastes, as directing sociological attention to social appearances' (Meltzer, Petras and Reynolds 1975: 73).

Re-reading Goffman and the criticism of his work in the 1990s imposes a recognition of an intuition present at the beginning but masked by the structure of feeling of the time. The defence of the dramaturgic approach included the valuing of a frame of analysis which allowed researchers to 'read' the meaning of action in the perceptions held by observers of the action. The dramaturgic perspective was valued for placing 'social behaviour in real life encounters' at the centre of its attention. It was seen as presenting 'a sociology of the common man' (Meltzer, Petras and Reynolds 1975: 70). The criticism of Goffman's work centred around the almost exclusive concern with 'expressive forms' at the expense of substantive content; the lack of attention to the efforts people make to change or even modify the structures they inhabit; and the 'functional necessity of performances' in the maintenance of social order. Perhaps the most interesting criticism of Goffman offered by Meltzer, Petras and Reynolds is that 'the dramaturgical approach ignores the macrocosm within which its micro-level concerns are imbedded' (Meltzer, Petras and Reynolds 1975: 72). Goffman, like Baudrillard, analysed only the present as an on-going round of social occurrences. The empiricist assumptions of his work ensured the absence of unwanted intrusions from the past.

In important ways, Goffman's work anticipated later work in semiotics and cultural studies. The exploitation of the I–me split echoes the splitting in semiotics of the sign into signifier–signified. The location of meaning outside the self, in the creative work of observers rather than in the actor 'himself', now flags both semiotics and reader-response theory. The attempt to know the macrocosm from the perspective of micro-level concerns echoed Marxist interest in the relation between the generic and the particular, and between superstructure and base. The relation of the generic and the particular was demonstrated by Goffman to be not a simple one of context, but a complex interactivity – more like symbiosis than co-habitation.

On the negative side, Goffman's work, like all symbolic interactionist work, is about explaining the self. The object of Goffman's analysis was 'man'. He advocated the use of participant observation in a managerial mode – to make individual motivation easier to read, to determine the relative interplay of context and personality in an interaction. While the dramaturgic perspective permitted a dual focus by the researcher, the simultaneous exploration of the situations and contexts of action as well as the motivations for action, nevertheless, it was work designed to explain and evaluate the quality of a 'self'. Its central focus was in many respects what one might call managerial therapy. The discrepancy between the actor's view of his/her actions and the perceptions of him/her by others may be used by 'the analyst' to 'reveal the way in which interactants construct, through their own acts, the "reality" they project "out there"' (Meltzer, Petras and Reynolds 1975: 72). But Goffman appears not to have been overly concerned by the meaning of this 'discrepancy', which is a much more contemporary concern. In fact, it could be argued that in Goffman's work there is an echo of existentialism, a denial of the distinction between the generic and the particular, a desire to abolish difference in the very act of creating it (Goffman 1959: 81–2).

Goffman's 'sociology of the common man' presumed an approach to the textualisation of everyday life in which the everyday and the generic became synonymous through the elaboration of a theatrical metaphor, immortalised in Shakespeare's phrase from *As You Like It*: 'All the world's a stage...and one man in his time plays many parts'. If 'all the world's a stage' then performance is obligatory; a logical necessity of being. Non-performance is, by definition, non-existence. The use of the 'life as theatre' analogy, in which life is 'what you see', 'what is staged', 'what is performed', is magically seductive. Like a visual illusion in which one is continually forced to choose between ground and foreground, knowing that seeing both at once is impossible; obsession with acts of perspective can create a temporary amnesia in the obligatory observer. An illusion of knowing 'the totality' is suggested by knowledge of multiple perspectives. One sees more than one point of view synchronically, or so it seems. The everyday is available from at least three perspectives: analyst/observer, performer, and audience.

The theatre of Goffman's analysis stemmed from the elaboration of the performer and audience in interaction, from the simultaneous explanation of both and neither. The actor 'makes sense' to the audience, the audience licenses the performance, evaluates, and in some respects, accounts for it. For while apparently explaining human motivation, and apparently providing guidelines for the evaluation of performance, Goffman had all the time been describing techniques for the maintenance of a definition of situation. The theatrical façade, a scaffold which supports both situation and performance, was itself a construction which cannot be explained by Goffman's theory. Beyond the analogy, everyday life remains a concept without definition, non-text. Goffman's key construct, 'the maintenance of a single definition of the situation', the issue which demands an account of society, power and social action, cannot be explained within the analogy.

> And so here the language and mask of the stage will be dropped. Scaffolds, after all, are to build other things with, and should be erected with an eye to taking them down. This report is not concerned with aspects of theatre that creep into everyday life. It is concerned with the structure of social encounters – the structure of those entities in social life that come into being whenever persons enter one another's immediate physical presence. The key factor in this structure is the maintenance of a single definition of the situation, this definition having to be expressed and this expression sustained in the face of a multitude of potential disruptions.
>
> (Goffman 1959: 246)

At this point, in the closing phrases of *The Presentation of Self in Everyday Life*, the impossibility of this very act of closure is obvious. If the scaffold, and the power structures it represents, is dismantled, the meaningfulness of a definition of situation based on its premise also disappears, as does the rationale for impression management and the rationale for the actor. For if the scaffold is removed, everyday life ceases to be part of the dramaturgic domain, the situation changes and the self as actor ceases to be. Goffman, in the end, demonstrated the symbiosis of self–everyday life while attempting to justify the separability of its constituent elements.

... and consciousness

Agnes Heller's *Everyday Life* is, by contrast, a text about consciousness of being, an attempt to explain everyday thinking and its impact on understanding and action. For this analysis, we might say her object of study was a relation in which the generic and the particular are united in a life which is always an expression of its times. Heller described everyday life as the 'objective fundament of every social action, institution, of human social life in general' (Heller 1970: xi). Everyday life was not to be reduced to the 'life world', to a 'natural' attitude in opposition to institutionalised or rational thought. Heller understood everyday life as encompassing '*different* attitudes, including reflective–theoretical attitudes' (Heller 1970: xi). In her writing, everyday life is presented primarily as thought or attitude within situational determinants. 'In our everyday lives, we can have recourse to higher objectivations, and as well we can test and query norms and rules which are "taken for granted"' (Heller 1970: xii). It was the attitude to everyday life, the frame of mind with which it is apprehended, the orientation adopted to its living that interested Heller. She expressed her aim as being to demonstrate 'how everyday life can be changed in a humanistic, democratic, socialist direction'. For this reason, she argued for 'the possibility of a change in attitudes on the grounds that the attitude essential for the change for the better does exist, and that it only needs to be generalized' (Heller 1970: x). In making everyday life a 'text' in this way, by endowing it with an intelligence, Heller stressed its necessary relation to both person and situation: it is impossible to live without an everyday. In this sense, everyday life was suggested as a universal. However, Heller also constructed everyday life as 'particular', as produced within the socio-cultural and historic specificity of each particular life.

The 'attitude essential for the change for the better' took the form of a concept Heller named 'individual personality' which she contrasted with the 'particularistic person'. The 'individual personality' was an ideal, the product of the right sort of engagement with the world, a 'conscious' engagement in Marxist terms. The 'particularistic person' was tied to the cares and woes of the world and incapable of understanding the higher significance of their actions. The 'individual personality', by contrast, is attuned to the objectivations and homogenisations which characterise a socio-historical context, accounting for the ways the heterogeneity of everyday life results in the homogeneity of social life. Heller argued that through 'individuality' generic ways of thinking become part of the person. 'Particularity', by contrast, is like a mode of experiencing which characterises everyday life and is shaped by the immediacy of the demands for action which daily confront a person, as well as by the nature of that confrontation.

Heller suggested that heterogeneous forms of everyday activity are ordered and guided by objectivations. 'The paradigm of objectivation' makes it possible to understand how 'species essential activity in itself' is an objectivation which is unified yet articulated. The sphere of objectivation was considered to 'regulate everyday activity'. It consisted of three realms – human artefacts, tools and products; custom and habit; language. Objectivation combined sense-making with pragmatism; and sense-making was seen as regulatory, and in this sense 'communal'. The distinction between the everyday and the generic, between the particular and the homogeneous, addressed as analogy in Goffman, became the nucleus around which Heller's analysis revolved. In defining everyday life, Heller named its constituent elements: 'If individuals are to reproduce society, they must reproduce themselves as individuals. We may define "everyday life" as the aggregate of those individual reproduction factors which, *pari passu,* make social reproduction possible' (Heller 1970: 3).

Social reproduction was argued to begin with reproduction of 'the concrete person' as the necessary precondition for the reproduction of society. Persons learn 'within certain degrees of tolerance', varying degrees of 'competence *vis-à-vis* the system of objects, habits and institutions of our surroundings' (Heller 1970: 4). Falling short means failure to attain person status. Heller was interested by the ways the requirements for person status changed with the transformation from a communal to what she termed a 'more dynamic, i.e. non-communal society' (Heller 1970: 5). Such different modes of social organisation presented an 'organizational framework of everyday life'. For Heller, 'everyday life moved turbulently in a world of heterogeneous actions'. It 'demanded heterogeneous skills and capabilities'. The chaotic, turbulent, wave-like activity which characterises everyday life was presented as a process of homogenisation; the heterogeneous activity in which objectivation is created and recreated.

Heller demonstrated a significant move beyond the understanding of everyday life available in Goffman. In seeking to demonstrate the relation between 'man' and society, between base and superstructure, between the particular and the generic, Heller was more self-consciously aware than Goffman of the need to address the incommensurability of particularity and homogeneity, though she presented a fairly predictable reading of it in Marxist terms. For example she suggests that

> Everyday life always takes place in and relates to the immediate environment of a person. The terrain of a king's everyday life is not his country but his court. All objectivations which do not relate to the person or to his immediate environment, go beyond the threshold of the everyday.

(Heller 1970: 7)

For Heller, an 'everyday' and the person who inhabits it are not separable. Goffman's 'self' was imagined as separable from the frame of the personal everyday, and so could wander from set to set, stage to stage, play to play. Everyday life was envisaged by Goffman as a never-ending setting, the source of innumerable possibilities for writing narratives about the self, for changing oneself, for being whatever the situation at hand demanded. Goffman advocated life survival tactics where history accounted for the situation but not for the person. The everyday possessed generic qualities located in the theatre of situation. The development of selfhood called for different methods of acting, a conforming desire to stay employed, to please the audience, to act to the crowd, to fatten the wad in the theatre manager's wallet. For Heller, the 'everyday', even in its own generic form as concept, was marked by a particularity which bore the mark of the historical specificity of a particular person. Heller's everyday could not be conceptualised separately from the person who made it. The terrain of an everyday must be imagined from the perspective of a particular person, must be informed by a consciousness of the person's place in the world. Heller's 'everyday' possessed generic qualities only to the extent that the person had modified his 'particularity' with 'individuality'.

The individuality, then, is the person who has a conscious relationship with the generic, and who 'orders' (naturally within the given conditions and possibilities) his everyday life on the basis of this conscious relationship. The individual is that person who synthesizes within himself the contingent singularity of particularity and the generality of the species.

(Heller 1970: 20)

The person can thus be seen to embody and to live the nature/culture split, to live out the contradictions between base and superstructure in the course of the conduct of their everyday life. Everyday life is the making of a way of operating within the contradictions of capitalism, contradictions which can take on an iconic dimension, as in impersonation, but more usually generate the type of activity I have described as 'improvisation' because it defies the prescriptive overtones of 'negotiation'.

In analysing her work on everyday life, one is conscious of Heller's meticulous establishment of 'the everyday' as a generic category. While ontologically 'the everyday' may be 'particular', Heller specified the species essential aspects of it which allowed her to describe and evaluate 'the everyday' generically. She put forward a rather discomforting classification of everyday life and took upon herself the articulation of the 'everyday' implications or perspectives suggested by the foundational concepts of Marxism: class consciousness, the economy, labour, morality, religion. Her strongly articulated understanding of universality and foundational concepts based in species essentiality and the Marxist theory of needs accompany a problem met first in Goffman. Both Heller and Goffman attempted to develop a concept of the everyday which is simultaneously separate from 'man' and part of 'him'. In Heller, everyday life was a sphere of action patterned by objectivations and an attitude to that action. Everyday life was somehow separate from, yet identical with the person, like an interlocking Venn diagram in which the greater the overlap between the everyday and consciousness of it, the more developed the individual. Heller's writing on everyday life elaborated the idealised vision of the individual which characterised the Frankfurt School and paid homage to Lukács. Heller's work is a reminder that the process of becoming generates and sustains the relation between self and everyday life and, by extrapolation, that between audience and text. Both are linked to the development of political and national identity and invariably involve processes of personal, social, or cultural transformation.

Dreamworlds and domesticity

In Lefebvre's (1971) account of everyday life, modernity was considered the realm of public male culture, and everyday life the realm of its feminine other – domesticity. Because of their exclusion from public life, Lefebvre considered women the keepers of this realm of domesticity – a sort of female proletariat and the likely authors of modernity's disintegration. Women's interests in popular magazines, fortune telling and astrology were taken to demonstrate the way that cultural residues, like a commitment to occultism and non-rationality, persist as a way of life within modernity. Men's interests in such pastimes and their susceptibility to suggestion were ignored. Lefebvre presented everyday life as an emotional projection – a process for endowing make-believe with a personal 'reality' or for adapting make-believe to 'fit' the processes of living. Everyday life became the means by which the dreams of modernity and capitalism were enacted as a daily struggle to subdue nature and to transform its unruliness.

In this activity, Lefebvre suggests, the dreams of modernism and consumerism, actualised in the administrative organisation of the 'bureaucratic society of controlled consumption', present themselves as reality and challenge ordinary people to enact their mythology and ideology as personal reality. For the modernist project, the dreams that counted were the dreams of the administrative classes. In Lefebvre's analysis, texts embody such dreams and have become a technology which assists the enactment of bureaucratic control. Through their management, production, distribution and exploitation, the glossy dreams of commodity culture have proliferated, becoming a realm of anti-rationalist activity in which discourses about the inadequacy of modernism can be pursued.

Lefebvre's dissatisfaction with the progress of modernism and the capitalist enterprise has much in common with the criticism of popular culture produced by Williams and Hoggart in the late 1950s and early 1960s. All three writers subscribe to a nostalgic idealisation of what the everyday-once-was which borders on pre-modern pastoralism. In their work, the domestic, the everyday, and the private were understood to support the production of the performances that are work, extra-ordinary and public. Lefebvre examined the everyday, noted its symptoms and diagnosed trouble. For example, he observed that

> If we probe into the private lives of the members of this society we find that they are, in many cases, fortune-tellers, witches, quacks, star-gazers...indeed, one has only to read the papers; it is as though people had nothing in their daily lives to give them a meaning, a direction, apart from publicity, so they fall back on magic and witchcraft. Perhaps they hope in this roundabout way to *adapt* their desires, discover and orientate them. Thus the rationality of economism and technicity produces its opposite as their 'structural' complement and reveals its limitations as restricted rationalism and irrationalism pervade everyday life, confront and reflect one another.
>
> (Lefebvre 1971: 83)

For Lefebvre, everyday life offered the ultimate critique of modernity by being the repository of its remainders: 'restricted rationalism and irrationalism'. Control of the cosmos – the zone of ambiguity between science and astrology – had become, he argued, essential for the maintenance of social control and for the promotion of understandings of personal, ethnic and national identity. But scientific knowledge is now so complex that cosmologies are routinely co-opted as public explanation for the achievements of modernity rather than as its undoing. Dreams of power once imagined as possible only through witchcraft and sorcery are reinvented in the ultramodern dreams of science – eternal youth (plastic surgery and HRT); transubstantiation (chemistry); mutation and aberrant coupling (genetic engineering); foretelling the future (diagnosis); miracle cures (medical science). The same old dreams are recast as the achievements of science.

Lefebvre's reflections on the 'complementing and compensating' relation between the cult of the Cosmos and the 'more "human" cult, that of Eros' (Lefebvre 1971: 84) have developed in slightly different directions from those he anticipated. The cult of the Cosmos has again been attributed human form as doctors publicise themselves as magicians and scientists as wizards, while the 'human' cult of Eros has been transformed by science. During the 1980s, the obsessive eroticism of the 1960s became a fetishistic narcissism which relies on body sciences to inform the care and development of the body machine. Rather than undoing rationalism, the non-rational justified itself as that which must be 'rationalised'. The free-love zone, the domain of the body in 1960s eroticism, has been cleaned up and landscaped, trimmed to scientific proportions to comply with the dreams of extreme economic determinism.

In the 1980s, a desire, epitomised in the public profile of Elle 'the Body' McPherson, for what you can make of yourself replaced the desire for what you can be in 'communion'. Body disciplines eclipsed the desirability of desire. New perverse pleasures have been institutionalised as addictions – to diet or exercise regimes; to the disciplines which deny desire. In the 1990s, new political desires were promoted – for 'World Peace', a 'New World Order', global environmentalism and cosmic harmony. Such dreams incorporate the celebration and exaltation of the particularity and diversity of 'poor down-trodden everyday life' and the regeneration of communalism – but not of 'love'. The diverse, the particular, and the local have become 'causes célèbres' which generate new themes in the quest for what one can be 'in communion'. Supposedly purposeless procrea-activity has given way to committed communal narcissism. When there is no other international commodity to generate foreign currency, a community can always package and sell itself as a tourist destination. All sciences, all heritages, all loves double as money-making ventures to pay for themselves.

In Lefebvre's work we are confronted with the transformative power of the relation between modernism and capitalism. As Craig Owens has commented, there is a wilful refusal in the rhetoric of the Right to recognise the excesses of contemporary society as a product of capitalism itself. As he suggests,

> permissiveness is not an index of immorality or degeneracy... but an essential factor in the dis-accumulative economy, the extensive regime of postwar capitalism or consumer society – which must promote consumption, expenditure, self-indulgence, the gratification of every desire as our fundamental economic obligation.
>
> (Owens 1987: 22)

Yet even the destruction of everyday life (a process to which Owen also draws attention) and its replacement by public performances, requires that its public expression – public eating, dressing, playing and exercising (even Princess Diana goes to the gym), and increasingly public sleeping and begging – should occur in inhabitable spaces. What is left of life, 'poor downtrodden everyday life', private life, has become a property of personhood, especially as outside work takes over the home. With the destruction of the distinction between public and private, the old infrastructure (the housekeeper and the regimes of domesticity) of everyday life has been replaced by personal responsibility.

The media, television especially, generate an ambiguity essential to the colonisation of the space between the generic and the personal which erases the everyday. Television creates an apparently 'workable' space of direct cultural interaction between person and superstructure where the intervention of the everyday and its rituals of regulation become redundant, a luxury few can afford. Each person, particularly in 'multi-cultural' nations like Australia and the USA, now has multiple and conflicting cultural and personal allegiances and obligations which they must be free to meet. Since the primary local structure of the past – the family – has crumbled as a significant social institution, the person is now a primary focus for the tolerance of diversity.[5] Living with diversity generates a nostalgic longing for past simplicities and cultural imperatives which justify fundamentalist simplicities.

Operating

Where communally imagined uniformity in the past produced a unified 'self', the diversity of the present creates the self as a complex of competing identities. The commensurability of institutional affiliations, accumulated as national identity and registered epistemologically as Mead's 'generalised other', Freud's superego, Lacan's big Other, no longer exists. The time when nation, corporation and institution, and family, all confirmed symbolically the same identity, the unified 'self', and the nineteenth-century ideal of the male 'individual' has passed. Less permanent structures that are often little more than alliances, like work groups, friendship groups or mixed households and other 'types' of contemporary corporate significance, have replaced the homologous structures of the past – the family organisation that echoed commercial, educational or ecclesiastical organisation, that in turn echoed national organisation (cf. Brunsdon and Morley 1978). The homological coherence of contemporary society, the assumptions which supported notions of cultural totality (Williams 1980a; Hall 1980b), have been shaken by the necessity for rapid movement of capital. The category of the family itself is in the process of becoming a series of transitory and variable structures for the maintenance of emotional comfort and psychological health. The zone of ambiguity produced by media engagement increasingly transposes everyday life to a public 'out there'. Everyday life has become synonymous with what's on television or radio, what's in the newspapers or magazines, what's on at the cinema or what's in the shops. All that is left is the person finding a way 'to be', operating electronically and commercially programmed pathways, locked into or out of 'trajectories' that might lead somewhere or nowhere (de Certeau 1984: Introduction).

When reading de Certeau I am reminded first of Lévi-Strauss, of an understanding of the person as a 'place' where discourses of the individual and of discourse itself collide, or pass each other by. In Lévi-Strauss there are no 'vectors of direction', no 'velocities' and no 'time variables' (de Certeau 1984). The person is a crossroads, constructed by the complexity, scale and busy-ness of the metropolis. In place of the 'individual', Lévi-Strauss proposed a meeting of discourses where people are the sites of this encounter. Time and place usurp the person who experiences the discursive encounter, lives it, and perpetuates the discourses, changing them according to the specificity of the crossroad in history.

De Certeau's work marked a break with the focus on the individual. He proposed that 'systems of operational combination' cohere in a culture, and bring to light its 'characteristic models of action'. Like a cultural meteorologist, his orientation is by wind direction, weather conditions, the barometer and satellite pictures. In explaining the speed and direction of cultural production, its cumulus and precipitation, de Certeau proposed two ways of understanding the world, two modes of cultural engagement: transport and consumption. Both these ideas were prefigured in Lefebvre. It is obvious that in *this* world, construction – what we are making ourselves, how we make ourselves, what we build where to shelter from life's storms – matters.

Transportation (writing–reading) and construction (consumption–production) are, for de Certeau, the models for agency and accumulation in the metropolis. They are the 'new' objects of study. Instead of describing where we are or what we are doing, we now focus on how the 'what' is being done 'where'. The focus is on performance, as in Goffman, but with a twist. In

Goffman the performance was believed to explain the actor, but in de Certeau performance is much more. It is an expression, not just of person, but of place and time as well. Performance is always an expression of culture.

To live requires much more than passive consumption, more than interpretation, more than accidental insight. It requires ways of getting out and about, a textual transportation system. Such a transportation system is not likely to be uniform (confined only to pedestrianism – the strolling gait of a flâneur, the dilettante dabbling in literature), but variable, depending on the passion associated with its pursuit. Being now involves a range of media engagements – we plod through the newspaper or stand by for the evening news on TV or radio; fly through a course on computer programming in the hope of a new job or cruise to sexual fulfilment with a *Joy of Sex* video. The point is that the co-optation of texts is motivated. Texts help us to move, change, become, to transcend the limitations of our location or to stay the same, to resist change. The world of texts is not always dedicated to progress. It is subject to traffic jams, detours, signalling systems. Texts can take us in entirely the wrong direction, enforce detours or lead us astray as easily as set us off on the right foot. Life travel is three-dimensional; it involves time, space and motion. Writing–reading is movement not only in the space of engagement, but also through time: time taken to write, and time taken to read, or view, or listen, as well as time represented – ages, generations, lifetimes – and the real time to enactment.

> The readable transforms itself into the memorable: Barthes reads Proust in Stendahl's text; the viewer reads the landscape of his childhood in the evening news. The thin film of writing becomes a movement of strata, a play of spaces. A different world (the reader's) slips into the author's place.
>
> (de Certeau 1984: xxi)

Construction, by contrast, creates/recreates the world. It makes the seen world in substance, shape and size. Production–consumption is an accumulative mode of performance, a way of adding weight to structure. It constructs the material world and the impetus and means for operating in it. De Certeau explored its creative dimensions, illicit usage and resistant acquiescence. Production–consumption produces the everyday world of objects.

In his account of consumption, de Certeau explored the relation between everyday life and consumerism, including the importance of the ways 'the weak make use of the strong' in acts of consumption. He noted that the logic of the control of everyday life originates in the functionalism of consumption, while the critique of the quality of everyday life is posed in terms of the particularity of meanings of consumption. The resistance inherent in consumption, demonstrated in the ways in which the homogeneous quality of products is bent to the particular demands of everyday practice is of intense interest for the understanding of media audiences. The meaning of consumption is linked to the 'trajectories', 'strategies' and 'tactics' which characterise the incorporative quality of consumption. The understanding of everyday life in de Certeau is environmentalist – space, time, action, climate – place in perpetual becoming, re-making, re-writing as sites or signs of significant past action. It embraces the inspired strategy or endured tactic employed to engage the living metropolis. Its politics can be seen in this context to be survival.

De Certeau linked 'systems of operations' (like transportation systems or public utility delivery systems like electricity or water) which take shape in semi-planned conditions of exigency, accident, the blind expansion of unplanned and haphazard growth of the city/metropolis to personal trajectories, tactics and strategies by which people find their way socially, culturally, intellectually. In writing–reading, a way is found to traverse temporal, geographical and imaginative space. In de Certeau's work, everyday life is the terrain, the ground under one's feet and the scenery and experiences encountered. People are still upright on the map, finding their way, walking the streets or boarding the trains, but what they do is ordered according to a cultural environmental ordering evident in figures of engagement – the shopper reading a magazine in the supermarket queue; morning exercise plus the Sony Walkman; writing letters on a laptop at the hairdressers; everyday life as *modus operandi*.

Precursors and parallels

These discussions of everyday life are not recent. Precursors abound and parallel the examples I have cited. Nineteenth-century guides to house-keeping parallel Lefebvre's domestic definition; ideas from eighteenth-century devotional tracts, guides to the maintenance of mental health, are echoed by Heller. Both Williams and Hoggart in the 1950s and 1960s explored similar themes to Lefebvre and Heller. All addressed the post-World War II collusion of modernism and capitalism which transformed the world into which they had been born. All sensed, perhaps mourned, the passing of that world as its comfortable domesticity changed to frenetic metropolitanism. There are parallels with post-modernist writers as well. A tantalising comparison is suggested of Goffman and Baudrillard. Goffman's optimistic New World embrace of the usefulness of the superficial contrasts wonderfully with Baudrillard's unrelentingly pessimistic Old World fear of the façade without substance; both opportunistically exploit the world of images and impressions inherent in their chosen analogies – the everyday world as theatre, the everyday world as television. The collusion of modernism and capitalism produced the glossy surfaces of contemporary culture – a *corpus delicti*, an offensive but compelling body, evidence of the work of shifty characters caught up in shady relations. In such places audience is a relation of complicity in which people actively live and make the cultural imaginary, the web of intrigue which the complex contemporary Text has become.

NOTES

1 *Father Knows Best* began as a radio serial in 1949 and was broadcast as an American situation comedy between 1954 and 1963. Episodes began when Jim Anderson arrived home from work and quietly set about solving all the problems accumulated by his wife, Margaret, and three children, Betty, Bud and Kathy. Jim was an insurance salesman (Brooks and Marsh 1992: 297–8).
2 *Married... with Children* (1987–present). This programme is a black parody of the idealised family sitcoms of the 1950s and 1960s (Brooks and Marsh 1992: 556–7).
3 Brooks and Marsh note that *Love and Marriage*, the programme's theme song, was written by Sammy Cahn and Jimmy Van Heusen, and recorded by Frank Sinatra in 1955 (Brooks and Marsh 1992: 556).
4 Stephen Greenblatt has described the psychology of the 'occupation' of the New World in great detail in *Marvellous Possessions: the wonder of the new world* (1991).
5 Carrithers, Collins and Lukes (1985) provide a fascinating discussion of the 'category of the person' across cultures which leads Lukes to conclude that 'individualism' is a necessary and inescapable category of modernisation and capitalism. He concludes, for example, that 'We may, with Taylor and Hollis, reject individualistic ways of conceiving the person that are typical of the first picture. But these are the ways by which we are culturally formed and they inevitably colour our every attempt to interpret the worlds of others or to seek to change our own' (ibid: 300). However, where Lukes sees a unified 'individualistic', ethnic or nationalistic framework defining this development, I am pointing to the disruption of the everyday world and the implications of the destruction of the old, national, uniform framework for new experiences of personhood.

Conclusion

Critical awareness about the way objects of study are defined and about the ways power may be shared in research has changed the expectations now held of cultural studies audience research.[1] Understandings generated initially by the growth of reader-response criticism and reception aesthetics, and by the epistemological turn in anthropology, have been further transformed by post colonial theory and by greater awareness of the complex ways research power can be handled. The emphasis has shifted both from 'man' as the object of study and from the oppositions which previously characterised Marxist and consumerist theory to the complex ways texts and people interpellate each other in the creation of new ways of doing and making. In the audience context this emphasis on the performance and production of culture has justified new metaphors being attached to the explanation of old interest in the prototypical base–superstructure relation. The shift has extended beyond the recognition that audiences are active, to an understanding that people cannot but make culture in the very acts of consuming it and living it. In the variety of its modes and undertakings, consumption realigns, reforms and transforms the present. The activity of audience need no longer be conceived as responsive, but can now better be understood as symbiotic or interactive. Freeing audience activity from the bonds of responsiveness means that the coercive nature of the practice of power by media corporations and the political machinery of manipulation employed by governments and military can be better defined and understood.

What we previously called 'audience research' now extends beyond both the traditional paradigms and reception into studies of cultural participation and the processes of inter-culturalism and inter-communalism. The recognition that relations can be objects of study has also been dramatically affected by the emergence of post-colonial studies (Trinh 1989) which point to the pitfalls of administratively authored research and unquestioning Western perspectives. The similarities between the way that the power of the mass audience has been co-opted by the industrial and administrative ordering of mass communication, and the exploitation and dispossession of

STAFFORDSHIRE
UNIVERSITY
LIBRARY

the colonised – those currently feeling the weight of administrative discipline in the name of regional development – cannot be ignored. Post-colonial studies suggest the relevance for audience–text research of ideals and ethics which again radically alter the role of the researcher, pushing beyond the administrative and governmental interests which identify 'man' as the object of study and delineate a more ecological orientation in which the audience is at last recognised as an interacting and integral part of the culture.

One way to make such understanding part of research culture is to take up the insights gained from approaching audience research as translation – as a process in which the viewer can be attributed a more active and motivated role in cultural production of the research process. The viewer is not only necessary to critical research about the meaning of the media and its texts, but absolutely essential to it; not an informant only, but a collaborator in the business of building an account of mediation. The viewer speaks a language of media experience and at least some of the (academic) language of the researcher whose role it is to translate that language into another text – a text which delivers the media for public scrutiny. Models linked to theories of post-coloniality and researchers who understand themselves and their collaborators in research as the products of media occupation of their cultural worlds are essential.

'Audience' – phenomenon or relation?

Because this is a crucial issue in how we research audience, description of the distinction between a phenomenal understanding of 'the audience' and a relational approach seems important. The question from mainstream audience research which the cultural studies research most frequently adopted was the injunction to explain why a particular television programme was so popular. The question, as we have seen in previous chapters, represents a crossroads for research. In answering this question the researchers usually pursued both cultural and psychological objectives. *A Country Practice* was shown to be 'quality soap'; *Dallas* was shown to embody a 'tragic structure of feeling' which addressed the 'melancholy imagination' cultivated in the audience; *EastEnders* was demonstrated to offer compelling opportunities for audience engagement in its construction. In other words, each study offered an account of the principles of spectatorship enacted in the production of the programme before pursuing the viewers judgements about the programme. Description of the quality of the programme could have been (and was) done without any reference to the audience research. The audience research allowed the researcher to engage with another discourse – that on the character, quality and rationality of the audience. In general, the cultural studies audience research dealt with the audience–text relation as accumulation – a textual account of the audience added to a qualitative assessment of the views of the audience. The audience was still approached phenomenologically rather than as part of the relation. By borrowing the question of popularity from mainstream media criticism, the cultural studies audience research bought into the objectification of the audience and the expectation that their role was to explain the audience. Instead of placing themselves in the problematic, as is possible with relational research, and being able to act with their research participants, the researchers imagined the participants phenomenologically as 'others' – the researchers were unwittingly co-opted to the administrative ends of programme producers and government agencies.

Models like 'encoding/decoding': (i) set in place the theoretical and methodological precursors necessary for the identification of cultural 'objects' with varying manifestation and meaning; (ii) marked the beginning of a movement beyond economistic delineations of social theory based on individualism; and (iii) consolidated the ideas in time and space, and lent a materiality to their theoretical development. Yet they were unable to escape the ideology of the audience enacted in the public and commercial discourses which frame recognised audience research practice. A central tenet of this discourse was the idea that audiences are a natural phenomenon, and should be researched 'naturalistically' (for example, Lindlof and Meyer 1987).

The problem is that people are not audiences by nature but by culture. A person can be a consumer of ice creams but will never be the audience of an ice cream. A person can both consume and use a refrigerator or an automobile, but trying to be its audience would be to risk incarceration in a mental institution. We invoke the theatre of the absurd by contemplating giving audience to an ice cream or a refrigerator. We learn to act and to think of ourselves as audiences in certain contexts and situations – these always possess a textual dimension which eclipses the mechanical or operational functions of the medium. From a research perspective, 'audience' is always context- and text-bound.

Deciding when a person is in a relation of audience and when that relation ceases is problematic. In some contexts, the audience–text relation might exist only during the time–space of viewing. But it is highly likely that the relation will continue outside this context, as the viewer experiments on a personal problem with a soap opera tactic – dresses like, speaks like or acts like a character. Such activity might even be based only tangentially on the programme – on, for example verbal reports of a fictional incident or on press reports of the real life of an actor who plays a favourite character. The activities encompassed by 'audience' escape well beyond the bounds of viewing/reading tied to the text. Viewing/reading is not a necessary condition of audience but merely one of its forms. As a result, the possibilities for the enactment of 'audience' must be explored in each research context. From a textual perspective, the relation defies both its audiences and its producers, broadcasters and sponsors, for by the continual articulation of the text outside the situation of engagement, it multiplies itself into new forms which address different audiences – newspaper articles and advertisements, magazine promotional features, product licensing, fan clubs, schoolyard discussions, and everyday gossip. The performed text outstrips the broadcast text in both significance and vitality, even though the two remain linked.

Attempts to define the audience–text relation, to attribute to it the status of object, are artificial but necessary. The relational approach points outwards, to broader cultural continuities. Just as people as audiences cannot be separated from personal, social and cultural continuity, so texts cannot be isolated from their broader cultural significance, or from the history of that significance. The audience–text relation is a chimera which can only ever be apprehended partially. We think we are seeing reality when what we see is more like a holographic reflection, changing as our own point of reference changes and dependent on our ability to see – on the quality of our vision. Audience is a shifty concept.

The shifty character of the audience

My first attempt to address the shifty character of the audience (Nightingale 1984) led me to propose that the audience could only be understood as a complex set of relations linked in a structured system of mass communication. At that early stage, I thought of mass communication, perhaps naively, as a sort of interlocking system of audience relations. I hoped that I could control its shifty character by pinning it down. I considered three relations likely to be particularly relevant: audience–industry, audience–medium and audience–text. In terms of these relations, the 'audience' can be seen to be implicated at different levels of abstraction and in different types of action in the system of mass communication. The nature of 'audience' depended for its defining characteristics on the other term of the relation. If analysed in accordance with Foucault's typology of social technologies (Foucault 1988: 18, 19), audience–industry, the most administratively regulated of these levels, can be seen to involve the interaction of technologies of domination and production, while audience–text involves the interaction of technologies of sign systems and of the self. Given the prevalence of addiction metaphors attached to discussions of television viewing (Nightingale 1993b: 282), audience–medium relations can be expected to combine technologies of domination and of self. As Foucault notes:

> ... these four types of technologies hardly ever function separately, although each one of them is associated with a certain type of domination. Each implies certain modes of training and modification of individuals, not only in the obvious sense of acquiring certain skills but also in the sense of acquiring certain attitudes.
>
> (Foucault 1988)

In other words, studying audience in this way should demonstrate that technologies of all four types are in simultaneous operation and that what we mean by 'audience' changes in accordance with the mode of operation of the technology. The definition of the research problem must be undertaken with care and due consideration of the complex field in which the relation operates in order to ensure that appropriate research design is planned.

For policy research, examination of the audience–industry relation as a technology of production, by means of which audience–text links are produced as marketable commodities, would seem a necessary beginning. Treating the audience–industry relation as a technology of power, by contrast, could lead to a research focus which investigated the ways in which people are coerced to apply consumer and commodity ideas and ideals to the analysis of their own interests.

Audience relations

Four qualities seem particularly important for the conceptualisation of audience as a relation:

1 Audience relations are based on symbiotic interaction. Audience relations are not another way of talking about a correlation between two objects or of analysing the variance between the occurrence of two things. The dimensions of an audience relation are linked by definition and/or logical necessity. By linking a person to a text, media industry, medium, and/or to a system of publicity the components of audience are invoked. In the 1990s the specialisation of the elements which produce 'audience' are proliferating with new media and the onset of media convergence increase the variety of ways audience may be expressed.

2 Consumption and use are necessary but not sufficient explanations of audience relations. 'Consumption' and 'use' guarantee a performative quality to audience, though the 'performance' always exceeds consumption or use. This excess is related to processes of combination and association. As de Certeau has observed, the practices of popular culture 'bring into play a "popular" *ratio*, a way of thinking invested in a way of acting, an art of combination which cannot be dissociated from an art of using' (de Certeau 1984: xv). Audience relations retain elements of giving patronage or service but may also offer freedom of expression, as when someone is given the right to speak in being 'given an audience'. The performance of an audience relation involves, at least potentially, a greater range of activities than using or consuming.

3 Audience relations always involve the exercise of power – someone always has the power to offer 'audience' and someone else must respond by accepting or rejecting that offer. There is no requirement that audience

relations be democratic – frequently, especially in broadcasting, they are not. The power structure of the relation always affects the nature and quality of its performance.

4 Perhaps most importantly in mass communication, audience relations are what I will call, again following Michel de Certeau, 'operational', and their operationalism is linked to the power structures which govern the relation. In the audience–text relation this operationalism encompasses the transformation of the heterogeneous, haphazard particularity of the everyday into personal narratives which conform to generic cultural ideals. Audience relations are ways of transforming particular potential into examples of cultural ideals and vice versa. In this sense the relation is always shady, always a compromise, even if sometimes a fortunate coincidence.

As relational research, audience research should have been freed from the shackles of its empiricist past and be madly embracing the new possibilities of union with literary theory and philosophy. There is some evidence that this has and will continue to happen, but there is even more evidence that the traditional empiricist approaches are being put back on like comfortable old shoes because funding for easily understood projects driven by political, educational or policy agendas is the only funding available. I would suggest at least three reasons for this: the crisis of theory and discipline; the problem of misrecognition where new audience research is not understood as a form of research; and the difficulty of reading the ideology of methods.

Crises of theory and discipline

The crises of theory and discipline are perhaps the easiest to explain of the obstacles facing cultural studies audience research. The problem can be simply stated – which theory? which discipline? These questions were more easily answered when Marxist political economy was the dominant academic theoretical perspective and researchers had only to choose between its varieties – between Lukács, Gramsci, Althusser and Benjamin. This is no longer the case and it is open to debate whether political economy, the philosophy of being, literary theory, feminist theory, or psychoanalysis should provide the inspiration for research. The question of audience raises so many philosophical problems that using theory to analyse rather than to inform research is the much easier, but dangerously empiricist, option. As interdisciplinary practice it presents itself in diverse forms, especially when some of those forms include cases where the researchers/critics propose themselves as the audience being researched (see Jauss 1982).

Recognising new audience research

Coming to terms with the diversity of the research produced when multiple theoretical and interdisciplinary perspectives are in the field is one of the challenges of cultural studies audience research. The uniformity which characterised audience research traditions in the 1960s and 1970s, and which was related to their indebtedness to psychology, has disappeared. Today audience questions are being addressed as integral parts of quite diverse research agendas which encompass both the arts and popular culture as well as marketing and management. So the diversity of theory currently used to inform research about audience leads to its being less easily recognised as such. This problem of recognition also affects how the research is read – whether as audience research or as textual research, as intercultural research or as an area study, or simultaneously as several of these. Increasingly it seems that two types of work – traditional audience research (I count the edited collections by Buckingham (1993) and Schlesinger et al. (1992) as examples of traditional research using qualitative methods) and writing about audience theory (I count Morley (1992), Ang (1996), and of course this book as examples) – seem unequivocally to be recognised as about audiences. When post-modern audience theory is put into practice it creates the problems of misrecognition to which I have already alluded. The extremely ironic situation is that post-modern audience writing and research creates its own audience and readership problems and will continue to do so until enough people are practising it to form a new reading community. The breadth of theoretical and philosophical referencing, the ways audience reflection and discussion about texts are integrated with the researcher's reflections and discussion about the same and additional texts, and the integration within the writing of other critical and theoretical writing place unusual demands on both reader and researcher (see Walkerdine 1990; Nightingale 1996).

Reading the ideology of methods

Such problems of recognition have another dimension which I link to the absence of critical consideration of the ideology of methods used in research. The assumption that people are able to give an account of their audience activities in a language which will conform to the researcher's expectations should be questioned, but seldom is. I am concerned particularly with the survey and the interview as ideological constructs in which the research participant is constructed in inferiority. In the cultural studies audience research I have discussed in this book, the inability to question the ideology of the methods used was obvious in the difference between the ways production personnel were treated (as authorities or artists) while the research participants were asked only to reflect and comment. In other words, continuation of the use of interviews rather than discussions, of surveys and questionnaires rather than open and intuitive exploration of audience as an experience, perhaps visually rather than verbally signalled, perpetuates not only the social and cultural distinctions between researcher and viewer, but also the administrative or managerialist stance in research. This problem was described by Walkerdine (1986) as the anguish felt in recognising that the family she observed failed to recognise her working-class background and did not take her to their hearts and treat her as one of themselves. But the use of managerialist research techniques and strategies by working-class (or any class of) researchers makes the politics of the research situation clear – the researcher, not the participant, is the collaborator.

The ideology of research methods – particularly of qualitative research methods – was addressed briefly and obliquely by Marcus (1986) and by Marcus and Fischer (1986) who advocated the use of juxtaposition and defamiliarisation. Marcus and Fischer suggested that we should be looking for research techniques and strategies which demonstrate our own strangeness at the same time that they teach us more about the research participants. This type of research is difficult, because the impetus to fetishise the other and to feel reassured by an account of our own 'normality' can prove almost irresistible. In a same-culture and audience research context strategies for defamiliarisation could, nevertheless, prove useful in demonstrating the 'strangeness' of the commercial imperatives to package people as commodities and to deliver them to advertisers as prospects; or to demonstrate the strangeness of academic interests in audience compared to the concerns of ordinary people.

NOTE

1   I have in mind work like Paul Willis's *Common Culture* (1990), Robinson et al.'s *Music at the Margins*, Ien Ang's *Desperately Seeking the Audience* (1991), and to some extent John Fiske's *Power Plays, Power Works* (1993), though many other examples could be cited. In all these examples, possibilities for cultural participation are mapped, and policy options explored.

Bibliography

Abercrombie, N., Hill, S. and Turner, B. S. (1986) *Sovereign Individuals of Capitalism*, London: Allen and Unwin.

Adorno, T. (1945) 'A social critique of radio music', *Kenyon Review* 7, 2: 208–17.

Allen, R. C. (1983) 'On reading soaps: a semiotic primer', in E. A. Kaplan (ed.) *Regarding Television: critical approaches – an anthology*, Frederick MD: University Publications of America Inc. and American Film Institute.

Allor, M. (1988) 'Relocating the site of the audience', in *Critical Studies in Mass Communication*, vol. 5, no. 3: 217–33.

Alvarado, M. and Buscombe, E. (1978) *Hazell: the making of a television series*, London: BFI/Latimer.

Ang, I. (1985) *Watching Dallas: soap opera and the melodramatic imagination*, London and New York: Methuen.

—— (1991) *Desperately Seeking the Audience*, London: Routledge.

—— (1996) *Livingroom Wars: rethinking media audiences for a postmodern world*, London: Routledge.

Atkinson, P. (1990) *The Ethnographic Imagination: textual constructions of reality*, London and New York: Routledge

Barthes, R. (1973) *Mythologies*, Frogmore, St Albans, Herts: Paladin.

—— (1977) *Image, Music, Text*, London: Fontana, Flamingo (1984).

Baudrillard, J. (1983) *In the Shadow of the Silent Majorities . . . or The End of the Social and Other Essays*, New York: Semiotext(e).

Benjamin, W. (1979) 'The work of art in the age of mechanical reproduction', in *Illuminations*, Glasgow: Fontana/Collins.

Bennett, J. (1981) *Oral History and Delinquency: the rhetoric of criminology*, Chicago and London: University of Chicago Press.

Bernstein, B. (1971) *Class, Codes and Control* (vol. 1), London: Routledge and Kegan Paul.

Berry, C. (ed.) (1985) *Perspectives on Chinese Cinema*, Ithaca NY: China–Japan Program, Cornell University.

Boot, C. and Glover, G. (1987) 'The South London Photo Co-op', in S. Bezencenet and P. Corrigan (eds) *Photographic Practices: towards a different image*, London: Comedia.

Bowlby, R. (1985) *Just Looking: consumer culture in Dreiser, Gissing and Zola*, New York and London: Methuen.

Brooks, T. and Marsh, E. (1992) *The Complete Directory to Prime Time Network TV Shows: 1946–present*, New York: Ballantine Books.

Brown, M. E. (1990) 'Feminist culturalist television criticism – culture, theory and practice', in M. E. Brown (ed.) *Television and Women's Culture: the politics of the popular*, Sydney: Currency Press.

Brunsdon, C. (1987) 'Men's genres for women', in H. Baehr and G. Dyer (eds) *Boxed In: women and television*, New York and London: Pandora Press.

Brunsdon, C. and Morley, D. (1978) *Everyday Television: 'Nationwide'*, London: BFI.

Buckingham, D. (1987) *Public Secrets: EastEnders and its audience*, London: BFI.

—— (1993) *Reading Audiences: young people and the media*, Manchester and New York: Manchester University Press.

Burgin, V., Donald, J. and Kaplan, C. (eds) (1986) *Formations of Fantasy*, London and New York: Methuen.

Burke, P. (1978) *Popular Culture in Early Modern Europe*, Aldershot, England: Wildwood House Limited.

Carrithers, M., Collins, S. and Lukes, S. (1985) *The Category of the Person*, Cambridge, New York, Melbourne: University of Cambridge Press.

Chambers I. (1975) 'A strategy for living: black music and white subcultures', in S. Hall and T. Jefferson (eds) *Resistance Through Rituals: youth subcultures in post-war Britain*, London and Birmingham: Hutchinson and CCCS.

—— (1985) *Urban Rhythms: pop music and popular culture*, London: Macmillan.

—— (1986) *Popular Culture: the metropolitan experience*, London and New York: Methuen.

Clifford, J. (1986) 'Introduction: partial truths', in J. Clifford and G. Marcus (eds) *Writing Culture: the poetics and politics of ethnography*, Berkeley and Los Angeles: University of California Press.

Clifford, J. and Marcus, G. (eds) (1986) *Writing Culture: the poetics and politics of ethnography*, Berkeley and Los Angeles: University of California Press.

Cohen, P. (1980) 'Subcultural conflict and working-class community', in S. Hall et al. (eds) *Culture, Media, Language*, London: Hutchinson.

Cohen, S. and Young, J. (eds) (1981) *The Manufacture of News: deviance, social problems and the mass media*, London and Beverley Hills CA: Constable and Sage.

Corner, J. (1980) 'Codes and cultural analysis', *Media, Culture and Society*, 1980, 2: 73–86.

Cox, S. (1991) *The Addams Chronicles*, New York: Harper Collins.

Craik, J. (1987) 'Soft soap', in *Australian Left Review*, No. 102, Nov/Dec 1987: 34–7.

Crary, J. (1992) *Techniques of the Observer: on vision and modernity in the nineteenth century*, Paperback edition. Massachusetts Institute of Technology, USA: MIT Press.

Curran, J. and Gurevitch, M. (eds) (1991) *Mass Media and Society*, London: Edward Arnold.

de Certeau, M. (1984) *The Practice of Everyday Life*, trans. S. Rendall, Berkeley: University of California Press.

—— (1986) *Heterologies: discourse on the other*, trans. Brian Massumi, Minneapolis: University of Minnesota Press.

De Fleur, M. L. and Ball-Rokeach, S. (1975) *Theories of Mass Communication* (third edition), New York: Longman Inc.

De Lauretis, T. (1984) *Alice Does-N'T: feminism, semiotics, cinema*, Bloomington: Indiana University Press.

—— (1987) *Technologies of Gender*, Bloomington and Indianapolis: Indiana University Press.

Douglas, M. (1991) 'Jokes', in C. Mukerji and M. Schudson (eds) *Rethinking Popular Culture: contemporary perspectives in cultural studies*, Berkeley, Los Angeles, London: University of California Press.

Dyer, R., Geraghty, C., Jordan, M., Lovell, T., Paterson, R. and Stewart, J. (1981) *Coronation Street*, London: BFI.

Eco, U. (1974) *Does the Public Hurt Television? RAI, Broadcasters and their Audiences: Volume 1 – Introductory Reports*, Turino: Edizioni Radiotelevisione Italiana (Proc. XXV Prix Italia, Venezia 1973).

—— (1979) *The Role of the Reader: explorations in the semiotics of texts*, London: Hutchinson.

—— (1986a) *Travels in Hyper-Reality*, London: Picador.

—— (1986b) 'Towards a semiological guerilla warfare', in *Travels in Hyper-Reality*, London: Picador.

Elam, K. (1980) *The Semiotics of Theatre and Drama*, London and New York: Methuen.

Elsaesser, T. (1981) 'Narrative cinema and audience oriented aesthetics', in T. Bennett et al. (eds) *Popular Television and Film*, London: BFI and Open University Press.

Ewen, S. (1976) *Captains of Consciousness*, New York: McGraw-Hill.

Fish, S. (1980) *Is There a Text in this Class? The authority of interpretive communities*, Cambridge MA and London: Harvard University Press.

Fiske, J. (1982) *Introduction to Communication Studies*, London: Methuen.

—— (1987a) *Television Culture*, London: Methuen.

—— (1987b) 'British cultural studies and television', in R. C. Allen (ed.) *Channels of Discourse: television and contemporary criticism*, Chapel Hill and London: University of North Carolina Press.

—— (1993) *Power Plays, Power Works*, London and New York: Verso.

Foster, H. (ed.) (1982) *The Anti-Aesthetic: essays on postmodern culture*, Port Townsend, Washington: Bay Books.

—— (1987) *Discussions In Contemporary Culture*, Dia Art Foundation, Seattle: Bay Press.

Foucault, M. (1970) *The Order of Things*, New York: Vintage Books.

—(1977) 'What is an author?' in *Language, Counter-memory, Practice*, trans. Donald Bouchard, Ithaca NY: Cornell University Press.

—— (1979) *The History of Sexuality. Volume One: an introduction*, Harmondsworth: Penguin.

—— (1988) 'Technologies of the self', in L. H. Martin, H. Gutman and P. H. Hutton (eds) *Technologies of the Self: a seminar with Michel Foucault*, University of Massachusetts Press, London: Tavistock.

Frank, R. E. and Greenberg, B. (1974) *The Public's Use of Television*, Beverly Hills and London: Sage.

Frith, S. (1978) *The Sociology of Rocks*, London: Constable.

Gerbner, G. and Gross, L. (1976) 'Living with television: the violence profile', *Journal of Communication*, 26, 2: 173–99.

Gitlin, T. (1978) 'Media sociology: the dominant paradigm', *Theory and Society* 6: 205–53.

Goffman, E. (1959) *The Presentation of Self in Everyday Life*, Harmondsworth: Penguin 1978.

Gorden R. L. (1987) *Interviewing: strategy, techniques and tactics*, Chicago: Dorsey Press (4th edn).

Gray, A. (1987) 'Behind Closed Doors: video-recorders in the home', in H. Baer and G. Dyer (eds) *Boxed In: women and television*, London: Pandora.

Greenblatt, S. (1991) *Marvellous Possessions: the wonder of the new world*, Oxford: OUP.

Grimshaw, R., Hobson, D. and Willis, P. (1980) 'Introduction to ethnography at the centre', in S. Hall et al. (eds) *Culture, Media, Language*, London: Hutchinson.

Grossberg, L. (1988) 'It's a sin: politics, postmodernity and popular culture', in L. Grossberg, T. Fry, A. Curthoys and P. Patton (eds) *It's a Sin: essays on postmodernism, politics and culture*, Sydney: Power Publications.
—— (1989) 'The context of the audience and the politics of difference', *Australian Journal of Communication* 16: 13–35.
Guiraud, P. (1975) *Semiology*, London: Routledge and Kegan Paul.
Hall, S. (1980a) 'Encoding/decoding', in S. Hall et al. (eds) *Culture, Media, Language*, London: Hutchinson.
—— (1980b) 'Cultural studies: two paradigms', in *Media, Culture and Society* 2: 57–72.
Hall, S. and Jefferson, T. (eds) (1975) *Resistance Through Rituals: youth subcultures in post-war Britain*, London and Birmingham: Hutchinson and CCCS.
Hall, S., Hobson, D., Lowe, A. and Willis, P. (eds) (1980) *Culture, Media, Language: working papers in cultural studies, 1972–1979*, London and Birmingham: Hutchinson and CCCS, University of Birmingham.
Halloran, J. (1970) *The Effects of Television*, London: Panther.
Halloran, J. D., Elliott, P. and Murdock, G. (1970) *Demonstrations and Communication: a case study*, Harmondsworth: Penguin.
Halloran, J. and Nightingale, V. (1982) *Young TV Viewers and Their Images of Foreigners: a summary and interpretation of a four-nation study*, CMCR University of Leicester: Prix Jeunesse.
Hardt, H. (1992) *Critical Communication Studies: communication history and theory in America*, London and New York: Routledge.
Hartley, J. (1987) 'Invisible fictions: television audiences, paedocracy and pleasure', in *Textual Practice*, vol. 1, no. 2, summer 1987: 121–38.
Hebdige, D. (1975) 'Reggae, Rastas and Rudies', in S. Hall and T. Jefferson (eds) *Resistance Through Rituals: youth subcultures in post-war Britain*, London and Birmingham: Hutchinson and CCCS.
—— (1979) *Subculture: the meaning of style*, London and New York: Methuen.
—— (1981) 'Towards a cartography of taste, 1935–1962', *Block*, No. 4, 1981: 39–56.
Heller, A. (1970) *Everyday Life*, London: Routledge and Kegan Paul.
—— (1979) *A Theory of Feelings*, Assen, Netherlands: Van Gorcum.
Hobson, D. (1980) 'Housewives and the mass media', in S. Hall et al. (eds) *Culture, Media, Language*, London: Hutchinson.
—— (1981) 'Now that I'm married...', in A. McRobbie and T. McCabe (eds) *Feminism for Girls*, London: Routledge and Kegan Paul.
—— (1982) *Crossroads: the drama of a soap opera*, London: Methuen.
Hodder, I. (1986) *Reading the Past: current approaches to interpretation in archaeology*, Cambridge: Cambridge University Press.
Hodge, B. and Tripp, D. (1986) *Children and Television: a semiotic approach*, Cambridge: Polity Press.
Hoffman, E. (1989) *Lost in Translation: a life in a new language*, New York: Penguin Books.
Hoggart, R. (1973a) *Speaking to Each Other. Volume One... about society*, Harmondsworth: Penguin.
——(1973b) *Speaking to Each Other. Volume Two... about literature*, Harmondsworth: Penguin.
Howitt, D. and Cumberbatch, G. (1975) *Mass Media, Violence and Society*, New York: John Wiley.
Hunter, I. (1993) 'Setting limits to culture', in G. Turner (ed.) *Nation, Culture, Text: Australian cultural studies and media studies*, London: Routledge.

Jakobsen, R. (1989) *Question and Answer: forms of dialogic understanding*, trans. M. Hays, Minneapolis: University of Minnesota Press.
—— (1992) 'On linguistic aspects of translation', in R. Schulte and J. Biguenet (eds) *Theories of Translation*, Chicago and London: University of Chicago Press.
Jauss, H. R. (1982) *Towards an Aesthetic of Reception*, trans. E. Bahti, Minneapolis: University of Minnesota Press.
Jenkins, H. (1993) *Textual Poachers: television fans and participatory culture*, London and New York: Methuen.
Jones, A. R (1986) 'Mills and Boon meets feminism', in J. Radford (ed.) *The Progress of Romance: the politics of popular fiction*, London: Routledge and Kegan Paul.
Kaplan, E. A. (ed.) (1983) *Regarding Television*, Los Angeles: American Film Institute.
Katz, E. and Lazarsfeld, P. (1955) *Personal Influence*, Glencoe IL: Free Press.
Katz, E., Blumler, J. and Gurevitch, M. (1974) 'Utilisation of mass communication by the individual', in J. Blumler and E. Katz (eds) *The Uses of Mass Communications: current perspectives on gratifications research*, Beverly Hills and London: Sage.
Kress, G. (1983) 'Media analysis and the study of discourse', in *Media Information Australia* 28 May 1983: 3–11.
Kuhn, A. (1987) 'Women's genres: melodrama, soap opera and theory', in C. Gledhill (ed.) *Home is Where the Heart Is: studies in melodrama and the woman's film*, London: BFI Publishing.
Lacan, J. (1977) *The Four Fundamental Concepts of Psycho-Analysis*, Harmondsworth: Penguin.
Lasch, C. (1980) *The Culture of Narcissism*, London: Abacus, Sphere Books.
Lefebvre, H. (1971) *Everyday Life in the Modern World*, trans. Sacha Rabinovitch, London: Allen Lane and Penguin.
Lévi-Strauss, C. (1978) *Myth and Meaning*, London: Routledge and Kegan Paul.
—— (1986) *The Raw and the Cooked: introduction to a science of mythology*, Harmondsworth: Penguin.
Lewis, L. (ed.) (1992) *The Adoring Audience: fan culture and popular media*, London and New York: Routledge.
Lindlof, T. R. (ed.) (1987) *Natural Audiences: qualitative research of media uses and effects*, Norwood NJ: Ablex Publishing.
Lindlof, T. and Meyer, T. P. (1987) 'Mediated communication as ways of seeing, acting and constructing culture: the tools and foundations of qualitative research', in T. Lindlof (ed.) *Natural Audiences: qualitative research of media uses and effects*, Norwood NJ: Ablex Publishing.
Livingstone, S. (1991) 'Audience reception: the role of the viewer in retelling romantic drama', in J. Curran and M. Gurevitch (eds) *Mass Media and Society*, London: Edward Arnold.
Lovell, T. (1972) 'Sociology of aesthetic structures and contextualism', in D. McQuail (ed.) *Sociology of Mass Communications*, Harmondsworth: Penguin.
—— (1983) *Pictures of Reality: aesthetics, politics and pleasure*, London: BFI.
Lukes, S. (1985) 'Conclusion', in M. Carrithers, S. Collins and S. Lukes (eds) *The Category of the Person*, Cambridge, New York, Melbourne: University of Cambridge Press.
Lull, J. (1990) *Inside Family Viewing*, London: Routledge.
Maccoby, E. E. and Wilson, W. C. (1957) 'Identification and observational learning from films', *Journal of Abnormal and Social Psychology* 55: 76–87.
Macdonell, D. (1986) *Theories of Discourse: an introduction*, Oxford: Blackwell.
McGuigan, J. (1992) *Cultural Populism*, London and New York: Routledge.

McLeod, J., Kosicki, G. and Pan, Z. (1991) 'On understanding and misunderstanding media effects', in J. Curran and M. Gurevitch (eds) *Mass Media and Society*, London: Edward Arnold.

McQuail, D. (ed.) (1972) *Sociology of Mass Communications*, Harmondsworth: Penguin.

—— (1983) *Mass Communication Theory: an introduction*, London: Sage.

McRobbie, A. (1981) 'Just like a Jackie story', in A. McRobbie and T. McCabe (eds) *Feminism for Girls*, London: Routledge and Kegan Paul.

McRobbie, A. and McCabe, T. (eds) (1981) *Feminism for Girls: an adventure story*, London: Routledge and Kegan Paul.

Malinowski, B. (1954) *Magic, Science and Religion, and Other Essays*, New York: Doubleday Anchor Books.

Marcus, G. E. (1986) 'Contemporary problems of ethnography in the modern world system', in J. Clifford and G. E. Marcus (eds) *Writing Culture: the poetics and politics of ethnography*, Berkeley and Los Angeles: University of California Press.

Marcus, G. E. and Fischer, M. (1986) *Anthropology as Cultural Critique: an experimental moment in the human sciences*, Chicago and London: University of Chicago Press.

Marcus, G. (1991) *Dead Elvis: a chronicle of cultural obsession*, London: Penguin.

Mattelart, A., Delcourt, X. and Mattelart, M. (1984) *International Image Markets: in search of an alternative perspective*, London: Comedia.

Meltzer, B., Petras, J. and Reynolds, L. (1975) *Symbolic Interactionism: genesis, varieties and criticism*, London: Routledge and Kegan Paul.

Meyer, E. (1987/88) 'Letters or the autobiography of writing', *Discourse* X, 1, Fall–Winter 1987–88.

Meyrowitz, J. (1986) *No Sense of Place: the impact of the electronic media on social behaviour*, New York and Oxford: Oxford University Press.

Modleski, T. (1982) *Loving with a Vengeance: mass-produced fantasies for women*, New York and London: Methuen.

Moran, A. (1982) *Making a TV Series: the Bellamy project*, Sydney: Currency Press.

—— (1993) *Moran's Guide to Australian TV Series*, Sydney: AFTRS; Sydney: Allen and Unwin; London: University College London Press; Concord MA: Paul and Company Publishing Consortium Inc.

Morley, D. (1980) *The 'Nationwide' Audience: structure and decoding*, London: BFI.

—— (1981) 'The Nationwide audience: a postscript', *Screen Education* 39, Summer 1981: 4.

—— (1986) *Family Television: cultural power and domestic leisure*, London: Comedia.

—— (1992) *Television, Audiences and Cultural Studies*, London: Routledge.

Morley, D. and Silverstone, R. (1988) 'Domestic Communication – technologies and meanings', paper presented to 1988 International Television Studies Conference, London, July 1988.

Morris, M. and Patton, P. (1979) *Michel Foucault: power, truth and strategy*, Sydney: Feral Press.

Muir, A. R. (1988) 'The status of women working in film and television', in L. Gamman and M. Marshment (eds) *The Female Gaze: women as viewers of popular culture*, London: Women's Press.

Mulvey, L. (1981) 'Visual pleasure and narrative cinema', in T. Bennett et al. (eds) *Popular Television and Film*, London: BFI and Open University.

Newcomb, H. (1974) *TV: The Most Popular Art*, New York: Anchor Press.

—— (ed.) (1976) *Television: the critical view*, New York: Oxford University Press.

—— (1978) 'Assessing the violence profile of Gerbner and Gross: a humanistic critique and suggestion', *Communication Research* 5, 3: 264–82.

Nightingale, V. (1984) 'Media audiences – media products?' *Australian Journal of Cultural Studies* 2, 1: 23–35.

—— (1986) 'What's happening to audience research?' *Media Information Australia* 30: 18–22.

—— (1989) 'What's "ethnographic" about ethnographic audience research?', *Australian Journal of Communication* 16: 50–63.

—— (1992) 'Contesting domestic territory: watching Rugby League on television', in A. Moran (ed.) *Stay Tuned! An Australian broadcasting reader*, Sydney: Allen and Unwin.

—— (1993a) 'Industry measurement of audiences', in S. Cunningham and G. Turner (eds) *The Media in Australia: industries, texts, audiences*, Sydney: Allen and Unwin.

—— (1993b) 'The vulnerable audience – effects traditions', in S. Cunningham and G. Turner (eds) *The Media in Australia: industries, texts, audiences*, Sydney: Allen and Unwin.

—— (1994a) 'Improvising Elvis, Marilyn and Mickey Mouse', *Australian Journal of Communication* 21, 1, July 1994: 1–20.

—— (1994b) 'Shifty characters and shady relations', *Media Information Australia* 73, August 1994: 40–4.

—— (1996) 'Adsick, lovesick, homesick', in M. Devers (ed.) *Australia and Asia: cultural transactions*, London: Curzon Press.

Noble, G. (1975) *Children in Front of the Small Screen*, London and Beverly Hills: Constable and Sage.

O'Sullivan, T., Hartley, J., Saunders, D. and Fiske, J. (1983) *Key Concepts in Communication*, London and New York: Methuen.

Owens, C. (1987) 'The birth and death of the viewer: on the public function of art', in H. Foster (ed.) *Discussions in Contemporary Culture*, Dia Art Foundation, Seattle: Bay Press.

Palmer, P. (1986) *The Lively Audience: a study of children around the TV set*, Sydney: Allen and Unwin.

Panati, C. (1991) *Panati's Parade of Fads, Manias and Follies: the origins of our most treasured obsessions*, New York: Harper Collins.

Parkin, F. (1971) *Class Inequality and Political Order: social stratification in capitalist and communist societies*, New York and London: Praeger Publishers.

Paz, O. (1992) 'Translation: literature and letters', in R. Schulte and J. Biguenet (eds) *Theories of Translation*, Chicago and London: University of Chicago Press.

Pearson, G. and Twohig, J. (1975) 'Ethnography through the looking glass: the case of Howard Becker', in S. Hall and T. Jefferson (eds) *Resistance Through Rituals*, London and Birmingham: Hutchinson and CCCS, University of Birmingham.

Philo, G. (1990) *Seeing and Believing: the influence of television*, London and New York: Routledge.

Postman, N. (1982) *The Disappearance of Childhood: how TV is changing children's lives*, London: W. H. Allen, Comet Books 1983.

Pratt, M. L. (1986) 'Fieldwork in common places', in J. Clifford and G. E. Marcus (eds) *Writing Culture: the poetics and politics of ethnography*, Berkeley and Los Angeles: University of California Press.

Radway, J. (1984) *Reading the Romance: women, patriarchy and popular literature*, Chapel Hill and London: University of North Carolina Press.

—— (1988) 'Reception study: ethnography and the problems of dispersed audiences and nomadic subjects', *Cultural Studies* 2, 3: 358–76.

Radway, Jean (ed.) (1986) *The Progress of Romance: the politics of popular fiction*, London: Routledge and Kegan Paul.

Roberts, B. (1975) 'Naturalistic research into subcultures and deviance', in S. Hall and T. Jefferson (eds) *Resistance Through Rituals*, London and Birmingham: Hutchinson and CCCS, University of Birmingham.

Robinson, D. C., Buck, E. B. and Cuthbert, M. (eds) (1991) *Music at the Margins: popular culture and global cultural diversity*, Newbury Park, London and New Delhi: SAGE Publications.

Rock, Paul (1979) *The Making of Symbolic Interactionism*, London and Basingstoke: Macmillan Press.

Rosaldo, R. (1986) 'From the door of his tent: the fieldworker and the inquisitor', in J. Clifford and G. E. Marcus (eds) *Writing Culture: the poetics and politics of ethnography*, Berkeley and Los Angeles: University of California Press.

Said, E. (1983) 'Opponents, audiences, constituencies and communities', in H. Foster (ed.) *The Anti-Aesthetic: essays on postmodern culture*, Port Townsend WA: Bay Books.

Schlesinger, P., Emerson Dobash, R., Dobash, R. P. and Weaver, C. K. (eds) (1992) *Women Viewing Violence*, London: BFI.

Schramm, W. (1954) *The Process and Effects of Mass Communication*, Urbana: University of Illinois Press.

Seiter, E. E. (1988) Women writing soap opera: the careers of Irna Phillips and Jane Crusinberry'. Paper presented to Society for Cinema Studies Conference, Montana University, July 1988.

Sinyard, N. (1988) *The Best of Disney*, London: Twin Books, copyright Walt Disney Company.

Sless, D. (1986) *In Search of Semiotics*, London: Croom Helm.

Smythe, D. (1981) *Dependency Road: communications, capitalism, consciousness and Canada*, Norwood NJ: Ablex Publishing Corp.

Sprinker, M. (1987) *Imaginary Relations. aesthetics and ideology in the theory of historical materialism*, London: Verso

Suleiman, S. and Crosman, I. (1980) *The Reader in the Text: essays on audience and interpretation*, Princeton NJ: Princeton University Press.

Tolson, A. (1986) 'Popular culture:. practice and institution', in C. MacCabe (ed.) *High Theory/Low Culture: analysing popular television and film*, Manchester: Manchester University Press.

Tompkins, J. P. (1980) *Reader Response Criticism: from formalism to post-structuralism*, Baltimore and London: Johns Hopkins University Press.

Traudt, P. and Lont, C. (1987) 'Media-Logic-In-Use: the family as locus of study', in T. R. Lindlof and T. P. Meyer (eds) *Natural Audiences: qualitative research of media uses and effects*, Norwood NJ: Ablex.

Travaglia, J. (1993) 'The memories file', in *Growing Up Italian in Australia*, Sydney: State Library of NSW.

Trinh, T. Minh-ha (1989) 'Outside in, inside out', in P. Pines and P. Willemen (eds) *Questions of Third Cinema*, London: BFI.

Tulloch, J. (1982) 'Back to the audience', *Australian Journal of Screen Theory* 11, 12: 128–33.

Tulloch, J. and Alvarado, M. (1983) *Doctor Who: the unfolding text*, London: Macmillan Press.

Tulloch, J. and Moran, A. (1986) *A Country Practice: 'quality soap'*, Sydney: Currency Press.

Tulloch, J. and Turner, G. (eds) (1989) *Australian Television: programs, pleasures and politics*, Sydney: Allen and Unwin.

Turner, G. (1986) *National Fictions: literature, film and the construction of Australian narrative*, Sydney: Allen and Unwin.

—— (1993) 'Moving the margins: theory practice and Australian cultural studies', in G. Turner (ed.) *Nation, Culture, Text: Australian cultural and media studies*, London and New York: Routledge.

Turner, V. (1977) 'Frame, flow and reflection: ritual and drama as public liminality', in M. Benamou and C. Caramello (eds) *Performance in Postmodern Culture*, Madison WI: Coda Press.

Turow, J. (1991) 'A mass communication perspective on entertainment industries', in J. Curran and M. Gurevitch, *Mass Media and Society*, London: Edward Arnold.

Veblen, T. (1899) *The Theory of the Leisure Class: an economic study of institutions*, New York: Macmillan.

Walkerdine, V. (1986) 'Video replay: families, films and fantasy', in V. Burgin et al. (eds) *Formations of Fantasy*, London: Methuen.

—— (1990) *Schoolgirl Fictions*, London and New York: Verso.

Wartella, E. (1979) 'Children and television: the development of the child's understanding of the media', *Television Programming for Children: a report of the children's television taskforce*, Washington DC: Federal Communications Commission.

—— (1987) 'Commentary on qualitative research and children's mediated communication', in T. R. Lindlof (ed.) *Natural Audiences: qualitative research of media uses and effects*, Norwood NJ: Ablex.

Williams, R. (1974) *Television: technology and cultural form*, London: Fontana.

—— (1975) *The Long Revolution*, Harmondsworth: Pelican.

—— (1977) *Marxism and Literature*, Oxford: Oxford University Press.

—— (1980a) 'Base and superstructure in Marxist cultural theory', in *Problems in Materialism and Culture*, London: Verso Editions and NLB.

—— (1980b) 'Literature and sociology', in *Problems in Materialism and Culture*, London: Verso Editions and NLB.

—— (1980c) 'Social environment and theatrical environment: the case of English naturalism', in *Problems in Materialism and Culture*, London: Verso Editions and NLB.

—— (1981) *Culture*, Glasgow: Fontana.

—— (1984) *The English Novel from Dickens to Lawrence*, London: Hogarth Press.

—— (1985a) *Keywords: a vocabulary of culture and society*, London: Fontana.

—— (1985b) *Culture and Society*, Harmondsworth: Penguin.

Williams, V. (1986) *Women Photographers: the other observers 1900 to the present*, London: Virago Press.

Williamson, J. (1986) 'The problems of being popular', *New Socialist* 41: 14.

Willis, P. (1977) *Learning to Labour: how working class kids get working class jobs*, Aldershot: Gower Publishing.

—— (1978) *Profane Culture*, London: Routledge and Kegan Paul.

—— (1980) 'Notes on Method', in S. Hall et al. *Culture, Media, Language*, London: Hutchinson.

—— (1990) *Common Culture: symbolic work at play in the everyday cultures of the young*. Milton Keynes: Open University Press

Willmott, P. and Young, M. (1957) *Family and Kinship in East London*, London: Routledge and Kegan Paul.

Wilson, T. (1993a) 'Television and political public relations: towards an historical analysis', paper presented to Sixth Australian History and Film Conference, Melbourne.

—— (1993b) *Watching Television: hermeneutics, reception and popular culture*, Cambridge: Polity Press.

Wolff, J. (1981) *The Social Reproduction of Art*, London: Macmillan.

Young, S. (1988) 'Feminism and the politics of power: whose gaze is it anyway?' in L. Gamman and M. Marshment (eds) *The Female Gaze: women as viewers of popular culture*, London: Women's Press.

Young, T. R. (1985) 'Public opinion, mass opinion and social opinion: the constitution of political culture in the capitalist state', in V. Mosco and J. Wasco (eds) *Popular Culture and Media Events*, New York: Ablex.

Zipes, J. (1979) *Breaking the Magic Spell: radical theories of folk and fairy tales*, London: Heinemann Educational Books.

Žižek, S. (1992) *Enjoy Your Symptom! Jacques Lacan in Hollywood and out*, New York and London: Routledge.

Index

Abercrombie, N., Hill, S. and
  Turner, B.S. 37–8
'active viewing' 7–9, 89–90
administrative audience research 4
Adorno, T. 75
advertising 3–4; revolutionary
  potential of 35
aesthetics, and popular culture 75–6
agency 29–30
agency, as subjectivity 30
Allor, M. 11, 20n.
Althusser, L. 21, 40, 41, 42, 150
Alvarado, M. and Buscombe, E. 21
Ang, Ien 5, 48, 92n., 99, 151; on
  fantasy 119; on identity 105; on
  ideologies of mass culture and
  populism 104; theorisation of
  discursive formations 86;
  Desperately Seeking the Audience
  20n., 152n.; *Watching Dallas.
  soap opera and the melodramatic
  imagination* ix, 58n., 59, 61,
  76–82
anthropology 53, 114; in traditions
  of ethnography 115–17
anti-foundationalism 57
archaeology 53, 114
argot 116
Atkinson, P. 39n.
audience active 7–9; breaking down
  into structured categories of
  viewers 69; constituency theories
  of 10; critique of mass audience
  12–13; definition of 10–12;

familial and personal
  performances 8; inclusion in 84,
  85–6; as lifestyle groups 10–11,
  20n.; performance of 95;
  positioning of 87–8; rule-
  following activities 8; symbiotic
  relationship with text 16, 149;
  under-theorisation of 86
audience research, administrative 4;
  audience research, development
  of viii–xii, 145–6; pedagogic
  aims x; 'personal influence'
  model 4, 5
audience–industry relations,
  Crossroads 71, 73–4, 91n.; as
  technology of production 149
audience–text relation, context
  147–8; expressions of xii
audio-visual codes 35
aural codes, and televisual discourse
  33–4
Australia, Aboriginal calls for
  autonomy 45, academic
  scholarship 42; immigration and
  'metropolitan experience' 12
authorial intention 84
authorship, of signs of subculture
  116

Barthes, R. 1, 50, 87; distinction
  between 'work' and 'text' 32; on
  interdisciplinarity 59; on role of
  researcher 104; on three types of
  reading 102

03527981